DISABILITY

DISABILITY

A LIFE COURSE APPROACH

MARK PRIESTLEY

polity

First published in 2003 by Polity Press in association with Blackwell Publishing Ltd, a Blackwell Publishing Company.

Editorial office:
Polity Press
65 Bridge Street
Cambridge CB2 1UR, UK

Marketing and production:
Blackwell Publishing Ltd
108 Cowley Road
Oxford OX4 1JF, UK

Distributed in the USA by
Blackwell Publishing Inc.
350 Main Street
Malden, MA 02148, USA

Library of Congress Cataloging-in-Publication Data
Priestley, Mark, 1963–
Disability : a life course approach / by Mark Priestley.
    p. cm.
    Includes bibliographical references and index.
    ISBN 0-7456-2512-6 – ISBN 0-7456-2513-4 (pbk.)   1. People with disabilities.   2. People with disabilities – Social conditions.   3. People with disabilities – Cross-cultural studies.   4. Sociology of disability.   5. Life cycle, Human.   I. Title.
    HV1568.P75 2003
    305.9'0816 – dc21

                                                                    2002012895

Typeset in 10.5 on 12 pt Sabon
by SNP Best-set Typesetter Ltd, Hong Kong
Printed and bound in Great Britain by MPG Books Ltd, Bodmin, Cornwall

For further information on Polity, visit our website: http://www.polity.co.uk

CONTENTS

ACKNOWLEDGEMENTS

The writing of this book was undertaken as part of a personal programme of research under the title 'Disability, Social Policy and the Life Course', made possible by a three-year Research Fellowship Award from the UK Economic and Social Research Council (number R000271078). I am also indebted to numerous people who have assisted me in the theoretical development and practical research leading up to this book. In particular, I owe a great deal to all the staff and students of the Centre for Disability Studies at the University of Leeds, for creating such a vibrant and challenging environment within which to work.

INTRODUCTION

Understanding disability, and our social responses to it, presents a number of challenges, not only to students and academics, but also to policy makers and activists concerned with social change. I hope that this book will help to further that understanding. By adopting a life course approach, the book offers an alternative framework for thinking about disability as it affects people of all generations and at all points of life course transition. This perspective is important, because it highlights how disabling societies and practices affect people of different generations in different ways (e.g., children, young people, adults or older people). It also allows us to consider some important disability issues at the very beginning and end of the life course (i.e. at birth and death). This in turn enables us to see more clearly how societies organize generational boundaries and life course transitions in a collective way, and how this shapes our understanding of disability in the social world.

Adopting a life course approach raises a number of significant questions. Why, for example, have states gone to such lengths to limit or prevent the birth of disabled children? Why have disabled children been so often excluded from mainstream education? What is the significance of youth culture and youth transitions for young disabled people? How does the expectation of an 'independent' adulthood – for example, in relation to employment or parenting – contribute to the production of disability in modern societies? Why are older people with impairments rarely seen as disabled in quite the same way that younger adults often are? Why are different moral standards applied to the death and dying of disabled and non-disabled people? By examining such questions in the context of theory and current debates, the book shows how our understanding of disability is framed by a particular view of life course progression and its social organization in contemporary societies.

Who this book is for

This is primarily a book for students and teachers of disability studies in universities and colleges. It is written and presented so that it may be used in courses in disability studies and related areas – either as a textbook or as supporting material. However, the issues covered in the book have a significance that carries far beyond the classroom, and there is also a great deal that will appeal directly to professionals, policy makers and interested lay readers. For those more familiar with the field, adopting a life course framework offers a new way of thinking about some important aspects of contemporary disability theory and debate. In this way, I hope that the book offers a significant development in both learning and thinking about disability issues.

What this book is about

This book is about disability, about the ways in which people with perceived impairments, of all ages, are excluded from full participation in contemporary societies. It is about the practices, policies, cultures and social structures that give rise to this exclusion, and about disabled people's resistance to them. In particular, it is about the way in which contemporary societies organize the relationship between disability and the life course, and how this affects people of different ages and generations. The material in the various chapters includes theoretical analyses of generation and the life course and suggests how these can inform our understanding of disability. There is also a large amount of illustrative material on specific disability issues, with an emphasis on using examples to encourage argument and debate.

What this book is not about

This is primarily a book about challenging disabling barriers and practices. It is not a book about impairment or medical issues; nor is it primarily a book about the personal experience of disabled people's lives (although it is very much informed by that experience as represented in the writings and cultures of disabled people). There are a number of published accounts relating directly to disabled people's life experiences, which may be useful in complementing this book. For further source material on biography and life history research with disabled people, it may therefore be useful to read this book in conjunction with the edited collection *Disability and the Life Course: Global Perspectives* (Priestley 2001).

How to use this book

The material in the book is organized using a sequential life course approach – roughly speaking, from the cradle to the grave, or, more accurately, from 'womb to tomb' (via birth, childhood, youth, adulthood, old age and death). The chapters have been arranged so that they may be read either sequentially, starting from the beginning, or as individual, free-standing units. Each chapter identifies specific themes and explores relevant issues. There are numerous examples and references to relevant source material, suggestions for further reading, discussion points and learning exercises in all of the main chapters. The first chapter provides some background and discussion on the general concepts that are applied throughout the book, and it may be useful to look at this first.

A note on terminology

The term 'disability' is used in this book, as it is within the disabled people's movement, to refer to the many ways in which people with perceived impairments are excluded from full participation in society, due to physical and social barriers. This kind of definition is now widely used in international policy making, but it has its origins in the writings of disabled people (e.g., within the Union of Physically Impaired Against Segregation in the UK and within Disabled Peoples' International). These developments are discussed in more detail in chapter 1.

This approach forms the basis for what has come to be known as the 'social model', or the social interpretation, of disability. It emphasizes that people become disabled through encounters with disabling barriers, rather than through any necessary causal connection with their individual level of physical or cognitive functioning. The implication is that disability, as social disadvantage, is produced by social and cultural processes, and that its effects may be reduced or eliminated by building a more inclusive society.

A *life course approach*

The argument presented in this book is based on the belief that we can learn a great deal about disability debates by examining them within the context of the life course. Here, the life course is understood as a central organizing principle in modern societies, rather than as a description of individual life careers. In this sense, adopting a life course approach to disability means examining the ways in which disabled lives are understood, organized and governed within societies – from the regulation of birth and reproduction to the social organization of death and dying (and all points in between). One of the weaknesses in the existing disability literature is that there has been a tendency to focus on a fairly narrow range of issues, often those affecting adults of working age. As we will see, there may be good reason for this, since our understanding of the roles and responsibilities of adulthood tells us a great deal about why people with perceived impairments have been so often excluded from full citizenship in modern societies. However, it is by no means the whole story. Using the life course as a conceptual framework is a productive approach, because it forces us to consider a wider range of issues, affecting people at all points of life, rather than focusing on those that are relevant only to a minority.

Contemporary theorizing about disability has tended to emphasize the collective experiences of disabled people, as an oppressed group in society, and this has been very productive. However, there are also dangers in over-simplifying the collective experience when we know that disabling societies affect different people in different ways. For example, there have been increasing claims that the disability experience may be markedly different for men and women, for people with different kinds of impairment, for people from different ethnic backgrounds, and in different cultural contexts. In this context, a life course approach suggests that disability also carries a different significance for people of different ages and stages of life. Just as gender theorists have shown how much can be gained by distinguishing between disabled women and disabled men, so a life course approach suggests that we might gain a great deal by starting to think more carefully about 'disabled children', 'disabled adults' or 'disabled elders', for example.

For this reason, a life course approach to disability requires us to add in the concept of *generation*. Generation, in this sense, is about more than just age. It involves thinking about the ways in which important generational categories (like childhood, youth, adulthood or old age) are constructed, and how the boundaries or transitions between them are governed through social relations and social institutions. Applying a generational analysis to disability highlights the different significance of particular issues at different points in the life course. A good example here is the apparent lack of critical debate about disability issues in old age. The likelihood of impairment increases with age, and in Western industrialized societies the majority of disabled people are over retirement age. Yet, older people are rarely considered as 'disabled' in quite the same way that younger adults and children often are (even within more radical debates on disability rights). Understanding these anomalies is possible only if we consider the relationship between disability and generation.

More generally, thinking about disability in terms of generation and the life course offers a way to make links with some important themes in contemporary social theory and research. Recent developments in social science have highlighted two significant trends in this respect. First, social scientists have become increasingly interested in using generational concepts to investigate social divisions. We have seen, for example, the emergence of a new and critical sociology of childhood, a renaissance in youth studies, and a renewed interest in social gerontology. Understanding the structural significance and cultural meanings of these generational categories has been presented as a key task for social science. Second, there has been a significant 'biographical turn' in social-scientific writing that emphasizes the importance of thinking about the life course and individual life projects (see Rustin 2000). Here, the emphasis has been to examine the uniqueness of lived experience within its social and cultural context. There has been an increasing amount of work in disability studies that reflects this more general trend.

To summarize, adopting a life course approach involves thinking about disability issues from the very beginning to the very end of life. It involves thinking about the way in which life course transitions are organized at a collective level within societies and about the generational significance of disability issues as they affect people of different ages. It adds a new dimension to our understanding of the category of disabled people, and has the potential to offer new ways of thinking about a wide range of disability debates (in a similar way to the introduction of a gendered analysis). Generational and life course analyses also offer a way to link disability debates with some important developments in contemporary social science.

Outline of the following chapters

The opening chapter provides a conceptual basis for the book, by introducing the key concepts of disability, generation and the life course. Both disability and generation are shown to be important social categories in regulating and governing our understanding of the 'normal' life course in modern societies. The discussion draws on literature from both disability studies and life course studies in order to highlight some important parallels in the way that normality is constructed through disability and generation. The discussion outlines the major challenges to these constructions, and shows how both disability and generation are widely used in contemporary debates about personhood, citizenship and entitlements. This analysis suggests that the historical construction of an idealized and gendered adulthood has a particular social significance in marginalizing the experiences of children, elders and disabled people (of all ages).

Chapter 2 begins at the beginning, by examining birth and the right to life, using examples of policy and practice in a variety of countries to explore current debates on disability and eugenics. These include both state-sponsored programmes to limit the birth of disabled children and individual birth decisions by parents. Issues of selective screening and abortion in information and consumer societies are particularly significant in this context. The chapter examines international policy debates in their sociological context, also noting how the disabled people's movement has mobilized around this issue. These examples show how the development of new biotechnologies, the rationing of scarce welfare resources, and the persistence of eugenic ideologies combine to influence the way we think about the birth of disabled children. The increasing diversity of life-style in a globalizing world is contrasted with the increasing use of eugenic technologies to police its boundaries.

Chapter 3 explores the relationship between disability and childhood. The discussion begins by introducing a number of theoretical approaches to childhood studies (such as developmental theories, socialization and the 'new' sociology of childhood). This review shows how traditional approaches have consistently disadvantaged disabled children by normalizing child development and reinforcing concepts such as 'developmental delay'. Structural approaches suggest that there are some important similarities in the way that both disability and childhood have been produced as social categories within modern societies (e.g. in terms of dependency). There are also parallels in the social construction and treatment of children and disabled people. Both have been denied attributions of agency or competence; both have been subject to differential mechanisms of surveillance and control by more powerful adults. There is also a sense in which disabled adults, particularly those with learning difficulties, are often perceived as eternal children. However, increasing claims to human rights for both children and disabled people pose challenges to this view.

Chapter 4 introduces the concept of youth and examines transitions from childhood to adulthood. The emergence of youth as a distinct generational category has aroused interest in thinking about youth cultures and identities (e.g. in relation to leisure consumption, the youthful body and expressions of sexuality). These debates take on a particular significance for young disabled people. Transitional approaches to youth show how life course progression has become highly organized at the collective level in modern societies, and enormous social investments have been made to ensure that we make 'proper' transitions, particularly from childhood to adulthood. Similarly, major social institutions have emerged to manage the problems arising from 'improper' transitions (e.g. the perceived failure of disabled people to achieve an independent adulthood). There is also a sense in which disability has been constructed as a kind of enduring adolescence, and this imagery has been reproduced in a variety of policy debates. For example, transition policies have consigned many people (often with learning difficulties) to a series of unresolved transitions in which true adult status is neither envisaged nor attained. Understanding more about the hopes and expectations we hold for young people helps to illuminate some important debates about disability and society.

Chapter 5 examines the key concept of adulthood: what it means in different societies and how this shapes our understanding of disability. The discussion explores ideas about independence, autonomy and competence in order to illustrate how the gendered ideals of independent adulthood underpin disabling assumptions and social institutions in modern societies. In particular, the examples of employment and parenting are used to illustrate some key arguments about the relationship between disability, citizenship and civil rights. At the same time, significant changes in technology, gender roles, working practices, the family and the nation-state have increasingly put in question our assumptions about adult roles and responsibilities. Thus, the discussion draws on claims and practices developed within the international disabled people's movement to critically examine the concepts of individualism, autonomy and interdependency in a changing world.

Chapter 6 explores the relationship between disability and old age. Both structurally and culturally, disabled people have often been constructed in similar ways to older people (e.g. as similarly 'dependent' on adult labour). Impairment and disability are also key to understanding issues of identity and the ageing body. In industrialized societies, the majority of disabled people are over retirement age. Disability is thus a fact of life for many older people, if not something of a social norm. Despite this demographic truism, or perhaps because of it, older people with impairments are rarely regarded as 'disabled' in the way that children, young people and adults often are. Disability policy making has focused on issues affecting those of working age or below, and older people have been underrepresented within the disabled people's movement. The chapter introduces some of the main theoretical approaches to thinking about old age, and draws on international debates about older people's rights, to examine the policy implications of a 'society for all ages'.

Chapter 7 concludes the overview of life course progression by turning to issues of death and dying, and the hotly debated territory of the right to life (discussed in chapter 2). The chapter begins by reviewing theoretical approaches to dying, life expectancy and the cultural construction of a 'good death'. This review highlights the normalization and increased regulation of death in modern societies, in the context of consumerism in information societies. Taken in a global context, disability is very much a life-and-death issue. Disabled people face an increased risk of death from lack of access to resources, from violence and murder, from the denial of life-saving medical treatment, and from legalized killing in the form of euthanasia. Using case-study examples, such as the Nazi Holocaust and physician-assisted suicide, the discussion examines policy interventions in the death of disabled people in contemporary societies. In so doing, it draws attention to debates about the worth or 'quality' of disabled lives, and the contribution of the disabled people's movement in challenging traditional assumptions about the normal life course.

The book ends with a short conclusion, drawing together lessons from the various chapters. Here, the emphasis is on reviewing the potential contribution of a life course analysis to the development of disability theory and indicating directions for future research. In many ways, the book raises more questions than it answers, and this is its intention, not only to raise awareness of contemporary disability issues but also to stimulate further discussion and debate.

SUGGESTIONS FOR INITIAL READING

There is now a substantial and diverse literature within the field of critical disability studies, and much of this is referenced within the subsequent chapters. For an introduction to some of the key approaches, and to the development of disability studies as a discipline within social science, it may be useful to review some texts. Oliver's *Understanding Disability* (1996) is a useful overview of the relationship between disability theory and practice (see also Priestley 1998), and Morris (1991) offers an accessible introduction to some of the key ideas. Barnes, Mercer and Shakespeare (1999) provide an excellent account of developing ideas and critiques within the field of sociology, while Linton (1998) explores some of the tensions in establishing disciplinary boundaries. To appreciate the range of recent contributions and approaches to disability studies, it may be useful to consult *The Handbook of Disability Studies* (Albrecht, Seelman and Bury 2001).

SOME USEFUL INTERNET SITES

There are also a large number of relevant Internet sites that may be useful in supporting further discussion of the issues raised in this book. Specific suggestions are included at the end of each chapter. However, the following general resources may be helpful.

- Centre for Disability Studies: *www.leeds.ac.uk/disability-studies* (includes access to an extensive online archive of disability writings)
- Disability-Research Discussion List: *www.jiscmail.ac.uk/lists/disability-research.html* (a major international forum for online debate)
- Disabled Peoples' International: *www.dpi.org* (international umbrella organization representing the views and priorities of the disabled people's movement)
- Disability Awareness in Action: *www.daa.org.uk* (an important international campaign and information network)

- Disability World: *www.disabilityworld.org* (regular publications on disability issues around the world)
- Cornucopia of Disability Information (CODI): *www.codi.buffalo.edu*
- Independent Living Virtual Library: *www.independentliving.org/htdig/libsrch.html*
- *Disability and Society* (academic journal): *www.tandf.co.uk/journals/carfax/09687599.html*
- *Disability Studies Quarterly* (academic journal): *http://www.cds.hawaii.edu/dsq*
- Society for Disability Studies: *www.uic.edu/orgs/sds*

1

CONCEPTS

This opening chapter provides an introduction to some of the key concepts used in the book – disability, generation and the life course. A distinction is drawn between individual and social models of disability, and the discussion draws attention to the complexity required in explaining disability as a social phenomenon. Four key themes are identified as significant in dealing with disability issues: the body, identity, culture and social structure. The concept of generation is introduced, as an important dimension of social stratification, with reference to different theoretical approaches. The argument suggests that it may be useful to think about relationships of power between different generations as a kind of 'generational system', analogous to gender or class relationships. Finally, the concept of the life course is reviewed, highlighting its importance in contemporary social thinking. This discussion examines the life course in terms of both individual biography and collective social organization. The argument shows how societies and social institutions regulate gendered patterns of life progression, based on shared cultural rules. However, social changes resulting from greater individuation and a more critical understanding of disability challenge these traditional views of what a 'normal' life might be.

Disability

Since disability is the main focus throughout this book, it is not necessary to provide more than a brief introduction here. The emergence of disability studies as an academic discipline has been both rapid and extensive, but has its roots in the activism and experiences of disabled people. It is therefore no coincidence that developments in disability theory have taken place alongside the emergence of an international disabled people's movement, campaigning for equality and full participation in all spheres of social life and human rights. Indeed, the kinds of models and thinking that have allowed academics and researchers to engage in a new and radical reappraisal of disability issues over the past twenty or so years spring directly from ideas developed within disability activism (Driedger 1989; Campbell and Oliver 1996; Fleischer and Zames 2001).

Undoubtedly, the most significant achievements (both academically and politically) have arisen from the development of a social interpretation, or 'social model', of disability that highlights the shortcomings of more traditional and individualistic approaches. Thus, social scientists have increasingly come to view disability as the product of complex social structures and processes, rather than as the simple and inevitable result of individual differences or biology. This historic shift of emphasis, from the individual to the social, has allowed both activists and academics to promote a fundamental and far-reaching critique of the way in which societies disable people with perceived impairments, and to envisage the possibility of more enabling social alternatives. Grasping the underlying distinction between individual and social models of disability is therefore key to understanding contemporary disability debates.

One way to understand this distinction is to think about the life experiences of disabled people. There is now a great deal of evidence to show how people with impairments are often excluded or disadvantaged in important areas of social life, such as education, employment, family life, political participation and cultural representation; or in access to goods and services, like transport, housing, information and so on (e.g. Barnes 1991). One of the big challenges for disability researchers and theorists is to explain how and why this happens. The traditional view within social science and medicine was to assume that someone with an impairment would inevitably find it difficult to perform various 'normal' activities and, as a consequence, would also have difficulty in fulfilling normal social roles (e.g. Parsons 1951). Thus the kind of social disadvantage commonly associated with disability in modern societies was viewed largely as *an individual problem caused by impairment*. From this perspective, the most appropriate social response was either to correct the impairment or to help the person 'come to terms' with it, by negotiating different (less valued) social roles (e.g. Nirje 1969).

By contrast, a social interpretation of disability turns this whole idea on its head, questioning the assumption that there is any necessary causal relationship between having an impairment and becoming disabled. For example, it is clear that the experience of disability varies for different people, in different cultures, and in different periods of history (e.g. Ingstad and Reynolds Whyte 1995). Thus, people with apparently similar biological characteristics might become more or less disabled depending on social circumstance. This implies that the disadvantage often associated with disability might be a social rather than an individual phenomenon, something that is not biologically determined but produced by particular social processes. Crucially, this view suggests that it is not physical, cognitive or sensory impairments that cause disability, but rather the way in which societies fail to accommodate natural aspects of difference between people (e.g. Zola 1989). Consequently, a social interpretation of disability tends to relocate the 'problem' from the individual to society. Disability can then be viewed as *a social problem caused by social processes.*

Individual and social models

These contrasting ways of thinking about disability have been developed more formally in the disability literature as two competing models, commonly known as the 'individual model' and the 'social model'. Traditionally, individual approaches dominated academic understandings of disability, especially in the medical and therapeutic literature. However, it is now social interpretations that largely define the boundaries of contemporary 'disability studies' (Albrecht, Seelman and Bury 2001; Davis 1997; Linton 1998). This distinction between individual and social models of disability was first articulated in an academic context by Oliver (1983) and has been developed at length since then. However, the original impetus came from ideas developed within the disabled people's movement. In particular, Oliver drew directly on a distinction made in the 1970s by activists within a British organization called the Union of Physically Impaired Against Segregation (UPIAS). In an exchange of ideas with other, more mainstream lobby groups, UPIAS argued that 'Disability is something imposed on top of our impairments by the way we are unnecessarily isolated and excluded from full participation in society. Disabled people are therefore an oppressed group in society' (Union of Physically Impaired against Segregation/Disability Alliance, 1976: 3).

Although the original members of UPIAS were building on their experiences as adults with physical impairments in an industrial society, they were also aware of the wider social significance of their claims. Yet, they could scarcely have been aware of the impact that these ideas would have on disability politics in the following twenty-five years. The UPIAS interpretation of disability influenced not only disabled academics like Oliver, but also the definitions adopted by the international disabled people's movement in the 1980s and, through this activism, the formulation of a radical policy agenda for full participation and equality in the twenty-first century.

From the UPIAS definition flows much of what we now understand as the social model of disability. Looking at the wording in more detail, there are four important points. First, the interpretation offered by UPIAS acknowledges that some people do have impairments, but points out that disability is something different, 'imposed on top'. Second, it suggests that disability is about exclusion from full participation in society. Third, and most important, this exclusion is neither necessary nor inevitable (by implication, we could imagine a society in which people with impairments were not disabled). Fourth, it makes sense to think of disabled people as an oppressed social group, and not simply as the victims of individual and tragic circumstance (for a discussion of the UPIAS document, see Oliver 1996).

Social model approaches to disability focus on explaining the social processes and forces that cause people with perceived impairments to become disabled, as a minority group in society. There have been different approaches to this task. For example, some writers have argued for a political economy of disability that explains the oppression of people with physical impairments or learning difficulties as a product of industrial capitalism (Finkelstein 1980; Ryan and Thomas 1980). Here, the emphasis is on identifying structural forces and material relationships of power arising from the division of labour and the factory-based waged economy that excluded many people from participation in paid labour. This was also an argument developed more formally by Oliver (1990). Other writers have emphasized the role of culture and ideas in shaping disability labels and social roles (e.g. Ingstad and Reynolds Whyte 1995; Shakespeare 1994; Ustun et al. 2001). Such approaches often emphasize traditional beliefs and folklore or the continuing reproduction of disabling images in the mass media. However, the differences between cultural and structural approaches tend to be a matter of emphasis, and most social model writers accept that both material and cultural forces play a part in creating the collective social experience of disability (Barnes 1996; Finkelstein 1991; Oliver 1990).

> Hence disability, according to the social model, is all the things that impose restrictions on disabled people; ranging from individual prejudice to institutional discrimination, from inaccessible buildings to unusable transport systems, from segregated education to excluding work arrangements, and so on. Further, the consequences of this failure do not simply and randomly fall on individuals but systematically upon disabled people as a group who experience this failure as discrimination institutionalised throughout society. (Oliver 1996: 33)

A complex phenomenon

For my part, I have found it helpful to distinguish different approaches to disability under four broad headings, using the distinction between individual and social models and also a distinction between materialist and idealist explanations. Broadly speaking, individual model approaches tend to focus on either biological or psychological explanations of disability, while social model approaches tend to focus on either cultural or structural explanations. This typology was originally developed in some detail in an earlier published paper (Priestley 1998b), but it may be helpful to review the framework briefly here.

Within the individual model we can identify two parallel themes of enquiry: one focused on the measurable characteristics of the body and its physical or cognitive functioning (a biological model of disability) and one focused on the negotiated aspects of individual identity and adjustment (a psychological model of disability). Similarly, social model accounts tend to cluster around two types of explanation: one focused on the role of cultural values and representations (a cultural model of disability) and one focused on political economy and disabling environments (a structural model of disability). A simplified form of this typology is shown in figure 1.

It is not necessary to review these distinctions in detail here; suffice it to say that each of the four themes is evident in contemporary writing about disability. In this book, I have not taken a rigid stance on the kinds of writing used to illustrate the various chapters. The overall approach is grounded in social model explanations, both structural and cultural, but I have sought to include a good deal of reference to studies that are more individualistic (including many from the medical or therapeutic literature). For those unfamiliar with

	Materialist explanations	Idealist explanations
Individual models	biology	psychology
Social models	structure	culture

Figure 1. Four approaches to disability.

this diverse theoretical terrain it may be worth consulting the original article (Priestley 1998b) together with some of the reading materials identified at the end of this chapter.

It is important to understand that there is room for a considerable amount of overlap between the basic types outlined above. To take an example, it would be quite wrong to consider all approaches to disability based on the body or impairment as simply biological in their orientation. Indeed, social models of disability have been criticized for ignoring the embodied experiences of disabled people (e.g. Crow 1996) and for 'abandoning' the body to medical science (Hughes and Paterson 1997). Biology is relevant to understanding the body, but environments and social processes play a big part too. Indeed, even the physical characteristics of bodies are shaped by social factors, such as access to nutrition, patterns of work, accidents and cultural practices (see Abberley 1987). Beyond the merely physical dimension, the experience and representation of disabled bodies is also mediated through negotiations of identity, through language and through cultural representation (Corker and French 1999).

Likewise, it would be wrong to think of all approaches to disability based on identity as simply individual. The personal life experiences and identities of disabled people are not simply the product of individual cognitive psychology, but are deeply embedded in the

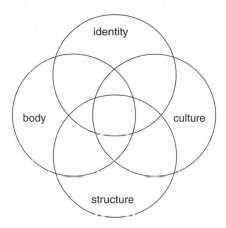

Figure 2. The complexity of disability.

social. Individual identities are negotiated with others in a social context, in response to cultural values and structural forces. They are narrated through language, and situated in social spaces and historical moments (Corker 2001). Consequently, explanations of disability that draw heavily on individually narrated experience or identities are often much more than simply psychological.

These kinds of examples suggest that it might be more appropriate to view the four theoretical approaches outlined earlier as overlapping areas of concern rather than as discreet conceptual 'boxes' fitting neatly into either individual or social models of disability. With this in mind, figure 2 provides a more useful framework for thinking about disability and its various representations in social science.

Looking at disability in this way, the complexities become more apparent. Many of the important questions we want to ask about disability deal with areas of overlap between different kinds of explanation or approach. For example, how do structural changes in the mode of production affect our collective cultural understandings of what it means to be disabled in a particular society? Thus, Burch (2000) illustrates how the unique socio-economic context of pre- and post-revolutionary Russia produced a different kind of 'Deaf identity' to that emerging in the USA and the UK, leading to alternative forms of 'subversive activity' to sustain Deaf culture. Similarly, taking another area of significant overlap, we might ask how far the adoption of disabled identities is influenced by embodied experience and how far by cultural or historical context (e.g. Kalekin-Fishman 2001). And so on.

This framework of multiple approaches is also useful when we think about disability in terms of generation and the life course (the primary focus of this book). For example, we could think about the way that a body and a sense of identity develop over the course of a life, within a particular structural or cultural context. This would involve quite a complex explanation of how biology and psychology interact with objective social positioning, power, language and culture. Keeping all of these factors in view at the same time is a significant intellectual challenge, but offers the potential for a more comprehensive account than could be gained by remaining within a single paradigm of enquiry (for a more detailed discussion of ontological pluralism in social-scientific thought, see Giddens 1984; Miller 1992; Rohrlich 2001). The interaction of different models, both individual and social models, has yet to yield a more general 'social theory' of disability; but such a theory would clearly need to explain the dynamic relationships between all of these contributory factors – biology, psychology, culture and structure.

Returning to the material in this book, it is relevant to note that we could also think about important generational categories (like childhood, adulthood or old age) within the same framework. For example, we could simply substitute the concept of childhood for disability in the model above, since theoretical approaches to childhood have also drawn on the diverse contributions of biology, psychology, culture and political economy (see chapter 3). A similar argument could be made about the generational category of old age (chapter 6), and so on. Indeed, these are recurrent themes throughout the book, drawing parallels between our understanding of disability and generation (the latter is explored further in the following section).

Key points and ideas for learning

To summarize, disability studies is a diverse and vibrant field arising from new and critical understandings of what it means to be disabled in modern societies. It owes its origins to the experiences and activism of disabled people, and has been developed within academia on the basis of a distinction between individual and social models of disability. However, it is important to look beyond this simple dichotomy and to note how different approaches emphasize different causal factors. Although there are many different approaches, it may be helpful to think of four over-lapping themes, focusing on the body, identity, culture and social structure. This typology also offers some interesting possibilities for examining the relationship between disability, generation and the life course.

QUESTIONS
- What is disability?
- What is the difference between individual and social model approaches?
- How do the body, identity, culture and social structure interact in shaping the experience of disability?

EXERCISE: A useful exercise is to examine a piece of writing or research about disability and determine how it might 'fit' within the typology outlined earlier. Does the author's position draw heavily on one of the four basic approaches, or does it contain aspects of two or more positions? How useful is the typology in highlighting the differences between particular authors or pieces of writing?

Generation

A second key concept used in this book is that of 'generation'. This concept is explored in some detail later with reference to childhood, youth, adulthood and old age, and it is not necessary to repeat those arguments here (see chapters 3–6). However, it is important to provide a brief introduction and to explain more clearly how the concept of generation is to be used, since this differs in some respects from the way it is often employed in life course studies and research.

Actual generations and cohort studies

The concept of generation was introduced into sociological theory by the German writer Karl Mannheim (1952). Mannheim noted that although people of the same generation were 'bound together' in some way, they could not automatically be considered as members of a concrete social group. Rather, he argued that generational location may be more similar to social class. Thus, although people are positioned within a particular generation (by virtue of their birth), they may or may not experience any sense of shared generational consciousness or identity. So, while generational location has a biological basis, it is more than this. Generation is also a social location, situated within a social structure and a historical time (i.e. different generations are exposed to different social influences and possibilities). However, Mannheim argued that 'actual' identifiable generations do emerge when there is some conscious bond between them. The identification of a generation in this sense involves a collective sense of identity in relation to other generations.

In this way, generations are often conceived as historical cohorts of similarly aged people who share significant formative experiences that have a lasting effect on their lives and identities, compared with those that went before or go after them. This approach has been widely used in life course research, particularly in explaining how different biographies and generational identities have been shaped by significant historical events (such as wars, economic depression and so on). Thus, Corsten (1999: 249) illustrates how the 'collective cognitive background or horizon of a generation' arises from a combination of biographical, historical and generational perspectives on time. As a consequence, people born into similar societies or families but in different historical epochs may develop divergent world-views and social values. These collective value differences may, in turn, exacerbate existing intergenerational differences and conflict (e.g. Scott 2000).

This kind of approach has been widely used to explain the apparently differing political values and actions of different generational cohorts. Here, a sense of generational consciousness is often seen as important for cohesion or social action at moments of historical importance. For example, Dunham (1998) draws on the experience of the anti-Vietnam War movement in California to demonstrate how younger people with the greatest 'generational consciousness' were also the most likely to participate in peace protest. Similarly, Cherrington (1997) uses Mannheim's approach to examine the distinctive political self-confidence of the 'reform generation' of young intellectuals in the democracy movement of 1980s China, while Misztal (1998) uses a cohort approach to explain the emergence of critical social theory amongst academics in the 1960s. From a disability perspective, Kasnitz (2001) applies a similar line of thought to explain some of the cohort factors involved in the emergence of political leadership within the US independent living movement.

However, political values and participation are by no means the only areas of concern for generational cohort studies, and there has also been a great deal of work examining changing patterns of education, employment, birth rates and family life over successive generations (for some examples, see Giele and Elder 1998; Hareven 1994). Drawing on intergenerational studies in the Netherlands, Diepstraten, Ester and Vinken (1999) conclude that values associated with personal relationships, such as upbringing, family life and sexuality, are actually more indicative of generational location than those associated with the public areas of politics or employment. Thus, the explanations offered by generational cohort studies, arising from Mannheim's approach, have been extremely useful in uncovering shifting patterns of social change, participation and the transmission of culture in contemporary societies. There is a great deal of scope for this kind of approach in disability studies too, examining the changing life experiences of disabled people and generational cohorts in different societies (for an application of some of these ideas, see Priestley 2001).

Generational categories and conflict

An alternative way of thinking about generation is to consider generational location in terms of broad, age-related categories in a society (such as childhood, youth, adulthood or old age). Looking at generation in this way, individuals and cohorts do not remain in the 'same' generation throughout their lives, but instead move through a series of transitions from one generational category to the next (e.g. from childhood to adulthood). This view of generation opens up a whole range of new questions – about the meaning of these categories, and about who is included or excluded from them. For example, when does 'childhood' begin and end? What does it mean to be an 'adult' in society? Has 'old age' changed?

This more categorical approach has been bolstered in recent years by a dramatic resurgence of interest in generational studies. For example, we have seen the development of a 'new sociology of childhood' (Brannen and O'Brien 1995), a renaissance in 'youth studies' (Coles 1986), and a critical reappraisal of approaches to social gerontology (Bengtson, Burgess and Parrott 1997). Such developments have shown how generational categories shift over time, how they are embedded within culture and shaped by structural processes of social change (e.g. changes in the mode of production and labour supply). Thus the social study of generation now provides the focus for a number of distinct sub-disciplines within the social sciences.

Thinking about the meaning of generational categories and the relationships between them also raises questions about generational inequalities, in terms of power and access to physical or cultural resources. In particular, studies of childhood and old age have highlighted the existence of significant intergenerational conflicts, contracts and bargaining (e.g. Caillaud and Cohen 2000; Collard 2001; Johnson 1995; Turner 1998). These debates have been mirrored in the widespread attention paid recently to generational rights and duties (e.g. in the United Nations Convention on the Rights of the Child). In some ways, the current preoccupation with generational inequalities in social science mirrors more traditional discussions of social stratification, linked to social class or gender, for example. It also raises questions about the way in which societies organize and regulate the boundaries of different generational categories and the transitions between them. Irwin (1999) reviews the development of such arguments, summarizing the general approach:

> In these perspectives life course differences are treated as an expression of inequality. Independent adulthood is the key to inclusion and relative advantage, whilst childhood, youth and later life are characterised as socially disadvantaged or marginalised positions. The young and the old are seen to experience exclusion from various forms of meaningful social participation and their voices are unlikely to be heard in contemporary society. In all these approaches life course stages, in particular as they cleave around the tripartite division between childhood (and youth), 'independent adulthood' and later life, appear to have a new significance as dimensions of inequality. (Irwin 1999: 692)

Foner (1988: 176) argues that, although generational inequalities cannot be understood solely in class terms, different age groups are stratified with 'different rights, duties, status, roles, privileges, disenfranchisements'. Age, she argues, is a particularly useful approach, because it alerts us to consider inequalities across the whole life span and not simply in particular age groups (such as those of working age). The purpose in this book is to do just that, with reference to inequalities arising from disability. This is important for two reasons. On the one hand, the similarities of inequality between disabled people of different generations have not always been recognized (e.g. there has been much more attention paid to disability rights for younger people with impairments than for older people). On the other hand, there are important distinctions to be made between the kinds of disability inequality experienced by people in different generations.

In a discussion of childhood sociology Alanen (1994) argues that the adoption of a generational analysis has much in common with developments in gender studies. In particular, she notes the analytical power that was gained by introducing gender as a relational and generalizable concept, one that offers a systematic approach to the examination of all aspects of the social world. Similarly, she suggests that generational concepts (such as childhood) are also relational, because they cannot exist except in relation to one another, and that they offer an important dimension for thinking about social relations more generally. Likewise, McDaniel (2001) argues that there are similarities in the way that generation and gender have emerged as 'social categories and identity signifiers', shaping public debates and public policy. Alanen concludes that it may be useful to think about a 'generational system', analogous to the gender system, at work in all aspects of the everyday social world and social relations. Thus:

> The assumption of the pervasiveness of the gender system implies that all social relations are 'gendered' – so feminists claim, and have substantiated the claim by producing much research. To acknowledge this has the effect of changing the focus from one turned exclusively on women to examining how gender shapes and is implicated in all kinds of social phenomena. . . . Can we accept that all kinds of social phenomena are not only 'gendered' but 'generationed' as well? (Alanen 1994: 37)

The analogy is a useful one, and it is precisely this question that influences the analysis of disability in chapters 3–6 of this book. When we look in detail at the way in which disability is produced and regulated within modern societies, it becomes clear that there are some very important generational dimensions, and that there is indeed a generational system at work. Thinking about disability in terms of generational categories (such as childhood, youth, adulthood or old age) helps us to understand more clearly how disability and impairment are produced, how they are socially constructed, and how they are regulated in significantly different ways across the life course.

Thinking back to the typology of disability theory introduced earlier, some of the same concepts can be applied to thinking about generation. Indeed, there are some striking similarities. Both disability and generation are important social categories. Both rely heavily on the application of labelling based on biological characteristics (e.g.

chronological age, physical and cognitive development, or bodily differences). Both disability and generation involve significant aspects of negotiated identity and accepted social roles. Both can be viewed as categories that are socially constructed through culture, and socially produced through structural changes in society. In this way, the typology used earlier – body, identity, culture, structure – works well in thinking simultaneously about the category of 'disabled' and about generational categories (such as childhood or old age). That is not to suggest that disability and generation are the same thing, simply that they are produced and regulated as social categories in very similar ways.

Key points and ideas for learning

To summarize, generation has become an increasingly important concept in social theory and research. This has been reflected in two areas of concern. First, there is a strong tradition of research examining the changing patterns of experience for particular generational cohorts. Second, there has been a growth of interest in studying generational location in terms of social stratification and inequality. Both disability and generational categories (such as childhood, youth, adulthood and old age) are socially produced, culturally constructed, and regulated through institutions and policies within societies. Relationships of power and conflict also exist between different generations and these play an important part in social stratification. Examining how this generational system works, and applying a generational analysis, offers a useful approach to learning more about social issues like disability.

QUESTIONS
- What are the main differences between people of different generations (e.g. children, adults and older people), and how do we know which generation we are in?
- Which generational groups are more or less dominant in modern societies and why?
- Does it make sense to talk about a 'generational system' within societies?

EXERCISE: It may be helpful to think more about these ideas before tackling the chapters on disability and generational location. One way to do this is by exploring an example in more detail (adulthood is a good example). Think about the way in which adulthood is defined and understood in society. How do we know that someone is an adult, rather than a child, for instance? What can adults do that children cannot? When does adulthood begin and end? Using the four headings of body, identity, culture and structure, try to identify which aspects of these differences are attributable to (a) chronological age or biology, (b) an individual's own sense of generational identity, (c) shared cultural traditions, (d) economic and structural influences. It may also be useful to list some examples of state policies and statutes that define who is regarded as an adult (are these related to a person's age, or to their competence in certain activities?).

The life course

The third key concept underpinning this book is that of the life course. The idea of a life course can be interpreted or understood in a number of different ways. In empirical research, it is often used to describe the life progress of individuals or cohorts over time. Many studies adopt quantitative methods, based on records of life events, although more qualitative and narrative methods have become increasingly popular. Life course methods are quite diverse, involving longitudinal or cross-sectional studies, retrospective or prospective accounts, and focusing on individuals or cohorts (for a fuller discussion of different approaches, see Giele and Elder 1998). For example, Mayer and Tuba (1990) advocate the use of 'life event histories' in chronologically mapping significant life events to explain changing roles and 'transformations of status' over the life course. A similar approach can be useful in identifying the significance of life events and social change for disabled people (e.g. Kasnitz 2001). More qualitative approaches have found increasing favour with researchers seeking to assert the value of 'authentic' narratives in the life histories of disabled people (e.g. Goodley 1996). Looking at individual lives over time is, I believe, a very useful way of expanding our understanding of disability and social change (Priestley 2001). However, the emphasis in this book is on thinking about life course concepts in a rather more general way, as a framework for assisting our understanding of contemporary disability debates.

Regulating the 'normal' life course

Traditional approaches to the life cycle tended to assume a fairly predictable progression through a sequence of life stages broadly linked to biological and chronological ageing (i.e. from birth to death via childhood, adulthood and old age). Consequently, the role of social institutions was seen largely as managing and supporting successful transitions from one stage to the next. For example, we could view historical changes in the social organization of the family, schooling, the labour market or welfare as institutional responses to the challenge of reproducing new generations and ensuring their successful passage through life (or in managing and containing those who 'fail' to make 'proper' life course transitions). Underlying this view, however, is an implicit understanding of the 'normal' life course, an idealized version of life patterns based on cultural norms and rules.

A useful approach is to critically examine some of our commonly held assumptions about progression through life and about the social institutions that regulate this. What, then, is an ideal life course, and what role do social policies and institutions play in policing it? In this ideal world, we are born healthy, we develop naturally as children and progress through education, we become independent young adults, we find work and partners to share our lives with, we establish our own homes and may have children of our own, develop a career, become old, and die a 'good death' (no doubt knowing that we would happily have done it all over again). Such idealized notions of the normal life are also highly gendered, with different expectations of proper work and family roles for women and men. Of course, 'real' life is not so straightforward, and such stereotypes have been brought into question by the emergence of a more contextual and socially constructed view of the life cycle (see Bryman et al. 1987).

However, social institutions continue to shape our understanding of a normal life and the 'problems' that arise when individuals or groups 'fail' to make proper progress through it. For example, from a social model perspective, we might view the history of public institutions and professions dealing with older and disabled people as a social response to these groups' perceived 'failure' to achieve or maintain the adult-centred life course ideals of independence and autonomy (Albrecht 1992; Finkelstein 1991; Oliver 1989). Similarly, Meyer (1988) argues that important social institutions arise in response to the transgression of shared 'cultural rules' associated with normal life course progression:

Individual life course problems are a matter of deep *collective* concern and much of the life course is explicitly and purposefully organized at the collective level in modern society. Improper or inarticulate sequencing, or unjust transitions or inattention to individual development rights, become major problems and institutions arise to manage them properly. The cultural rules of the life course are central elements of these and other major institutions. (Meyer 1988: 58, original emphasis)

Thus, Walker and Leisering (1998) argue that the 'quasi-biological' view of the life cycle has become increasingly outdated, and that the concept of 'life course' helps us to gain a better understanding of the ordering of our lives – driven by individual decision making, yet shaped by public institutions and policies. They argue that regimes of policy and practice play a significant role in structuring life course transitions and the relationships between different generational groups (e.g. through policies for education, social security, employment and pensions). Thus, they perceive a continuing connection between social policies and the construction or maintenance of normal life course progression. Indeed, Brückner (1995) argues that social policy has become 'life course policy', dealing as it does with the negotiation and management of risk over a lifetime (see also Falkingham and Hills 1995).

This is an important observation in the context of this book, since a critical understanding of disability challenges both life course institutions and the cultural rules that define what a 'normal' life means. This argument is then central to understanding the chapters that follow, which are primarily concerned with charting the social organization of life course transitions and their impact in producing and reproducing disability. For example, by understanding more about the social regulation of 'normal' birth, it is easier to appreciate why eugenic debates about who should be born are so hotly contested. Understanding our assumptions about 'normal' child development makes it easier to see why the education and care of disabled children is regarded as such a problem in modern societies. Similarly, understanding more about our idealized expectations of an autonomous adulthood (in relation to work or parenting, for example) helps to explain why disability debates so often focus on dependence and independence. Likewise, understanding more about 'normal' ageing helps to explain why older people with impairments are often overlooked in discussions of disability. These and related issues are discussed in the subsequent chapters. Here, the significant point is simply that we need to understand more about the social regulation of the normal life course in order to appreciate the significance of contemporary disability debates.

Uncertainty and biographical disruption

As mentioned earlier, it is important to distinguish between the apparent certainties of idealized life course models and the comparative uncertainties of 'real' lives. This, in turn, brings into question traditional assumptions about the predictability of 'normal' life course progression, and highlights the increasing fragmentation, uncertainty and biographical risk associated with more postmodern theories of society (e.g. Bauman 1995). Such accounts tend to stress the breakup of traditional life course pathways, based on class, gender or national stereotypes, for example, and the rise of individuation and choice in negotiating the risks of contemporary life (Beck 1992). Put simply: 'Where earlier agrarian and industrial societies provided social scripts, of deferential or collectivised kinds, which most individuals were expected to follow, contemporary societies throw more responsibility on individuals to choose their own identities' (Rustin 2000: 33).

Thus, Giddens (1991) sees the changing patterns of consumption in late modernity as indicative of a shift away from predictable life course trajectories and towards more individual biographical views of chosen 'life styles' or 'life projects'. Given the multiple narrative options and 'props' available to us in a consumerist society, from which we might construct and perform our individual life projects, there are seemingly unlimited possibilities for reflexive biography and 'choosing' our own lives. However, as Giddens (1991: 54) admits, this kind of reflexive self-identity remains contingent upon 'the capacity to keep a particular narrative going'. In this sense, we need to look beyond the individual to the kinds of resources that people are able to draw upon, and the kind of barriers they face in negotiating their lives.

Theoretical interests in biography and risk negotiation have been mirrored in life course research, and this has given rise to a growing stream of biographical writing in the social sciences (Chamberlayne, Bornat and Wengraf 2000; Luken and Vaughan 1999; D. Morgan 1998). Within this approach, much attention has been paid to the role of impairment and disability during life. For example, within medical sociology, particular emphasis has been given to the idea of impairment and chronic illness as 'biographical disruption' (see

Brown and Harris 1989; Bury 1982) requiring 'narrative reconstruction' (G. Williams 1984). In this sense, medical sociology has tended to view impairment as disrupting or subverting our assumptions and explanatory frameworks of the 'normal' life course.

S. Williams (2000) reviews this tradition, and asks whether the idea of biographical disruption remains useful in the context of late modernity. For example, where traditional life course assumptions become blurred through reflexivity, diversity and risk, so our assumptions about 'normal' biography are widened. More specifically, Williams argues that the use of biographical disruption in explaining disability and the life course relies on an 'adult-centred model of illness'. Thus:

> Biographical disruption . . . rests on problematic foundations concerning the 'shattering' of our taken-for-granted assumptions about our bodies, our selves and the world in which we live. In doing so, it fails to account for a range of other possibilities in which illness may already be a central part of one's biography, either from birth, early childhood or in later life. (S. Williams 2000: 60)

It also fails, he argues, to take adequate account of lay understandings about 'normal' illness and impairment during the life course (see Kelly and Dickinson 1997; Pound, Gompertz and Ebrahim 1998). In this sense, generational location and generational identity are very important (e.g. in the case of impairments accepted by many as 'normal' in old age). Consequently, Williams argues that age, timing and context are critical factors, and that we should seek to liberate biographical sociology from adult-centric preoccupations by extending its use to 'both ends of the life course'. This concern mirrors some of the arguments presented later in this book.

The limits of individual biography

Current interest in the individual aspects of identity and biography has contributed greatly to disability studies, by highlighting 'authentic' accounts of disabled people's life experiences. However, there is also a danger that biography on its own, or interpreted within an entirely post-structuralist framework, may lead us back full circle to thinking about disability simply as a life course risk to be negotiated by individuals. Such a move would clearly negate many of the theoretical and political advances gained by viewing disability as a social or collective phenomenon. So it is important to think carefully about the limits of biography in adopting a life course approach to disability issues.

As much feminist writing has consistently reminded us, individuals live relational and interdependent lives with others, together producing intertwined and reciprocally constructed biographies. For example, individual life stories are embedded within the ongoing dialogue of historically situated family histories (Vierzigmann and Kreher 1998). Similarly, numerous other people in circles and networks of interdependence contribute intimately to the construction and reconstruction of an individual biography – parents, peers, partners, carers, colleagues and so on. The use of biographical methods in studying the life course therefore requires a relational, rather than an individualist, view of the way that life course pathways and narratives are constructed.

Meyer (1988) goes further, arguing that the level of explanation offered by individual approaches is inadequate, demanding much more social context. For Meyer, preoccupation with individual models of the life course reflects the dominance of individualist values in Western societies, rather than any 'real' individuation within society. Thus, he expresses concern that individual approaches risk reproducing the cultural values of individualist societies in a rather unquestioning way:

> the modern institutionalized life course structured around the rights and development of the individual may be less a consequence of political and economic changes than a deliberate and grounded reflection of the collective cultural authority given the perspective of the individual. That is, in individualist societies, the elaboration of the structured life course may reflect the culture of individualism more than the efforts of natural individuals or the functioning of an individuating social organization. (Meyer 1988: 50)

The key point here is Meyer's recognition that the life course is not simply an individual matter, but something that is heavily institutionalized and organized within societies (through culture, policy and governance). A great deal of collective effort is invested in the social institutions and cultural processes that shape our progression through life – for example, in the way we manage education, work and care. This is what Meyer is implying when he talks about the 'institutionalized' life course. Within these institutional practices there is still plenty of room for the kind of reflexivity and resistance that biographical methods often reveal. However, that should not hide the fact that the available options for life course transitions and choices are also mapped out within societies at a collective level.

This kind of approach is particularly important if we want to understand disability issues from a social model perspective. Disability studies have been greatly enriched by disabled people's biographical writings and life experiences. None the less, these accounts have become politically meaningful and powerful because they have helped us to understand and challenge disabling barriers. They have been helpful because they enable us to understand more about the way in which disabling societies work, and how people have challenged disabling social relations in real world situations. Finding the connections between individual biography and social barriers is therefore an important task, if sometimes a difficult one. In this sense, biography becomes more than simply individual when it provides us with a window on the social world, or when it provides 'traces' of wider social relations and macro social change (e.g. Chamberlayne and Rustin 1999; Priestley 2001; Ulrich 2000).

Key points and ideas for learning

To summarize, life course concepts and life course research have played an increasingly important role in contemporary social thinking. At the individual level, the life course has been a useful tool in analysing biographical evidence of the risk and uncertainty associated with individuation in modern societies. More broadly, it has been helpful in conceptualizing the way in which 'normal' life progressions are organized and governed through social institutions, in response to structural forces and shared cultural rules. Within the biographical approach, impairment and disability have been widely viewed as disrupting normal life course pathways. Within the institutional view, disability has been presented as a social problem of 'failure' to make successful life transitions. A more critical understanding of disability offers the opportunity to question assumptions about the normal life course and to challenge the institutional arrangements that regulate its boundaries.

QUESTIONS
- Is there such a thing as 'a normal life', and what would it be like?
- How do social institutions (like the family, schools, the media and welfare) shape our expectations of a normal life?

- In what ways may disabled people's life experiences differ from the gendered 'cultural rules' of normal life course progression?
- Should disability be seen as a form of 'biographical disruption' or as part of the normal life course?

EXERCISE: It may be useful to think more about the relationship between individual biography and social institutions in shaping life course pathways. One way to introduce this idea is to critically examine biographical accounts of disabled people's lives. Using two or more pieces of autobiographical or biographical writing, identify the key turning points that had a significant impact on the person's life (both positive and negative). How many of these are presented as personal choices, and how many as external influences? How might life have been different in another time or another cultural context?

Summary

The preceding discussion provides an introduction to ways of thinking about disability, generation and the life course, and illustrates how these have been operationalized in social research. This review suggests that disability should be viewed as a social phenomenon caused by social processes, rather than an individual phenomenon caused by biological processes. However, disability is also a complex concept that can be interpreted on many levels, and it is therefore important to consider a number of possible approaches – for example, in relation to the relative significance of the body, identity, culture and social structure.

Similarly, the concept of generation is open to different interpretations. Here, it is used to define important social categories or life course stages (such as childhood, youth, adulthood or old age). Like the category of disability, these generational locations have been socially produced and culturally constructed. Generational boundaries and transitions are therefore partly about people's subjective perceptions of where they stand in relation to others, and partly about collective frameworks and expectations negotiated through policy and governance. Since there is also a generational system of conflict and power relationships, applying a generational analysis to important social divisions like disability can be a useful approach to studying inequality.

Thinking about the life course as a whole forces us to consider social issues as they affect people of all generations and throughout the life cycle (including birth and death). This is important when we consider disability issues, since it avoids an over-simplification of disabled people's collective experiences and the marginalization of issues affecting underrepresented groups (e.g. disabled children and older people). The life course can be considered as both an individual and a social construct. But the social approach is particularly useful in highlighting how societies and social institutions reproduce idealized notions of what it means to live a 'normal' life. In this context, critical disability studies and disability politics pose some significant challenges to our assumptions about normal life course transitions, and raise important questions about the policies and institutions that regulate them.

SUGGESTIONS FOR FURTHER READING

There is a wealth of literature within the field of disability studies, much of it dealing with the distinction between individual and social models of disability. For an introduction to these concepts it would be useful to read Oliver's (1996) *Understanding Disability*, especially chapter 2. This volume also contains a partial reproduction of the historically significant UPIAS discussion document *Fundamental Principles of Disability*. For an excellent introduction to the development of social thinking about disability, see *Disability: A Sociological Introduction* (Barnes, Mercer and Shakespeare 1999) or *Disability Studies Today* (Barnes, Barton and Oliver 2002). It would also be useful to look in more detail at the article discussed earlier in relation to theoretical typologies (Priestley 1998b). Linton's (1998) book *Claiming Disability* deals with some of the issues in defining disability and disability studies, while a more comprehensive overview of the discipline is provided in *The Handbook of Disability* (Albrecht, Seelman and Bury 2001).

Similarly, there is a considerable literature dealing with concepts of generation and the life course. For an introduction, it may be worth consulting *Methods of Life Course Research: Qualitative and Quantitative Approaches* (Giele and Elder 1998) or *Social Structures and Human Lives* (Riley 1988b), particularly the chapters by Meyer and Riley. A more directly relevant discussion may be found in Arber and Evandrou's (1993) *Ageing, Independence and the Life Course* or Hockey and James's (1993) *Growing Up and Growing Older*. For an application of these ideas to disability, there are a variety of useful contributions in the edited collection *Disability and the Life Course* (Priestley 2001).

2

BIRTHRIGHTS

Building on the concepts developed in chapter 1, this second chapter begins the life course analysis of disability debates by examining birth and the right to life. The governance and regulation of birth decisions provide a useful starting point by highlighting the way in which different human characteristics and lives are valued according to normative life course assumptions. Interventions that influence who will be born frame our understandings of human potential and citizenship, and recent debates have illustrated how disabled lives are often devalued in this way. Within a political context of scarce welfare resources, new technologies and old ideas have shaped the way we think about the birth of disabled children. The discussion introduces the concept of eugenics and its influence in public and personal decision making, including examples of eugenic practices (such as selective abortion and prenatal screening). It shows how birth decisions are increasingly influenced by the availability of new genetic knowledge, and why impairment and disability issues figure so prominently in the management of risk within knowledge societies. The chapter concludes by highlighting the political activism of disabled people on issues of diversity and the right to life.

Birth decisions and the value of lives

One of my purposes in adopting a life course approach in this book is to ensure the inclusion of disability debates across the whole of the life span, rather than focusing on those of importance only to particular generations. In order to do this, it is important to look critically at the way life begins, and how disabling barriers affect the life expectations and life chances of disabled people at birth (increasingly before birth, and even before conception).

Choosing our children

In chapter 1, the life course was identified as a matter of collective social concern, constructed through patterns of 'normal' life progression, framed by shared cultural rules, and regulated through social policies and institutions. In this context, the regulation of birth is a particularly important example. The way that societies govern who should be born tells us a great deal about the value placed on different human characteristics and different lives. Thus, the discussion and examples in this chapter deal with some important and sometimes difficult debates about the value of human life and diversity, and about the selection of who will live and who will not. Although these are not new debates, they have acquired a new significance and currency in contemporary societies.

In particular, the rapid development of reproductive knowledge and technologies expands the potential for intervention in the governance of birth choices. Parents, medical practitioners, policy makers and legislators are all involved in making decisions about who may be born. From a sociological perspective, it is tempting to view the increasing options for selecting birth characteristics as a function of reflexive modernization (presenting increased personal choices in the management of life course risks). However, it is also important to examine the boundaries and contexts within which such choices are made. For such decisions are influenced not only by personal 'choice' but also by professional discourses and state interests.

Birth rates have shown a historic and substantial decline on a global scale, in both industrialized and developing countries, although there are some significant anomalies (Attane 1998; Gajdos 2000; H. Kohler 2000; Salisbury 1998, 1999; Strickland and Tuffrey 1997). Indeed, it is clear that birth rates fluctuate in response to a range of factors associated with social and technological development (Hirschman 1994), including biology, demographic change, methods of fertility regulation, and state policies (Courbage 1994; Fargues 1997; Potts 1997). While no general theory explains all of the trends, the combination of increased technological knowledge and declining birth rates in modern societies has been taken by many to suggest that reflexive choices are now a more significant factor in deciding to have a child than, say, economic necessity, social pressure or chance (e.g. Buchanan et al. 2000; Eastwood and Lipton 1999; Stobel-Richter and Brahler 2001).

Given the emphasis on parental and social decision making, it is important to consider the kinds of birth decisions that are being made and the factors that influence them. This is particularly important in the context of disability, since there is evidence that birth choices are increasingly focused on knowledge about, and perceptions of, impairment. The possibility of finding out more about the biological characteristics of children prior to birth has increased the scope for deciding whether children with impairments should be born at all. But such choices are also embedded within cultural discourses of personhood and citizenship that influence how we think about the value of disabled lives, such as the perceived pressure on mothers to produce a 'normal baby' (Ettorre 2000). Although the genetic and medical technologies that inform birth decisions are relatively new, the underlying moral and eugenic arguments must be understood in a more historical context (these ideas are discussed in more detail later).

Determining which human characteristics are socially desirable or undesirable, and where we 'draw the line' between them, is therefore central to decision making about who should or should not be born (Buchanan et al. 2000; Wolbring 2001). In this context, impairment characteristics are generally seen as undesirable, and practices such as genetic counselling, prenatal screening and selective abortion are widely offered as a means to reduce the number of disabled children born. This in turn reinforces the low social and economic value attributed to the lives of those who do survive. For policy makers and disability activists alike, birthrights and bioethics have thus become hotly contested fields of current debate (see Shakespeare 1999).

> Worldwide, disability organizations, disability rights activists, and theorists have taken up the question of how the increasing use of prenatal testing and selective abortion affects the place of people with disabilities in the world. . . . However, the vast majority of theorists and health professionals still argue that prenatal testing, followed by pregnancy termination if an impairment is detected, promotes family well-being and the public health. To them, it is simply one more legitimate way of averting disability in the world. (Asche 2001: 306)

A *wrongful life*?

At the heart of these debates is an argument about whether it is right, or even acceptable, for a person to begin life with an impairment when such a life could be prevented. Birth decisions are, of course, not based on any knowledge of the actual life that someone with a particular biological characteristic might live. Rather, they rely on our imaginings of the kind of life they might live, based on current knowledge about how people with similar characteristics live in the world today. Thus, to confront birth choices at the beginning of the life course is also to confront the criteria we use to value different lives in society. As the subsequent chapters in this book will show, disabled people's lives have been widely devalued on many levels – as biologically inferior, as psychologically damaged, as culturally 'other', and as presenting an economic 'burden' to welfare capitalism. Consequently, it is hardly surprising that contemporary birth choices continue to be framed within a pervasive view of disabled lives as wrongful lives.

A graphic example of this view is provided by recent developments in medical litigation in Western industrialized societies. Within this context, there has been a dramatic increase in legal suits brought by parents concerning the 'wrongful birth' of disabled children (Gold 1996). These cases involve an action brought by the parents of a child born with impairment characteristics that could have been detected prior to birth (through screening). The implication is that medical diagnosis, genetic counselling and selective abortion could have prevented the birth (and that parents should be financially compensated for the task of raising a disabled child whom they did not wish to have). This may be accompanied by a parallel action, brought on behalf of the child, to compensate for their 'wrongful life' (Laudor 1994) – a life that, by implication, should not have been lived.

For example, a high-profile case in France generated substantial public debate when, in November 2000, the court awarded damages to Nicolas Perruche, a teenage boy born with multiple impairments after his mother contracted rubella during pregnancy (the mother argued that she would have had an abortion if the correct diagnosis had been given). Two similar rulings involving children with Down's syndrome led to widespread protest by the French disability community. In addition to public pressure, French gynecologists refused to carry out ultrasound scans for fear of liability, and the French Parliament was forced to introduce a bill overturning the court ruling and outlawing claims to wrongful birth. Legal actions for wrongful birth have been recorded in many other countries, but have been most prominent in North America. For example, at least twenty-five US state legislatures have now enacted laws recognizing claims to 'wrongful birth' or 'wrongful life' (for a more detailed discussion, see Waldman 1990). The legal literature has emphasized a need to clarify professional responsibilities in such cases (e.g. Norrie 1991; Petersen 1997; Shapira 1998; Um 2000). However, Shepherd (1995) argues that the increasing pressure to produce children without impairments means that parents too require legal protection, particularly when they choose to bear children with genetic differences.

The construction of a 'wrongful life', and its formalization in law, seems to go to the very heart of the debates in this chapter. Even when sophisticated states have grappled at length with the complexities of reproductive rights and medical technologies, they have eventually fallen back on a simplistic moral framework that characterizes life with impairment as wrong. Yet those who argue that we should prevent the birth of children with impairments wherever possible, and many do, are making a significant assumption about the relationship between impairment and disability (outlined in chapter 1). The assumption is that people born with certain *biological* characteristics, those defined by medicine as impairments, will inevitably go on to lead disadvantaged lives (and that this will also disadvantage the lives of their families and society as a whole). Asche (2001: 307) summarizes this view:

> First, people with disabilities are more costly to society than others, and society should use its resources for children and adults who will not have impairments. Second, either the lives of disabled children are so miserable that they are not worth living at all, or they are more miserable than the lives of nondisabled children are expected to be. Third, the lives of parents and family members will be harmed by the psychological, social, and economic burdens of caring for the child, and these burdens will not be offset by the expected psychic and social rewards of raising a child without a disability.

However, as Asche points out, social models of disability challenge the reasoning that underpins these assumptions, suggesting that oppression and disadvantage result primarily from *social* rather than *biological* causes. To recap on earlier arguments, it is not biological difference that causes disability, but our inability to accommodate human difference in society. From this position, it is not biological differences that need to be removed from the world, but disabling barriers; it is not disabled lives that are 'wrongful' but disabling societies.

Key points and ideas for learning

The economic pressures of population growth and new developments in medical knowledge have combined to increase the possibility and the incentive to make more choices about the birth of children. Looking at the ways in which societies govern and regulate these choices can tell us a great deal about the social value attributed to different human characteristics and lives. Disability has figured prominently in these debates, with an increasing emphasis on the social responsibility to produce 'normal' babies. Thus, the potential for greater 'choice' over the biological characteristics of future generations must be viewed within a social context, in which disabled births are increasingly characterized as 'wrongful' births, as lives that should be prevented. Such arguments draw on a variety of justifications relating to biology, identity, culture and economics. However, advances in disability politics and rights are beginning to challenge the assumption that people born with particular impairments will inevitably lead devalued lives. Consequently, it is important to examine critically those policies and practices that seek to prevent the birth of disabled children.

QUESTIONS

- What evidence is there that parents are now in a better position to 'choose' their children?
- Why is control over biological characteristics so important in making birth decisions, and should parents have the right to expect a 'normal' baby?
- Can there be such a thing as a 'wrongful birth'?
- Are life opportunities for disabled people today more or less affected by biological differences than they were in the past?

EXERCISE: Consider the competing arguments for preventing or supporting the birth of children with impairments. What would be the impact of any substantial increase or decrease in the number of people born with impairments? List these impacts using the following four headings: (a) the effect on the biological diversity of a society, (b) the effect on the self-identity of disabled people, (c) the effect on cultural values about disability, (d) the effect on the economy. It may be useful to debate the conflicting positions in a classroom or online discussion. Should children be born with impairments if this can be prevented? Is there any scope for some middle ground or compromise in this debate?

Eugenics, old and new

In order to understand the social implications of birth choices in contemporary societies, it is important to appreciate the historical significance of past practices. Social regulation to 'improve' the physical,
cognitive and moral characteristics of human populations has a long
history, but was most clearly expressed in the state-sponsored eugenic
movements of the last century. However, the apparent increase in
reflexive choice and risk negotiation in contemporary consumer societies suggests that it may be useful to distinguish between public policies and personal choices. The following sections provide an overview
of these debates, using examples to illustrate the complex relationship between public and personal eugenics.

A brief history of eugenics

The term 'eugenics' (from the Greek *eugenes*, meaning 'well born')
refers to philosophies for selecting the characteristics of people in a
population, and to practices for 'improving' the genome of that
population (specifically, deciding who should be born, who should
die, and who should reproduce). D. Galton (1998) traces early
eugenic influences to the writings of Greek scholars such as Aristotle
and Plato (see also Barnes 1996; Garland 1995). However, the development of eugenic thinking and its widespread practice during the
twentieth century can be considered as a more modernist project,
linked to the scientific revolution of the nineteenth century and to the
political development of the modern nation-state.

   The pioneer of modern eugenics was an English scientist named
Francis Galton (strongly influenced by his cousin Charles Darwin).
Galton became fascinated by human variation, and particularly by
variation in mental ability. In 1869 he published a book entitled
Hereditary Genius, in which he sought to show that 'natural abili-
ties are derived by inheritance, under exactly the same limitations as
are the form and physical features of the whole organic world'
(Galton 1869: 1). Galton wanted to see scientific knowledge of
human variation and ability used to increase the presence of 'good
genes' in subsequent generations. Although the causal logic behind
his conclusions left something to be desired, Galton's eugenic ideas
became enormously influential (see Galton and Galton 1998). The
idea that science could provide the basis for 'improving' populations
proved popular with politicians and social thinkers of the time, many

of whom had expressed concern about the poor health of their national populations and armed services.

The development of statistical methods gave further impetus to the measurement of human variation. In particular, Galton's emphasis on the mathematical modelling of 'deviation' from the 'normal' allowed for the cultural labelling of certain population groups as genetically inferior. For example, Trent (1998) highlights the display of disabled people as 'defectives' and 'primitives' at the 1904 St. Louis World's Fair in the USA. As Foucault (1977) argues, defining abnormal groups as 'the Other' is an important prerequisite in any process of normalization. So it was that the definition of people with certain impairments as statistically abnormal and inferior provided eugenicists with a scientific and moral justification for seeking to eradicate those characteristics from the population. As Selden (2000) concludes, eugenic attempts to 'improve' the populations of nation-states should thus be seen as a modernist project of normalization.

By the early twentieth century, scientific eugenic beliefs were widespread within modern societies, not only in Galton's native Britain but throughout mainland Europe, North America, Scandinavia, South-East Asia and South America. Early eugenic philosophies were highly racialized, and human capital or value was frequently represented in terms of 'racial types' – particularly in segregated and racist societies like the USA (Selden 1999). Eugenic societies were created in England, North America, Scandinavia, Italy, Austria, France, Japan and South America. Many of the leading eugenicists were active campaigners, seeking legislation to reduce non-white immigration and to reduce the presence of other 'inferior' peoples (for an account of developments in Britain, see Mazumdar 1992). So-called 'positive' eugenics promoted the procreation of the most desirable in society (e.g. through selective breeding or artificial insemination), while 'negative' eugenics sought to reduce the procreation of the least desirable (e.g. through segregation, abortion, birth control or sterilization). There is not room here to review these developments in detail, and numerous authors provide useful overviews (e.g. Kevles 1985). However, it is important to note that perceptions of impairment and disability figured prominently and consistently in eugenic debates throughout the world, alongside issues of 'race' and gender.

Policies to prevent the birth of disabled children were often justified on economic grounds. For example, the American Eugenics Society was keen to compare the apparently low cost of sterilizing or segregating people with learning difficulties with the high cost to society of supporting future generations of 'defectives' (see Larson

1995). Such arguments were persuasive to policy makers concerned with productivity and welfare expenditure. Thus, in Britain, D. Porter (2000) shows how eugenic concerns with 'mental deficiency' became a central organizing principle in the development of social policy from the late nineteenth century. Similar developments and objectives were apparent in other Western European countries, such as France, although developing later than in Britain or the USA (Drouard 1992).

It is important to see the rapid development of eugenic ideas in the context of imperialism and the modern nation-state. The spread of Western eugenic thinking, with its emphasis on national identity and 'racial' purity, generated some paradoxes for other countries. For example, although American eugenic thinking characterized Asian populations as genetically inferior, providing grounds for reduced immigration from those countries, Japanese scientists and policy makers appeared comfortable with the application of eugenic logic to their own population (Otsubo and Bartholomew 1998). Here, the focus was again on disability. Japan's National Eugenic Law (passed in 1940 and modelled on developments in Nazi Germany) sought to improve the 'quality' of the Japanese population by reducing the number of children born with inherited impairments. Although the law was reframed in 1948, as the Eugenic Protection Law, the emphasis on preventing 'defective offspring' remained until its amendment in 1966 (see Morita 2001).

The spectre of twentieth-century eugenics is most commonly associated with the imagery of mass murder and genocide under Hitler's administration of the German Third Reich, and Nazi doctors were certainly among the first to develop systematic approaches to measuring disabled people's lives in terms of economic 'value' (see Burleigh 1994, 1998). However, while the eugenic methods pursued by Germany in the 1930s and 1940s were clearly extreme, it is important to remember that they drew extensively on ideas that were current throughout the modern world, and which emanated largely from Britain and the USA. Indeed, Mehler (1997) argues that scholars have been misguided in characterizing eugenics as 'a marginalized or obsolete movement of the radical right', given that such ideas were so widely adopted by different groups in different countries (including, for example, prominent liberals, Communists and Catholics).

Public and personal eugenics

The brief review above might suggest that the widespread implementation of eugenic policies to control disabled births during the twentieth century exemplifies what social theorists would see as the key features of the modernist nation-state (Bauman 1987). For example, eugenic principles were based on categorizing different population groups using rational scientific methods. They reflected concerns with the strength of nations, based on a desire to maintain racial 'purity'. Eugenic concerns also mirrored the imperative for productivity, social order and social conformity inherent in the social relations of industrial capitalism. In addition, the methods used to monitor human characteristics and to implement eugenic 'solutions' arose from technological advances in the bureaucratic and hierarchical apparatus of the modern state (see Bauman 1989).

By contrast, it is harder to view current practices for the regulation of birth in quite the same way, since analyses of postmodern or late modern societies tend to emphasize reflexivity and consumer choice over uniformity and state control (Bauman 2001). In this context, birth decisions today are increasingly seen as individual negotiations of life course risk or as attempts to reduce biographical uncertainty (Beck 1992). It is therefore useful to distinguish between eugenic decision making at the individual level and that at the level of the state, although the two are closely intertwined. Birth decisions, in richer technological societies at least, are now more likely to be based on individual attitudes than mass state-sponsored programmes. This might suggest that we are witnessing a move away from traditional 'societal cultural eugenics' towards a new kind of 'personal eugenics' based on informed consumer choices (Wolbring 2001).

However, it is important to remember that parents are not the only ones involved in making reproductive decisions, and that doctors and other health professionals play a major role (Iredale 2000). Given the relative power of the medical profession, particular concern has been raised about the prevalence of eugenic thinking amongst those with such influence. For example, a survey of nearly 3,000 geneticists in thirty-seven countries (Wertz 1998) found widespread evidence that individual eugenics influenced the kind of advice and information available to parents (particularly in Asia and Eastern Europe). The study showed that negative views of people with congenital impairments were prevalent amongst geneticists, and that the spread of 'non-directive' counselling was the exception rather than the rule. But individual attitudes do not tell the whole story. Economic context is also important, particularly since the vast majority of future births, more than nine out of ten, will occur in developing countries (Galjaard 1997). Although there is great diversity in the majority world, structural economic pressures have led many states to express their desire to control population levels more directly, and to reduce the incidence of birth impairments.

Experiences in China provide a useful example in this respect, highlighting the complex relationship between public and personal eugenics. China is the world's most populous country, with more than 1.3 billion people, and there has been much public concern with policies for population control (Attane 1998; Thomas and Price 1996; J. Wu 1994). In addition, China has seen a higher than average incidence of children born with genetic impairments (Chen and Simeonsson 1993; Luo 1988). China's response has been to promote birth control and to instigate a formal policy of 'one couple, one child'. With only one chance available to parents, it could be argued that the social pressure to have a 'normal' child carries much greater weight for Chinese families (Harper and Harris 1986). In addition, parental decisions are heavily regulated by state policies. Consequently, 'personal' decision making by Chinese parents occurs in a structural context of economic imperatives to reduce population growth, and in a cultural context where state intervention in private life is an established norm.

The pressure on Chinese parents to exercise eugenic choices was bolstered, in 1994, by the introduction of the Infant and Maternal Health Care Law, which required physicians to perform premarital 'checkups' and to investigate potential genetic 'disease' (referring to any condition that might undermine a person's future independence). Where such conditions are 'considered to be inappropriate for child-bearing *from a medical point of view*', marriage is permitted only on the couple's agreement to contraception or sterilization (Article 10, emphasis added). Thus, the relationship between the medical profession and the state in promoting eugenics in the Chinese context has been viewed as particularly important.

In the cross-cultural study noted earlier, Chinese geneticists were identified as unusual in their strong support for state intervention in parental birth choices, and the vast majority agreed with the basis of existing laws on the use of abortion to eliminate impairment characteristics (Mao 1998; Mao and Wertz 1997). Indeed, more than 90 per cent agreed with the statement that 'it is not fair for a child to be brought into the world with a serious genetic disorder if the birth could have been prevented', while four out of five felt that disability would never be overcome for those with more severe impairments, even with social support (Mao and Wertz 1997). These findings also indicated a lack of awareness about disability policy. More than half the Chinese geneticists believed that there were no laws against disability discrimination in China, although, as E. Stone (1996) points out, such laws have existed for some time. Indeed, Article 3 of the 1990 Law on the Protection of Disabled Persons clearly states that 'Disabled persons shall enjoy equal rights with other citizens in political, economic, cultural and social fields, in family life and other aspects. . . . Discrimination against, insult of and infringement upon disabled persons shall be prohibited' (quoted in Stone 1996: 472).

In seeking to explain the views of Chinese geneticists, Mao suggests that:

> This may be because, although the rights of people with disabilities have been protected constitutionally in China, there are no Chinese laws specifying whether people with genetic conditions should be protected as disabled people. This survey also suggests that most Chinese still regard disabilities as a severe burden for both family and society. Population and disability issues are universal. As the history of the Western eugenics movement has shown, these issues are to some extent likely to produce a social 'medium' or environment for the 'birth and growth' of eugenics. (Mao 1998: 692)

In the West, there has been considerable concern about the eugenic potential of China's approach, both within the scientific community (Morton 1998; O'Brien 1996) and within disability studies (E. Stone 1996). However, the situation is complex. Eugenic policies on the birth of disabled children sit uncomfortably alongside public commitments to disability rights, while Western bioethics conflicts in many ways with traditional Chinese values (Lee 2001; Z. Wu 1994). Economic imperatives, as well as culture and politics, play a large part, and the strength of state regulation suggests that there is considerably less scope for parental 'choice' than might be assumed in many other countries (e.g. Lisker, Carnevale and Armendares 1999). As the Chinese example illustrates, it is often difficult to separate personal and public eugenics.

The case of selective abortion

The most obvious example of personal eugenic decisions to prevent the birth of children with impairments is the use of selective abortion. As R. Hubbard (1997) puts it, selective abortion involves significant decisions about 'who should and should not inhabit the world'. Debates around abortion are morally contentious, with many people taking principled and often irreconcilable stands – such as an absolute assertion of 'the right to life' or 'a woman's right to choose'. Abortion policies are hotly debated, and the resolution of moral conflict is rarely clear-cut, as recent debates over the legality of abortion in Germany have shown (Simon 2000). In practice, it would be difficult to separate any real life discussion of disability and abortion from these wider debates. However, taking a moral or feminist position on abortion *per se* does not necessarily involve having a view on disability and eugenics (for a discussion of these issues, see Sharp and Earle 2002). What is more important in the disability debate is to establish where the practice and regulation of abortion is applied *differently* to children with perceived impairments than to those without.

In this sense, personal abortion choices are commonly influenced by state policies. For example, in Britain the law on abortion is applied differently where 'there is substantial risk that if the child were born it would suffer from such physical or mental abnormalities as to be seriously handicapped' (Abortion Act, subsection 1.1.d). Although the risk of injury to the mother or any existing children can justify abortion up to twenty-four weeks, termination on the grounds that a child might be 'seriously handicapped' can, in theory, be carried out legally up until birth. This distinction has been the subject of much recent debate and, in June 2001 the UK Disability Rights Commission (DRC) considered a request from the anti-abortion group Life to advise Government that these aspects of the Act were discriminatory against disabled people. In a statement, the DRC concluded that:

> The Section is offensive to many people; it reinforces negative stereotypes of disability and there is substantial support for the view that to permit terminations at any point during a pregnancy on the ground of risk of disability, while time limits apply to other grounds set out in the Abortion Act, is incompatible with valuing disability and non-disability equally.

The situation in Britain is unusual, in that most countries do not allow later abortion on the grounds of impairment. However, in practice there is considerable scope for interpretation by medical staff. For example, drawing on research in Australia, Savulescu (2001) demonstrates that criteria for the late termination of pregnancy were applied inconsistently, and that the consequences for disabled people were potentially discriminatory and eugenic. The following case study illustrates this situation and highlights the uneasy relationship between personal decision making, state policies and the medical profession.

In July 2000 the coroner in Victoria, Australia, began an investigation into the late termination of pregnancy for a forty-year-old mother, who had chosen abortion when it was discovered that the foetus exhibited achondroplasia (often described colloquially as 'dwarfism'). The woman, who was thirty-two weeks pregnant when the termination was carried out, had threatened to commit suicide if hospital staff did not accede to her request (abortions are technically illegal in Victoria, but permitted where the mother's physical and mental wellbeing are at risk). The example of selective abortion for achondroplasia was also significant because the condition is not generally regarded as an extreme case. Indeed, it is not generally associated with fatality, with extreme suffering, or even with extreme exclusion from social participation (e.g. Shakespeare 1998). Many people with achondroplasia live full and happy lives, yet medical practitioners have been shown to have little objection to termination of pregnancy when it is detected, even though this generally involves late term abortions that would not be permitted for foetuses without those characteristics.

Following the termination in question, three senior medical staff were suspended pending an internal investigation, and there was a heated debate about the issues at an open meeting of hospital staff, attended by more than 200 people. The case attracted a good deal of media attention, and the following comments are some of those reported in the Australian press at the time:

> the fact that this was a late gestation pregnancy and that the foetal malformation present was not one that was lethal are matters that were substantive to our concern. (Professor Glenn Bowes, Hospital Medical Director)

> It makes me angry. It makes me sad. We're short. So what? Ultimately it comes down to a self-esteem issue. . . . It needs to be reinforced that dwarfism is not a death sentence and life remains very much full of promise. (Francis Kelly, chair of Short Statured People of Australia)

> It's time for the Australian hospital management to support doctors when they are making these decisions. (Professor Julian Savulescu, Murdoch Children's Research Institute)

> I would not see anything wrong. The woman counts for more than the foetus. (Dr John McKie, Centre for Human Bioethics, Monash University)

At the extreme end of the scale is the real fear that society will say, 'Why should we be paying out for expensive medical care for people when there was a choice for them not to have been born in the first place?' (Julian Gardner, Public Advocate)

Having a disability is just part of the rich and diverse community we live in and the real issue shouldn't be how we eliminate people with disabilities, it is how we embrace diversity in the community. (Phillip Ripper, Action for Community Living)

These examples provide a useful illustration of the range of arguments used to justify or challenge personal eugenics. Here we can see that there are a number of competing claims relating to the rights of different groups – people with achondroplasia, the mother, the doctors and the economic interests of society. Mirroring some of the core themes in this book, there are biomedical concerns, identity concerns, cultural concerns and structural economic concerns. Although selective abortion decisions in consumer societies are perhaps the most obvious example of personal eugenics, involving parents in individual risk negotiations, they are rarely 'free' choices. Economic, professional and state interests continue to play a role.

Key points and ideas for learning

To summarize, eugenic policies and practices are concerned with limiting the diverse characteristics of human populations by selecting and deselecting certain characteristics. Eugenic thinking has a long history, and can be seen in many societies throughout the world. However, important developments in science and state bureaucracies allowed eugenic thinking to find a more concrete expression during the twentieth century, particularly in modern nation-states. Disability issues figured prominently, and public programmes to prevent the birth of disabled children were widespread. More recent analyses have tended to emphasize the increasing significance of 'personal' eugenic decisions, involving consumer choices and individual risk negotiations by prospective parents. The case of selective abortion to prevent the birth of children with impairment characteristics is the most obvious example of personal eugenics. But the distinction between the personal and the public remains contested, because economic imperatives, cultural values and the power of the medical profession continue to be significant factors in shaping reproductive choices.

QUESTIONS
• Why did eugenic policies become so widespread in modernist nation-states during the twentieth century?
• Does it make sense to distinguish between 'personal' and 'public' eugenics?
• What are the main constraints and influences on parents' decision making about the birth of disabled children?
• Does the adoption of a disability rights perspective on birth decisions require a 'pro-life' position on abortion?

EXERCISE: Consider the Australian example of selective late term abortion discussed above. Using this summary and the illustrative comments as a starting point, consider the arguments that might be presented by different sides in an investigation of the case. Who might be called to give evidence? What might be the outcome of such an investigation? What should it have been? Consider using role-play for a classroom or online debate in the form of a mock enquiry into this or a similar case. It may also be useful to consult the Short Statured People of Australia (SSPA) website at *www.sspa.org.au* and the review of ethical issues in late-term abortions for foetal abnormality published by the Medical Practitioners Board of Victoria (available online at *www.dhs.vic.gov.au/ahs/report*).

New choices or old issues?

As mentioned in the preceding sections, recent developments in medical knowledge and technology have had a substantial bearing on eugenic debates. In particular, advances in genetic research offer the possibility of detecting and selecting a wide range of different biological characteristics. It is therefore important to ask how far these developments offer new consumer choices in the management of risk, and how far they may lead to a retrenchment of old eugenic ideas. The following sections consider the relevance of specific practices, such as genetic screening and pre-implantation diagnosis, and the wider implications of expanding genetic knowledge for disabled people.

Genetic screening and consumer choice

The practice of screening for impairment characteristics varies considerably between countries (e.g. Chadwick et al. 1998). However, two main areas of intervention are evident: screening to identify carriers of a genetic characteristic before conception (e.g. parental genes for sickle cell anaemia or cystic fibrosis) and screening to identify foetal characteristics after conception (e.g. muscular dystrophy or Down's syndrome). The purpose in both cases is ostensibly to provide parents with the wherewithal to make informed reproductive choices, so that they may decide whether to proceed with a pregnancy. Screening has become an increasingly popular option, and there is much support amongst doctors for programmes to detect genetic characteristics associated with impairment.

Recent advances in reproductive technology also introduce the possibility of *selecting* certain birth characteristics, rather than simply eliminating unwanted ones. The key examples here are in vitro fertilization and pre-implantation diagnosis ('test tube babies') and gene therapy ('designer babies'). The fact that such procedures avoid the thorny moral issue of abortion means that it is much easier for parents and doctors to make eugenic birth decisions. Here, the sense of consumer choice becomes very real, because there may be a number of actual genetic offspring to choose from (e.g. in deciding which egg to implant). Thus, King (1999) argues that the increasing preference for pre-implantation screening may be leading us towards a new kind of 'free-market eugenics'.

The efficacy of genetic screening is generally justified in two ways: in terms of costs and benefits, and in the provision of informed choice. Cost–benefit analyses suggest that the economic cost of screening and abortion compares favourably with the cost of supporting people who might otherwise be born with significant impairments (e.g. Vintzileos et al. 1998; Wald et al. 1992). The major criticism of such approaches is that they tend to define disabled people simply as a financial 'burden' to society, while failing to address their potential contribution. The second justification, that screening allows parents to make more informed reproductive choices, is also problematic, since this assumes that the information provided is both accurate and relevant. As we will see, this may often be a questionable assumption.

Public trust in the accuracy and certainty of medical knowledge has been increasingly brought into question within consumer societies (Illich 1975; Zola 1977), and knowledge derived from genetic screening is no exception. For example, although consumers may be preoccupied with gaining 'accurate' medical information (Wertz and Gregg 2000), some screening tests are notoriously unreliable (see Painton 1997). More critically, genetic screening presupposes that knowing more about *biological* characteristics provides sufficient evidence for parents to make birth choices. But this masks the fact that such choices should also be based on *social* considerations (e.g. on what we know about the life opportunities available to people with impairments in society). Thus, Asche (1999, 2000) argues that parents should have much more access to evidence from the disability movement that questions the assumed link between impairment and negative quality of life.

Reviewing the literature on prenatal screening for Down's syndrome, Alderson (2001) also questions whether parents or professionals have access to the full range of evidence, particularly where negative images are reproduced in clinical discourse and media representations. Thus, she concludes that a greater awareness of the social model of disability and its evidence base would support more informed choices and moral arguments. Similarly, Shakespeare (1998) emphasizes the social context of reproductive decisions, including the gendered and professionalized power relationships that surround screening processes. He draws attention to evidence suggesting that greater numbers of terminations result when mothers are reliant upon medical advice, and on obstetricians in particular, than when non-directive counselling is provided. Consequently, he concludes that:

> we should argue for the provision of positive information about disability, alongside the clinical material, in order that the choices made by prospective parents can be as informed as possible. Disability equality resources could be balancing the 'medical tragedy' information with more realistic accounts of living with a disabled child and, indeed, living as a disabled adult. (Shakespeare 1998: 681)

The assumption of 'informed choice' in birth decisions is therefore problematic when there is no parity in the kinds of knowledge available to parents, and particularly where reproductive choices are presented within a moral framework that devalues disabled lives. For mothers in particular, this raises the question of whether a woman's 'right to choose' includes the right to choose impairment (Bailey 1996; Rock 1996). Within the medical professions there is a widespread assumption that screening for impairment is offered to parents on the understanding that they will choose termination in the event of a positive test result. For example, leading British embryologist Bob Edwards was widely quoted when he argued that the availability of screening gave parents a moral responsibility to avoid the birth of disabled children: 'Soon it will be a sin of parents to have a child that carries the heavy burden of genetic disease. We are entering a world where we have to consider the quality of our children' (reported in *Sunday Times*, 4 July 1999: 28).

Such arguments highlight an important contradiction in the justification of screening for impairment before birth. On the one hand, screening is promoted as a way to provide parents with informed consumer choices in an information age. On the other hand, its acknowledged goal within biomedicine is to prevent the birth of children with impairments. Illustrating these conflicts, Jallinoja (2001) reviews a prenatal screening programme in Finland, identifying tensions for the staff between the programme's two stated objectives of 'preventing disability' and increasing maternal choices (nursing staff were particularly uncomfortable with the rationale of financial savings used to justify the recommendation of abortions).

Given the considerable influence of biomedicine over birth decisions, there must then be considerable doubt about the degree of real 'choice' offered by screening programmes (Farrant 1985; Harper and Clarke 1997). In the absence of more critical disability perspectives it is easy to see why negative cultural assumptions about the value of disabled lives often go unquestioned. Cunningham-Burley and Kerr (1999) argue that the medicalized discourses of contemporary genetics reinforce divisions 'between science and society', and that this has the effect of bolstering the 'cognitive authority' of clinicians and scientists, at the expense of more critical perspectives. Within this power–knowledge context, a little knowledge can be a dangerous thing, and an over-reliance on genetic knowledge can lead to a self-limiting, self-disciplining eugenics amongst would-be parents (Loeppky 1998). Thus, the expansion of national screening programmes for genetic characteristics, such as Down's syndrome or cystic fibrosis, has given rise to widespread concern amongst disability campaigners, parents and some health professionals about the potential for more widespread eugenic practice.

Normality and diversity in knowledge societies

As the screening debate illustrates, knowledge and information are key to understanding contemporary reproductive choices. More

generally, social theorists have argued that information and knowledge networks are defining features of post-industrial societies (e.g.
Castells 1996; Drucker 1993), in which knowledge relationships are
power relationships (Bohme 1997; Steinbicker 2001), with a significant influence on biographical decision making (see Delanty 2000).
In information societies, genetic knowledge is becoming ever more
important in the management of life 'risks'. In this context, the preceding discussion raises some important questions. For example,
what kinds of knowledge should be available? And what responsibilities exist to acquire the necessary information? The examples cited
earlier address some of these issues. But it is useful to reflect further
by examining the implications of expanding genetic knowledge for
disability and diversity in knowledge societies.

The most significant developments have arisen from the Human
Genome Project. This international, fifteen-year project was initiated
in 1990 by the US Government, in order to study and map the
detailed structure and characteristics of human genetics (with particular reference to understanding more about the function of human
genes in impairment and disease). Researchers in the UK recently
completed the task of mapping some three billion base pairs in
80,000 genes, providing a working 'map' of the entire human
genome. Much emphasis has been placed on the scale and complexity of this scientific challenge, but there has also been an increasing
concern with the social, legal and ethical implications (e.g. Greely
1998; Wattanapitayakul and Schommer 1999).

Fundamental to these debates, and of great significance to thinking about birth decisions relating to disability, is the question of who
should know about our genetic make-up and why. Takala and Gylling
(2000) identify four groups of people who may wish to gain information about our genetic make-up. They argue that genetic knowledge can be useful to individuals in helping to 'draw up our life plan'
and to family members with whom we might be genetically linked
(see Juengst 1999). However, they have greater reservations about the
rights of other groups, such as employers, banks and other commer-
cial interests (see Stepanuk 1998; Zimmerman 1998), or the wider
availability of screening information in society (Markham 1998).
They conclude that 'As long as people whose genes deviate from those
of the average individual are likely to face suspicion and discrimination, societies cannot legitimately force people to know about their
hereditary composition' (Takala and Gylling 2000: 174).

Access to genetic information raises particular concerns for minority genetic groups, including groups of disabled people, about confi-

dentiality and the potential for new forms of 'genetic discrimination' (Wattanapitayakul and Schommer 1999). Significantly, genetic knowledge offers the opportunity to prevent births not only where future impairment appears certain, but also where it appears possible in the future. For example, how should doctors respond to the knowledge that a foetus has a genetic predisposition to later life impairments such as Alzheimer's (see Kapp 2000). Prediction and the calculation of risk are thus key components in birth decisions based on genetic knowledge. Although proponents of the new genetics are optimistic about the power of 'predictive medicine' (Gilger 2000), the prediction of many conditions remains both difficult and uncertain (Turney and Turner 2000), particularly in relation to cognitive or behavioural characteristics (Balaban 1998).

Aside from these technical arguments there remains an underlying concern that the increasing currency of genetic knowledge reduces the social value of human lives to the level of biology. Thus, Fitzgerald (1998) concludes that we are witnessing an increasing 'geneticization' and 'commodification' of the self, with considerable implications for disabled people. Although the Human Genome Project was initiated within a 'culture of impartiality and empiricism', she argues that its impact devalues disabled lives (particularly within a climate of economic rationalism). Consequently, disabled writers have been concerned that the biological reductionism of genetic knowledge may offer an unwelcome return to medical and individualized models of disability (e.g. Newell 2000). In a similar way, Ettorre (2000: 409) notes the limited bodily discourse offered by the new 'genetic moral order': 'As a powerful way of injecting biology into social relationships, reproductive genetics constructs the idea that genetic capital, pedigree (i.e. "pure" breeding) and ultimately, social fitness can be ranked. But, of course, this ranking is carried out in already unequal social contexts in which gender and disability are devalued.' This she sees as a disciplining process in the management of women's reproductive bodies, exploiting the traditional eugenic language of 'defective genes' and cultural discourses of 'shame'. It is, she argues, a process that constructs a very limited view of the impaired body, and increasingly denies embodied agency.

More broadly, there is concern that the new genetic knowledge will impact not simply on individuals, but on identifiable social and ethnic groups, whose genetic capital is viewed as undesirable, or at the very least devalued (Greely 1998). For example, Dodson and Williamson (1999) raise concerns about the political, economic and ethical implications for indigenous peoples, while Tangwa expresses concern that regulation may impose a genetic normalization based on Western values:

> globalisation may simply translate into westernisation, given the Western world's dominance and will to dominate the rest of the globe. How is global bioethics to be possible in a world inhabited by different cultural groups whose material situation, powers, ideas, experiences and attitudes differ rather markedly and who are not, in any case, equally represented in globalisation efforts and fora? (Tangwa 1999: 218)

If the new genetics does pose a threat to global human diversity, then it is important to ask which characteristics are most likely to be targeted in eugenic birth decisions. This is not simply a technical scientific question, but is deeply embedded in social and cultural processes.

> Technologies are not neutral; they are social and political phenomena, and the field of bio/gene technology research is no different. It has the potential to fundamentally alter society, to divide us into two classes: those whose characteristics are in tune with expectations and those viewed as undesirable. Whenever it is detected that a human being is not measuring up to societal expectations, whether prior to birth or after, the 'offending' person will have his or her right to exist put at risk. Different characteristics will be targeted, depending on the cultural, political, philosophical, economical and spiritual background of any given society. (Wolbring 2001: 38)

Writing from a disability perspective, Wolbring asks how we can 'draw the line' between different characteristics, such as impairment, sex or sexuality (for a discussion on sexuality, see Gabard 1999). Medical ethicists have consistently sought to justify impairment selections, while opposing selection based on other characteristics such as sex. For example, the World Health Organization guidelines on prenatal diagnosis prohibit only screening for paternity or the sex of a foetus, the implication being that these would be unacceptable grounds for termination of pregnancy. As Henn (2000) argues, this leaves open the possibility for 'genetic consumerism' in selecting a number of other 'desirable' characteristics, such as intelligence or longevity.

The common distinction between screening for impairment characteristics and for other genetic characteristics has led to a polarization of the debate between disability activists and the scientific community (Shakespeare 1999). For example, these competing views were evident in a published exchange between Harris (1993) and Reindal (2000). Harris argued that aborting a foetus with significant impairment characteristics, or seeking to cure such impairment through gene therapy, did not amount to 'preferring' non-disabled over disabled lives. Rather, he argued that gene therapy offered the chance for the 'genetically weak' to give birth to the 'genetically strong'. In her reply, Reindal (2000: 93) disagreed, arguing that 'the very idea of "curing" disability is the core element in the discrimination of disabled people because the "curing ideal" resides in conformity and normalcy . . . in other words, full participation in society is found through cure or fortitude'.

In February 2000, representatives of disabled people's organizations from twenty-seven countries met in the UK for a conference organized by Disabled People's International Europe on disability, bioethics and human rights. The outcome was a joint statement entitled *The Right to Live and be Different* (Disabled People's International Europe 2000). In their statement, commonly referred to as the 'Solihull Declaration', delegates expressed concerns at the exclusion of disabled voices from bioethical debates and called for greater support in advocating alternative perspectives. Under the heading 'Richness in Diversity' the declaration includes the following claims:

> We are full human beings. We believe that a society without disabled people would be a lesser society. Our unique individual and collective experiences are an important contribution to a rich, human society.

> We demand an end to the bio-medical elimination of diversity, to gene selection based on market forces and to the setting of norms and standards by non-disabled people.

Drawing attention to the threat that biotechnological developments pose to disabled people's human rights (particularly the right to life), the declaration then makes six specific demands. These include:

> An absolute prohibition on compulsory genetic testing and the pressurising of women to eliminate – at any stage in the reproductive process – unborn children who, it is considered, may become disabled.

> That having a disabled child is not a special legal consideration for abortion.

> That no demarcation lines are drawn regarding severity or types of impairment. This creates hierarchies and leads to increased discrimination of disabled people generally.

Clearly, such claims cut to the heart of the issues debated in this chapter. In particular, they highlight an argument against the eugenic deselection of children with impairments, based on the value of human diversity and the universality of human rights to life.

Key points and ideas for learning

To summarize, rapid advances in genetic science have a substantial bearing on eugenic debates and birth decisions. The widespread use of genetic screening, arising from advances in scientific knowledge and the Human Genome Project, provides increasing opportunities for eugenic decision making that avoid the contested moral territory of abortion. In knowledge societies, genetic information is increasingly important in informing reproductive decisions and risk negotiation. However, such developments also resurrect old eugenic debates about which human characteristics are desirable and which lives are worth living. The biological reductionism of the new genetics has thus prompted considerable criticism from minority groups, including disability activists, concerned with issues of human diversity and human rights.

QUESTIONS
- Do advances in genetic knowledge and biotechnologies offer greater choices or greater constraints on decisions about the birth of disabled children?
- Does the greater availability of genetic knowledge place a new social responsibility on parents and professionals to avoid the birth of children who might develop impairments during their lives?
- To what extent should the new genetics be seen as 'eugenic'?

EXERCISE: Using the extracts from the Solihull Declaration, consider the implications of discussing disability and impairment in terms of (a) 'disease' and (b) 'diversity'. Are these 'extreme' positions? What alternatives are there? Should birth selection on the basis of perceived impairment be treated differently from the selection of other characteristics, such as sex, height or intelligence? Critically examine some of the suggested readings at the end of this chapter and identify the sorts of arguments used by the authors to support or contest the deselection of children who may face disabling barriers in their future lives.

Summary

The discussion in this chapter introduces a life course approach to disability debates by considering the social regulation of who will be born. The examples illustrate how states have applied different rules and different moral frameworks to regulate the right to birth of children with and without perceived impairments. Although the case of abortion, especially late-term abortion, provides the most graphic and challenging examples, eugenic birth decisions are framed by power–knowledge relationships. In knowledge societies, eugenic decision making relies on the ability to detect unwanted characteristics and on the availability of knowledge about their likely impact (on the child, the parent or on society more generally). Where unwanted characteristics are not detected prior to birth, prenatal selection is not an option, and this may explain the position of those who have argued for a ban on all prenatal screening.

Historically, there has been a shift of emphasis in the eugenic debate from state-sponsored programmes towards the consideration of personal eugenics. It is helpful to think of these trends as reflecting a shift from modernist to late or postmodern analyses of society. In this sense, the practice of personal eugenics offers a useful illustration of individual risk negotiation and reflexive consumer choice. However, the relationship between personal and public eugenics is complex, and decisions are often regulated by state policies or professional practices. In addition, birth decisions remain deeply embedded within cultural discourses that devalue the potential of disabled lives. Thus, the supposed value of life-style diversity in a globalizing world sits uneasily alongside the increasing use of eugenic technologies to regulate and control who should be born.

SUGGESTIONS FOR FURTHER READING

There is a wealth of literature concerning the development of eugenic thinking and practice. For an overview it would be useful to look at Kevles's (1985) book *In the Name of Eugenics*, or the article by Galton and Galton (1998). From a disability perspective it would be useful to compare the work of some prominent contributors, including Shakespeare's (1998) article on genetics and disability equality, Asche's (2000) book *Prenatal Testing and Disability Rights*, or Wolbring's (2001) chapter on 'drawing the line' between different genetic characteristics. On the specific question of abortion,

R. Hubbard's (1997) contribution is also a useful starting point, while Pfeiffer (2000) argues that medical model classifications of disability continue to play to the eugenic agenda.

There is a wealth of Internet sites devoted to the discussion of bioethics and eugenics, many directly related to disability equality issues. The following resources are therefore indicative, providing links to other relevant sites. In addition, it may be useful to consult some of the general disability resources noted in the introduction to this book.

- National Reference Center for Bioethics Literature at Georgetown University: *www.georgetown.edu/research/nrcbl/scopenotes/sn28. htm* (a good overview, with reference to various countries and sources)
- For historical information on the development of American eugenics, see *www.amphilsoc.org/library/exhibits/treasures/aes.htm* and *www.eugenicsarchive.org*
- Eugenics: *www.thalidomide.ca/gwolbring/eugenics.htm* (a comprehensive source of links to both pro-eugenic and anti-eugenic source material)
- The Pro-Choice Forum: *www.prochoiceforum.org.uk* (for debates on abortion issues)
- Human Genome Project: *www.ornl.gov/TechResources/Human_ Genome* (US government gateway to a wealth of information and links)

3

DISABILITY AND CHILDHOOD

Moving on from birth decisions and the right to life, this chapter explores the relationship between disability and childhood. The chapter begins with an introduction to theoretical perspectives, highlighting a tension between the 'new sociology of childhood' and traditional child development theory. As a generational category, childhood in contemporary societies shares much in common with the category of disability – for example, in the way it has been socially produced and culturally constructed. Historically, there are also parallels in the social regulation of children and disabled people. Both have been denied attributions of agency, competence and civil rights. Both have been subject to differential mechanisms of surveillance and control by more powerful, non-disabled adults through policy and institutions. There is also a sense in which disabled adults, particularly those with learning difficulties, have been perceived as eternal children. The final part of the chapter addresses two prominent public debates regarding the situation of disabled children in contemporary societies: children's rights and inclusive education.

Thinking about childhood

The framework adopted in chapter 1 suggests that there are important relationships between disability and generation, including the way they are constructed and governed as social categories. The discussion in this chapter returns to those core themes by analysing the specific relationship between disability and childhood. However, childhood itself is not a straightforward concept, and has been interpreted in different ways within academic writing and research. So, as an introduction, it is helpful to review the key theoretical positions as a context for thinking about the disability debates raised in subsequent sections.

Towards a new sociology of childhood

There have been some major developments in the theory and study of childhood, most notably in the development of a 'new sociology of childhood' (James, Jenks and Prout 1998; James and Prout 1997). Until recently, childhood remained largely untouched by the sociological gaze (Brannen and O'Brien 1995; Butler and Shaw 1996), and traditional approaches tended to study children indirectly, through institutions like the family, schools and welfare services, or through macro-level statistical analyses. However, by the 1990s, there was evidence of a more critical approach (see Cunningham 1995; Qvortrup et al. 1994). This new paradigm involved a fundamental reappraisal of the concept of childhood, in its social and historical context, an acknowledgement of children's rights, and a more active engagement with children themselves.

Thus, James, Jenks and Prout (1998) draw a distinction between our current understanding of Western childhood and what they describe as the 'pre-sociological' imaginings of children that dominated previously. In the latter category they identify five significant themes. These include historical portrayals of the child as evil (as amoral, undisciplined and self-gratifying) yet also innocent (angelic, romantic and uncorrupted). They note the construction of children's potential for growth and learning (either as a 'blank page' to be written on or as 'naturally developing') and the emergence of psychoanalytical theory, in which childhood was viewed as the unconscious foundation for adult dysfunction. Although these pre-sociological constructions present us with some contradictory images, they also share a certain similarity. Thus, 'The gathering principle for the set of models assembled here is that they begin from a view of childhood outside of or uninformed by the social context within which the child resides. More specifically, these models are unimpressed by any concept of social structure' (James, Jenks and Prout 1998: 10).

Although recognizing the role of environment and adult influence, traditional views overlooked the social significance of childhood as anything more than a stage on the road to adulthood. As Waksler (1991: 63) puts it, 'Children are viewed as in their very nature not grown up and thus *not something* rather than *something*.' The emphasis in both theory and policy was on mapping the pathways of child development to determine the kind of interventions that would ensure safe passage to adult status. Thus, Alanen concludes that:

> Two perspectives dominate: children are understood either as beings in a gradual process of growing up in order to become adults and members of society at some future time or, because of their present immature and socially unfinished condition, as problems and victims of, or nuisances to, the everyday running of the (adult) social order. The effect of both perspectives has been to keep children outside the proper concerns of sociology. (Alanen 1994: 27)

Where contemporary theorizing departs from these pre-sociological accounts is in the significance accorded to social context and structure. More recent theorizing has constructed childhood as a distinct social phenomenon, with structural significance and cultural meanings. James, Jenks and Prout (1998) suggest that four general approaches have contributed to this new approach. These they characterize as the 'social-structural child', the 'socially constructed child', the 'minority group child', and the 'tribal child'. Although it is not necessary to explore these concepts in detail, it may be helpful to summarize the key themes.

Childhood is recognized as a distinct generational location in all societies, so we can think of the 'social-structural child' as a global phenomenon (Qvortrup 1994). However, children also exist in relationships of power and conflict with other generational groups (notably adults). So it is also useful to think of children as a minority group with claims to personhood and citizenship. This view of the 'minority group child' has been highly influential in the debate over children's rights (discussed later). However, the difficulty with these approaches is that they present a view of childhood that is universal when, in fact, there are many cultural variations (Ariès 1962). In order to address this cultural relativism, it is therefore helpful to view childhood as a social construction. This allows us to look more closely at the situated experiences of children in different social contexts, and at children's agency in shaping those contexts. Linked to this view is the idea that children's worlds, with all their meanings, cultures and rituals, exist largely beyond the experience of adults. This view of the 'tribal child' suggests that children's lives and cultures can also be treated as anthropological phenomena, where children are the primary social actors (see James, Jenks and Prout 1998; Opie 1993; Opie and Opie 1959).

Following these theoretical developments, disability researchers have shown an increasing interest in the experiences and perspectives of disabled children themselves. For example, Watson et al. (1999) worked alongside disabled children in England and Scotland to examine their perspectives on everyday life. This study revealed high levels of adult surveillance in disabled children's lives and the complex nature of their interactions with others (e.g. in families, schools and leisure activities). Within these worlds of children, the attitudes of parents, professionals and peers also influenced the development of disabled children's self-identity (e.g. Priestley 1998c; Priestley, Corker and Watson 1999). Thus, Wolman and Basco (1994) found that self-esteem amongst disabled adolescents was more likely to be bolstered when parents treated them in age-appropriate ways and when they were more permissive about children's social participation.

Stoneman (2001) reviewed research on disabled children's relationships with their siblings and parents. Contrary to the negative assumptions of some researchers, she showed that such relationships are consistently as positive and interactive as those of non-disabled siblings. Yet, as time goes on and children grow older, the social and territorial gap between disabled and non-disabled children often widens (as a result of discrimination and disabling barriers). The enforced separation of disabled children from the everyday worlds of other children is therefore a factor in reinforcing negative or stereotypical attitudes amongst both peers and parents (e.g. Nikolaraizi and Reybekiel 2001; Russell, John and Lakshmanan 1999).

Placing the emphasis on children's perceptions and experiences, Davis and Watson (2001b) and Priestley (1998c) illustrate how disabled children encounter discourses of 'normality' and 'difference' in school, arising from institutional factors and everyday cultural practices. In particular, the construction of disabled children as a homogeneous group within institutions often overlooks the diversity and richness of their everyday lives. Thus, the new sociology of childhood, with its emphasis on listening to children's voices, calls into question policies and services that treat disabled children as a single category, denying the complexity of their identities and experiences (Priestley 1998a).

The tyranny of 'normal' child development

Our understanding of childhood in modern societies has been heavily influenced by child development theory. The work of influential child psychologists such as Piaget (1959) and Erikson (1968) provided a view of children as developing towards adult competences through a sequence of predictable stages. At the same time, biomedical knowledge and technologies offered an array of new tools for measuring children's bodies and minds against physical and cognitive norms. By defining childhood as a sequence of measurable stages towards adulthood, classical child development theory established a rigorous definitional framework of what it means to be a 'normal' child. In so doing, it marked out the boundaries of deviation from developmental norms, and provided the administrative basis for treating children with impairments as not only different but also 'sub-normal' or 'developmentally delayed'.

The normalization of child development has resulted in an array of standardized developmental sequences and timetables, against which children can be compared (e.g. in their physical growth and morphology, locomotion and physical co-ordination, speech and language, sensory perception, cognition and reasoning, intelligence, 'reading age' and so on). Such approaches have also spawned a burgeoning industry of assessment and evaluation in child health, welfare and education. Indeed, judgements about children's 'developmental delay' or 'failure to thrive' continue to provide the basis for determining interventions in children's lives, and are widely used to separate children into distinct administrative categories (such as the category of disabled).

> Judged against these normative yardsticks, the imperfectable bodies
> . . . of disabled children were inevitably constructed as inferior – as
> 'backward' or 'developmentally delayed'. Moreover, as children were
> exposed to ever more scrutiny, so children with impairments became
> disproportionately subject to new forms of surveillance, discipline and
> control (through institutional 'care', 'special' schooling, medical treat-
> ment, 'corrective' surgery, 'remedial therapy', eugenic abortions and
> genetic 'screening'). (Priestley 1998a: 208)

Discourses of normal child development are significant, because they impact directly on disabled children's lives (Bloch 2000). Yet, the application of child development theory in professional training is often over-simplified. Lubeck (1996), for example, suggests that teacher training based on a universalist modernist approach fails to deal with the sheer diversity of children's development (see also Stott and Bowman 1996). Thus, the validity of child development measures has come into question. For example, Pecheux (1999) suggests that predictive 'developmental timetables' have been too unequivocal and atheoretical to be of much use in common-sense or contextual understandings of children's development. Similarly, measures derived from the norms of the majority have been criticized for a lack of transferability to minority children (e.g. children of colour in the USA), and for failing to take proper account of factors such as social class, poverty, discrimination, oppression and segregation (e.g. Coll et al. 1996; Najman et al. 1992). In this way, more recent studies have begun to highlight alternative perspectives based on the social diversity of human development, rather than its biological universality (Hauser-Cram et al. 2001).

Thinking back to the beginning of this chapter, it is evident that classical child development theory and its associated practices owe much to a pre-sociological view of children as incomplete adults. It is then the perceived norms and competences of *adulthood* that define the goals and milestones of normal child development. Consequently, the idea that disabled children are 'developmentally delayed' is based on a socially constructed concern that they are 'failing', or may fail, to become the kind of autonomous adult citizens that modern societies appear to require (see chapter 5). The developmental emphasis has implications for disabled adults too. Indeed, the term 'developmental disability' has been widely appropriated to describe those with lifelong impairments, especially learning difficulties (Sandieson 1998; Smith 1999). The effect of such labelling is to define those who develop differently as underdeveloped or incomplete people, throughout their lives.

Early sociological approaches to childhood also focused on development, using the concept of socialization (the processes through which children learn to adopt adult norms and roles). The emphasis here was to understand the transmission of adult culture from one generation to the next, and how this might be achieved through the organization of socializing institutions like the family or schools (e.g. Parsons 1951). However, as James, Jenks and Prout (1998) point out, such an approach assumes that children are simply the passive recipients of adult influences, and that existing adult patterns of society are both fixed and desirable. Failure to assimilate to these adult norms is then regarded as social dysfunction. In this context, disabled children have been constructed as a significant social 'problem', giving rise to enormous investments in 'special' institutions and professions geared towards their assimilation into normal adult roles (or their confinement where this is perceived as unlikely). Thus socialization approaches have similar implications for disabled children to approaches based on developmental psychology. Yet, the focus for intervention has shifted – from correcting the biological or cognitive characteristics of the errant child to correcting the structures and processes of ineffective institutions.

In particular, there has been a strong focus on the effectiveness of institutions concerned with disabled children (in health and social care, child protection and schooling, for example). This preoccupation with institutions rather than children is reflected in the domestic sphere too, where disabled children's concerns have often been subsumed into collective notions of the 'disabled family' (Hurt 1981; Topliss 1979). It is then *families*, rather than *disabled children*, who are seen as the service users, emphasizing the supposed 'burden of care' for parents, particularly mothers (e.g. Baldwin and Carlisle 1994; Ferrari and Sussman 1987). The danger then is that the experiences of disabled children themselves may easily be overshadowed by the needs of adults and their institutions.

To summarize, understanding the construction and regulation of 'normal' child development helps to explain why disabled children continue to be regarded as a significant social problem, both individually and collectively. Judged against adult-centred and non-disabled norms, children with impairments are likely to be defined as 'failing' or as 'developmentally delayed'. However, contemporary critiques of classical child development theory and modernist socializing institutions suggest that social responses to childhood in contemporary societies must respond more flexibly to the diversity of human development.

Key points and ideas for learning

The way we now think about childhood as a social phenomenon differs in a number of ways from traditional and pre-sociological approaches. We are now less likely to view children simply as 'unfinished' adults, and less likely to view their development as simply biological or 'natural'. We are more likely to encounter explanations of childhood that emphasize cultural meanings and children's rights, and more likely to encounter the voices and experiences of children themselves. The development of a more critical, and socially situated, study of childhood has opened up a wealth of discussions, and the preceding review suggests a number of themes that may be directly relevant in considering the relationship between childhood and disability.

QUESTIONS
- To what extent should we think of child development as bio-logically determined or as socially constructed?
- What effect do models of 'normal' child development have on children with impairments?
- Why are children whose development differs from the norm viewed as a social problem, and what are the main challenges to this view?

EXERCISE: It may be useful to think more about the similarities and differences in children's development, and about the social signifi-cance for disabled children. Begin by making a list of the most important developmental 'milestones' in normal child develop-ment. Try to include examples that relate to physical development, cognitive development, social development and emotional devel-opment. For each milestone, consider what happens to children whose progress towards these milestones is regarded as 'delayed'. Think about the likely impact in terms of (a) the body, (b) the child's own sense of identity, (c) cultural attitudes towards such children, and (d) the economic implications for society.

Culture and structure

The preceding sections suggest that disabled childhoods are not simply biologically determined, but also culturally constructed and socially produced. In order to examine this argument, it is useful to draw parallels between the construction of childhood and disability. For example, there are many similarities in the ways that children and disabled people (of all ages) have been represented through culture – as innately evil, innocent, vulnerable or dependent upon non-disabled adults. Similarly, there are significant parallels in the structural location of childhood and disability – for example, as social categories exempt from participation in adult labour markets. This in turn may help to explain why children and disabled people have been subject to similar forms of adult surveillance and institutional regulation in modern societies.

Kill or cure

Historical responses to childhood impairment in Western societies appear to reflect long-standing cultural values. For example, Dutton

(1996) points to the preoccupation with bodily perfection and physical and intellectual fitness in ancient Greek culture. Garland (1995) notes these traditions, and identifies similar values and practices in ancient Roman culture. In that context, children born with significant impairment characteristics were viewed as undesirable, and frequently abandoned or killed, sometimes as a requirement of local states (Tooley 1983). However, as Barnes (1997a) points out, it is important to view such practices as more than simply 'cultural', since there were also significant structural and economic imperatives towards human perfection in these imperial slave societies.

Pursuing the cultural theme, Haffter (1968) draws attention to the portrayal of certain children in pre-Christian European folklore as 'changelings' (peculiar beings brought by demons or fairies to replace the 'real' child that should have been there). These myths also suggested that the proper child could often be returned if the changeling could be persuaded to interact, or if it was treated so badly that its non-human parents would take pity and reclaim it (e.g. by beating, burning, poisoning or exposing the child). Thus, the changeling myth both explained the birth of disabled children and absolved parents of their responsibility for bringing such a child into the world.

> It explains the presence of the abnormal child by supposing that it is not a human creature at all but a subhuman one which was not borne by the mother but surreptitiously substituted for the real child shortly after birth. . . . It was not merely that the powers of the underworld were made responsible for the misfortune; the whole struggle with the calamity was seen as a struggle with the powers of the underworld; they must be propitiated, outwitted or rendered docile by brutal methods. (Haffter 1968: 57–8)

Historical practices of infanticide and torture appear extreme, but they illustrate the degree of negative social value attributed to disabled children's lives in early Western culture. While institutional infanticide was largely outlawed in later Judeo-Christian and Islamic cultures, the construction of disabled children as unnatural and flawed remained deeply rooted. With the rise of scientific rationalism and medical knowledge, attention turned increasingly to the possibility of correction and cure. Thus, the cultural construction of disabled childhoods continued to emphasize a desire to resolve or eliminate impairment characteristics. Keith (2001) pursues these themes in her gendered analysis of disability in classical English fiction for girls, showing how impairment and disability featured as prominent and pervasive metaphors in the plot and narrative of children's fictional lives (see also Davidson, Woodill and Bredberg 1994). Reflecting on her reading, Keith notes that:

> At one point in my research for this book it felt like there was hardly a girls' novel since 1850 which didn't have a character who at some crucial stage defied their guardian and fell off a swing or out of a sled, became paralysed through tipping out of a carriage, or was suffering from some nameless, crippling illness from which they could, indeed must, be cured, . . . there were only two possible ways for writers to resolve the problem of their characters' inability to walk; cure or death. (Keith 2001: 5)

For these authors and their child characters, the prospect of future adult life as a disabled person was simply not an option. Since the child could not remain disabled, the narrative resolution required either a miraculous cure, usually resulting from a thorough moral examination of the self, or a premature death. There are numerous examples; suffice it to say that the construction of disabled childhoods as unnatural and requiring elimination, through death or cure, is a powerful tradition. As the examples in chapter 2 show, social interventions to prevent lives with childhood impairment raise eugenic concerns. For children who are born with impairment characteristics, there may then be considerable pressure to 'correct' the perceived abnormality, particularly in technological consumer societies.

Thus, Shakespeare and Watson (1998) argue that the main problem facing disabled children is that they live in a society that devalues their difference, viewing their existence as problematic, and ultimately undesirable. This view is then enacted in very real ways upon children and their bodies through intensive and often expensive programmes of therapy, surgical intervention and behavioural modification. They conclude:

> We may no longer follow the traditional route of abandoning or killing disabled children (in most cases), but we are keen to invest immense amounts of money in developing techniques to prevent them from being born. . . . If by any chance an impaired child slips through this screen, an array of techniques is available to intervene surgically and attempt elimination of the physical abnormality. The word orthopaedics, we may want to remember, derives from the Greek for 'child correction'. (Shakespeare and Watson 1998: 20)

In this context, we might question a wide variety of systematic attempts to make disabled children walk, speak or appear 'normally'.

Westcott and Cross (1996) examine some of these examples, and argue that we should consider such practices as serious institutional child abuse. Similarly, in her study of children's consent to surgery, Alderson (1993) highlights corrective procedures concerned less with ensuring disabled children's personal welfare or intrinsic quality of life than with enforcing their physical compliance with norms of appearance or conduct. Not only are such interventions socially problematic, but the effect on children's sense of themselves can also be very negative – for example, by reinforcing feelings that they are either unloved or inadequate (Middleton 1996: 37).

A useful example is provided by recent debates on the use of corrective surgery to change the facial characteristics of children with Down's syndrome (e.g. Glasper and Powell 1999). Reviewing the issue, Aylott (1999) argues that the increasing uptake of this surgery is a direct response to discriminatory social attitudes. R. Jones (2000) goes further, arguing that such procedures serve no clinical purpose other than the normalization of children's appearance, and that they are therefore analogous to other forms of mutilating child surgery, such as female circumcision. This argument appears to be supported by evidence that the acceptance of children with Down's syndrome has less to do with physical appearance than with opportunities for social interaction (e.g. Cunningham et al. 1991; Saviolonegrin and Cristante 1992). Thus, Aylott (1999) questions why there should be such an interest in normalizing surgery at a time when children with Down's syndrome are becoming more integrated, and when disability culture is challenging disablist attitudes in society. Social theorists have sought to explain consumer interest in cosmetic surgery and body modification as an expression of cultural resistance and human diversity (see Brush 1998; Featherstone 2000). However, cosmetic modification for disabled children appears to run counter to this more postmodern trend. Not only is children's agency denied when parents and doctors choose surgery for them (Alderson 1993), but enacting discourses of normalization on children's bodies appears to directly undermine claims to human diversity.

To summarize, the historical construction of disabled childhoods in Western culture has drawn heavily on images of the unnatural, the inhuman and the undesirable, justifying interventions to eliminate impairment characteristics through death or cure. Thus, institutional attempts to modify the physical appearance and behaviour of disabled children can be construed as significant cultural practices of normalization, reflecting modernist obsessions with conformity. However, such traditions and practices appear to sit uncomfortably alongside more recent claims to human diversity arising from both disability culture and reflexive consumerism.

Vulnerability and dependency

A second theme in the cultural construction of disabled childhoods is that of vulnerability and dependency. Here, the similarity between images of disability and childhood as dependent states is striking, including the construction of people with certain kinds of impairments as eternally 'childlike'. This is particularly evident in the historical construction and treatment of people with learning difficulties, where early attempts at institutional discipline and moral education were frequently justified through the representation of such people as innocent or untamed children (see e.g. Goodley 2000; Ryan and Thomas 1980). A similar line of argument might be applied to the historical construction of insanity and the institutional treatment of those so defined. Thus, in *Madness and Civilisation*, Foucault describes how hospital patients were characterized as children, and how institutional regimes contributed to the daily reproduction of their infantilization: 'Madness is childhood. Everything in the Retreat is organised so that the insane are transformed into minors. They are regarded as "children who have an overabundance of strength and make use of it" ' (Foucault 1967: 123).

Drawing on contemporary practices of institutional infantilization, Hockey and James (1993) conclude that the imagery of dependency is key to understanding the cultural otherness of children, older people and disabled people as 'non-persons' (i.e. non-adults). Indeed, perceptions of dependency are central in cultural parallels between childhood and disability, and the similar ways that children and disabled people have been governed through adult-centred policy and institutions. Here it is important to note that childhood dependency is not simply biologically determined, but also culturally constructed and socially produced (Shamgar-Handelman 1994: 251). The definition of childhood in any given society varies according to the extent of children's dependency on adults (e.g. the age at which children leave home or cease to be financially dependent on their parents). This in turn determines the extent of adult responsibilities to care for children and adult rights to exercise discipline over them. In the case of disabled children this is significant, since their dependency has been constructed as both longer lasting and qualitatively different from that of other children. Understanding constructions of dependence and independence is therefore important in thinking about the differential regulation of disabled children's lives.

In an early review of research on childhood disability and the family, Philp and Duckworth (1982: 48) suggested that parental rejection of some children with impairments was related to 'the child's failure to develop independence'. Yet, it might be more accurate to assert that such a tragedy-laden evaluation resulted from the impact of disabling barriers and the value attributed to independence, particularly in adult-centred Western societies. This is particularly relevant when we consider that parental perceptions of age-appropriate independence for children vary considerably within and between cultures. For example, Gannotti, Handwerker, Groce and Cruz (2001) examined parental perceptions of childhood impairment in Puerto Rico, and found differences from data collected in the USA. In particular, they draw attention to the relative value placed on interdependence, parental nurturing and protectiveness in Puerto Rico, arising from different social relationships between children and adults.

Similarly, Werner (1993) argues that sustainable relationships of interdependence between families and neighbours in self-reliant rural village communities offer a key resource for disabled children in developing countries that are largely absent in urban neighbourhoods. Moreover, he argues that the nature of the rural village economy offers greater opportunities for disabled children to fulfil meaningful, valued roles in work and collective subsistence. Likewise, other authors have pointed to significant differences in the cultural construction of childhood impairment, disability and dependency between Northern and Southern world contexts (e.g. Ingstad and Reynolds Whyte 1995; Rao 2001; E. Stone 1999; Zinkin and McConachie 1995).

To summarize, the expectation that children will develop consistently towards idealized goals of independence and autonomy is a powerful cultural force in Western societies, drawing on the high value attributed to adult individualism and personal competence (discussed in chapter 5). However, cultural values vary in this regard, and the way in which parents are socialized to think about child development reflects wider cultural meanings of what it means to grow and function through life in relationship to others. In order to develop these ideas, it is important to think not only about culture, but also about the structural significance of dependency associated with childhood and disability.

The social production of disability and childhood

The preceding sections highlight the significance of thinking about disability and childhood as cultural constructs, in terms of their otherness from independent adult social status. But, as discussed in chapter 1, explanations of disability that rely simply on 'culture' run the risk of obscuring the structural position of disabled people in modern societies – and the same is true of childhood. The development of social models of disability drew heavily on materialist analyses of capitalist societies, suggesting that changes in technology, social organization and modes of thought, arising from industrialization and competitive wage labour markets, acted to *produce* what we now understand as the social category of disabled people (see Oliver 1989, 1990). For example, Finkelstein (1980) argued that people with physical or sensory impairments were increasingly dislodged from adult labour markets with the development of mechanized and urban factory production. Similarly, Ryan and Thomas (1980) showed how changes in the skills and learning required of workers during the Industrial Revolution led to the dislocation of adults with cognitive impairments from labour force participation. The suggestion, then, is that disability emerged as a distinctive social category in modern economies due to structural changes in political economy (Priestley 1997; D. Stone 1984). As a consequence, disabled people became a substantial 'administrative problem' (Finkelstein 1991), fuelling the expansion of health and welfare institutions to govern and regulate their lives outside the traditional domain of adulthood (Albrecht 1992).

The social category of childhood can be viewed in very similar terms – as the categorical exemption of a section of the population from the adult labour market, arising from competing social claims and the regulation of labour. The most significant development here has been the transformation of children's work, in industrialized societies, from participation in the productive or domestic sphere to 'school labour' in preparation for adult productive roles (Qvortrup 1994). For Oldman (1994), this distinction is important because it highlights the different purposes of investing in child and adult labour. Whereas the latter is concerned with the accumulation of economic capital, the former is concerned with the accumulation of human capital – developing children's future capacity to labour as adults. This, he suggests, indicates that there are different 'generational modes of production' for children and adults, and that class relations exist between them. Oldman also draws attention to differences in the structural significance of adult work with children (e.g. in child care or teaching) and that with other minority groups (such as older people or disabled people). Thus, 'The essential difference between children and the elderly . . . is that the former and their child-workers are engaged in a distinctive type of production, that of making or preserving human capital in the minds and bodies of the children themselves' (Oldman 1994: 56).

Thus, although disability and childhood share some similarities, as socially dependent categories produced through relations of production and reproduction, their structural significance differs. Whereas social investments in childhood, like educational institutions, function as investments in future human capital and adult productivity, social investments in disability have traditionally functioned to maintain disabled people in a state of continuing dependency (see Oliver 1989). This raises considerable questions about the purpose of state investments in the present and future lives of disabled children (e.g. Tomlinson and Colquhoun 1995). For example, to what extent are investments in 'special' education geared towards the development of disabled children as human capital, or towards their continued dependency into adulthood?

Key points and ideas for learning

To summarize, both disability and childhood are significant social categories, culturally and structurally defined in relation to independent adulthood. Both are distinguished by perceptions of otherness based on assumed relationships of dependency. Culturally, there is a sense in which disability continues to be represented as a 'childlike' state, and this infantilization is reproduced through institutional practices of adult surveillance and care. Structurally, this dependency can also be explained by considering childhood and disability as exemptions from adult labour, arising from the social relations of production in capitalist economies. But there are important differences, since social investments in childhood dependency envisage the development of future human capital, whereas investments in disability have tended to reproduce and maintain 'childlike' dependency into adulthood.

QUESTIONS
- What are the dominant cultural images of disabled childhoods in literature and the media, and what do these images tell us about the place of disabled children in society?
- Why is the issue of dependency so important in understanding the relationships between children and adults, and between disabled people and non-disabled people?
- How far do state policies and investments in the lives of disabled children envisage their future potential as adults?

EXERCISE: Identify a range of examples from literature, television, film, newspapers, charity advertising and websites in which disabled children are depicted (in either words or pictures). Try to include both positive and negative representations, including examples from disabled people's organizations. For each, summarize in just a few words the underlying message that is conveyed – for example, by completing the sentence, 'Life as a disabled child is ...'. Consider using these statements and the examples as the basis for a classroom or online discussion.

Current debates

In considering the questions raised so far, it is important to note that state investments in disabled children's futures appear to be changing, with a greater emphasis on inclusive educational provision and future adult employment. Such developments have arisen in response to both political claims from the disability movement and to changes in technology and flexibility within the adult labour market. The final part of this chapter considers two themes that have figured prominently: the development of an international framework for thinking about children's rights and the debate over inclusive education.

Children's rights

The development of more critical approaches to childhood has occurred in parallel with significant policy developments, most notably in the adoption of the United Nations Convention on the Rights of the Child (UNCRC) in 1989. The significance of these developments should not be underestimated when we consider that, until recently, children were almost completely excluded from discussions about human rights. This exclusion appeared to arise from the commonly held assumption that children are in some way qualitatively different from adults, and that adult status is the primary measure of what it means to be a person or a citizen. However, Qvortrup questions this distinction:

> Is there behind the widespread contention that children are and must be treated differently from adults an idea that can be confirmed, that children and adults are ontologically different? Can in other words age – to the extent that age is systematically related to putative ontological differences – legitimately justify different treatment of children and adults? (Qvortrup 1994: 3)

Addressing similar concerns, Alderson (1993) notes how the international human rights agenda was conceived within a view of personhood and citizenship that relied on attributes such as rationality, independence and freedom. However, as she points out, such characteristics were also associated with a particular view of autonomous adulthood. Children (conceived as non-adults) were rarely recognized as having these adult attributes, and, consequently, were denied claims to adult rights. But there has been something of a paradigm shift in recent years, and children have been accorded increasing rights and responsibilities within national and international policy frameworks (Scott, Jackson and Backett-Milburn 1998). Although the bulk of institutional resources continues to be directed towards the care and control of children in their development towards adulthood, new ways of thinking about children's rights have led to a major reappraisal of policies and practices.

In particular, the near universal adoption of the UN Convention provides a useful basis for examining children's rights (the only two countries not to formally ratify the Convention were the USA and Somalia). The UNCRC asserts a range of human rights for all children, and sets out service standards against which states may be judged, including rights to survival, development, protection and social participation. Thus, it also offers a useful framework for evaluating state responses to the needs of disabled children (e.g. Morris 1998a). Using this approach, Save the Children Fund hosted a major project, beginning in 1999, collecting data on disabled children's rights from more than seventy countries to highlight both violations and good practice (International Save the Children Alliance 2001).

All the articles within the Convention apply equally to disabled children and non-disabled children. However, unlike other international conventions and declarations, the UNCRC explicitly includes disabled children, and Article 2 cites disability amongst the grounds for protection against discrimination. More specifically, Article 23 addresses the rights of disabled children directly, resting on the assertion that 'State Parties recognise that a mentally or physically disabled child should enjoy a full and decent life, in conditions which ensure dignity, promote self-reliance and facilitate the child's active participation in the community' (UN Convention on the Rights of the Child, Article 23.1).

While the Convention recognizes that disabled children have rights to receive 'special' support and services, the manner in which these are provided should always be 'conducive to the child's achieving the fullest possible social integration and individual development' (Article 23.3). This emphasis on community participation then calls into question the historical segregation of disabled children from the mainstream. In reporting progress on the Convention, the UN Committee on the Rights of the Child has drawn attention to a number of areas in which disabled children's rights continue to be violated or constrained, in discriminatory attitudes and in access to education, health or social care (see Hurst and Lansdown 2002). Some examples relating to the specific provisions of the Convention help to illustrate this.

Article 3 asserts that the primary consideration in all actions concerning children should be their 'best interest' – for example, in the provision of legal protection, care or services. But, as some of the examples cited earlier in this chapter illustrate, there are many instances in which disabled children are subject to adult decisions to normalize their appearance, or to place them in institutions, that might be considered as being primarily in interests of parents, professionals or governments rather than the children themselves. Similarly, the discussion in chapter 2 suggests continuing contradictions between eugenic state policies and Article 6, which affirms that 'every child has the inherent right to life'. Similarly, Article 9 states that a child 'shall not be separated from his or her parents against their will'; yet the organization of support for disabled children in many countries continues to rely heavily on segregated residential hospitals, treatment centres and schools, where involuntary separation is the norm.

Article 12 of the Convention asserts the right of children to be consulted and involved in decisions that affect their lives, while Article

13 provides the right to 'freedom of expression', including access to ideas and information. There is, however, a significant caveat here, open to disablist interpretation and potentially damaging to disabled children. Thus, 'States Parties shall assure to the child *who is capable of forming his or her own views* the right to express those views freely in all matters affecting the child, the views of the child being given due weight in accordance with the age and maturity of the child' (Article 12.1, emphasis added).

The danger, particularly for young children and children with cognitive impairments, is that disablist adult assumptions may be made about children's 'capability' in this respect. In particular, there is considerable evidence that children with learning difficulties or communication impairments are frequently denied the right to express their views and to participate in decision making that affects their lives (e.g. Morris 1998b). Involving disabled children in consultation and decision making can be time-consuming and resource-intensive (Ward 1997), and there are many children who require substantial accommodations in order to participate in information exchange. Thus, effective consultation requires specific resourcing to enable disabled children to participate (such as transport, accessible venues, alternative communication media, additional staffing and expertise, etc.).

Article 19 requires states to protect children from all forms of injury, abuse or neglect arising from their care within families or other social institutions. Yet, it is clear that disabled children have been subject to significant rights abuses in this respect, and rates of abuse and neglect of disabled children are often considerably higher than for non-disabled children (e.g. Waldman, Swerdloff and Perlman 1999). Westcott and Cross (1996) argue that our understanding of child abuse in welfare states has been built on the experiences of non-disabled children, and that significant disability issues have therefore been overlooked. Similarly, Morris (1998a) notes how widespread public concern with child abuse during the 1980s in Britain led to major policy developments, but largely failed to address the situation of disabled children.

Although disabled children's particular 'vulnerability' is socially constructed, it is important to recognize that real opportunities to abuse disabled children are often more readily available, because such children are subject to greater levels of adult surveillance and intervention than non-disabled children, particularly within institutions (Giese and Dawes 1999; Watson et al. 1999). In addition, disabled children may be subject to particular forms of institutional abuse (including medical treatment, corrective therapy, rehabilitation and so on). Where children are already disempowered, through institutional experiences and an absence of positive adult role models, the effects of abuse may go unchallenged, further undermining children's self-esteem. In addition, the impact on already disadvantaged minority groups, such as black disabled children, may exacerbate this effect (Bernard 1999). More generally, Westcott and Cross (1996: 2) suggest that the abuse of disabled children should be viewed within its wider social context. 'Just as the abuse of girls is part of the overall pattern of sexism, so the abuse of disabled children must first be understood as part of the position of disabled adults within society; that is, part of the overall pattern of disablism.'

The issue of adult surveillance and control is further highlighted by Article 16 of the UNCRC, which asserts every child's right to be free from arbitrary 'interference with his or her privacy, family, home or correspondence'. It is easy to see how medical, therapeutic and social interventions aimed at normalizing disabled children's lives might be regarded as an infringement of this right. There are numerous other debates that could be drawn from a closer examination of the UN Convention (for a detailed account, see International Save the Children Alliance 2001). For example, how do disabled children's daily experiences of education, leisure, community participation and family life match up to the aspirations and requirements of the international rights framework?

In considering such questions, it is important to note that the fulfilment of children's rights is contingent upon resource allocations within states. This is particularly significant, since the majority of disabled children live in developing countries, with often very limited access to economic and welfare resources (see e.g. Hyder and Morrow 2000; Zinkin and McConachie 1995; Wirz and Lichtig 1998). Poverty is then a real barrier to the achievement of children's rights, and impacts disproportionately on disabled children in the South. However, in terms of *relative* disadvantage, poverty is a significant issue for disabled children and their families in richer Northern societies too (e.g. Dowling and Dolan 2001; Rosman and Knitzer 2001). Thus, in order to address the issue of disabled children's rights, it is important to think beyond the biological differences between children, and the varied cultural responses to them, so as to appreciate how economic and structural factors shape the agenda. In a climate of scarce welfare resources, there are many competing claims for investments in social rights. Since disabled children are often seen as having low value, in terms of human capital and future productivity, it is perhaps unsurprising that they often fall far down the list of priorities for rights.

Education and schooling

Within the context of rights and resources, the issue of education and schooling provides a particularly useful example, one that has been subject to considerable debate and policy development. Referring back to the preceding discussion, Article 28 of the UNCRC affirms the right of all children to education. Yet, many disabled children, and disabled girls in particular, continue to be either denied this right or offered second-rate alternatives under the guise of 'special' education (e.g. Rousso and Wehmeyer 2001). While it would not be possible to provide a comprehensive discussion of educational debates here, the issues are extremely important in understanding social responses to childhood disability. At the heart of these debates is the distinction between segregated and inclusive education (e.g. Alderson and Goodey 1998; Cook, Swain and French 2001; Graves and Tracy 1998).

Different perspectives on disability generate different approaches to the education of disabled children. For example, Riddell (1996) suggests that the historic shift of emphasis from essentialist biological explanations to socio-material ones highlights significant tensions in the construction of special education. Thus, whereas essentialist perspectives suggest a child-deficit approach, based on the allocation of children to particular impairment categories in schools, constructionist analyses provide a critique of administrative segregation as reinforcing artificial boundaries and negative stereotypes. Materialist models of disability offer an additional perspective by explaining the structural and economic forces that shape particular patterns of school provision in different societies (for an analysis of different perspectives, see Clough and Barton 1999; Clough and Corbett 2000; Corbett 1998, 2001).

Historically, the development of 'special' education has been associated with the establishment of special schools and educational programmes that separate children with certain impairments from their non-disabled peers. However, there have been considerable challenges to this approach, arising from both educational theory and disability politics. Thus, the 1990 World Conference on Education for All in Thailand established an international agenda for universal educational access, culminating in 2000 with the World Education Forum in Senegal, and including a recognition that disabled people should be included 'as an integral part of the education system' (World Conference on Education for All 1990).

At the World Conference on Special Needs Education in 1994, representatives of governments and international organizations met to further this agenda in a global context. Reaffirming a commitment to inclusive education, the conference statement (often referred to as the 'Salamanca Statement') argued for the education of all children in inclusive 'regular schools' that respond to the full diversity of children's needs, regardless of impairment. Thus:

> Regular schools with this inclusive orientation are the most effective means of combating discriminatory attitudes, creating welcoming communities, building an inclusive society and achieving education for all; moreover, they provide an effective education to the majority of children and improve the efficiency and ultimately the cost-effectiveness of the entire education system. (United Nations Educational Scientific and Cultural Organization and Ministry of Education and Science 1994: 2)

Although there is a common rhetorical commitment to the principles of inclusion by states throughout the world, achievements in practice remain patchy and sometimes contradictory. For example, Kavale and Forness (2000) examine gaps between rhetoric and reality in the history of inclusion policy in the USA, while Lloyd (2000) points to the 'false promises' of recent inclusion policy in the UK. Even within countries that have similar populations of disabled children and similar levels of economic or political development, there are clear national differences in the way that education is organized. This may reflect economic and demographic considerations, the constraints of physical and social geography, and differing political or welfare regimes. For example, the introduction of compulsory schooling in the USA and the UK was a significant factor in shaping educational provision for disabled children. On the one hand, the requirement to attend school increased the number of disabled children accessing basic education. On the other hand, the institutional strain on schools seeking to provide standardized curricula to a wider range of learners led to the establishment of more special schools outside the mainstream (e.g. Yell, Rogers and Rogers 1998).

Taking a structural demographic approach, Meijer and Jager (2001) identify a relationship between population density and special education in fifteen European countries. Their data show how countries like Belgium, the Netherlands and Germany place up to three times as many children in segregated schools or special classes as countries like Greece, Italy, Portugal, Spain, Norway and Sweden (where the figure is less than 1 per cent). While acknowledging the significance of national policy traditions and regimes, they conclude that geographic and demographic factors have a considerable influence on the pattern of provision, particularly in the incidence of segregated schooling. In explaining these findings, they argue that:

> in countries with a low population density, segregation in separate, special schools has some clear disadvantages. First, large travel distances are a result, which are time-consuming. . . . Secondly, there are negative social consequences: children are taken out of their social environment and have less time for their friends in their own neighbourhood. Furthermore, special settings in sparsely populated areas are not very cost-effective. (Meijer and Jager 2001: 147)

While this may hold true in many rural, developing countries too, there are also cultural influences to consider. For example, the development of special educational institutions has often been shaped by Western influence. This may create tensions and cultural conflicts in determining the most appropriate pattern of provision (see e.g. Deng, Poon-McBrayer and Farnsworth 2001). Thus, Adnan and Hafiz (2001) examine policy and practice in Malaysia, arguing that confusion over definitions has resulted in educational practices that are both discriminatory and 'haphazardly planned' (see also Jelas 2000). Reviewing international developments since the 1990 World Conference, Tony Booth (2000) notes that disabled learners continue to be the most excluded from education. This raises particular concern in the poorer countries of the South, where limited resources present barriers, and where policies of universal schooling are less established than in the North. Importantly, Booth argues that educational inclusion cannot be viewed simply as a fixed goal, but rather as a never-ending process of responding to human diversity. In this respect, he acknowledges the significant and ongoing role played by organizations of disabled people and parents of disabled children in mobilizing claims to inclusive education.

These political challenges have also questioned the underlying rationale for schooling in contemporary societies, and for special education in particular (Biklen 2000). As discussed earlier, the key functional role of schooling is to invest in children as future human capital, and to socialize children into accepted adult roles. Within Western education systems in particular, preparation for individual adult autonomy in a market economy appears to be a significant educational goal (Cuypers 1991; J. Morgan 1996), and values such as 'competition' and 'selection' are prominent in the curricula and management of schools. However, the adoption of a more inclusive agenda, particularly for disabled children, raises many challenges to this framework. Thus, Barton and Slee (1999) conclude that it is important to reconstruct educational provision as an issue of redistributive justice beyond the confines of market forces.

Key points and ideas for learning

The brief examples included above highlight some of the most prominent contemporary debates about disability and childhood. The development of an international child rights agenda raises questions about the rights of disabled children, and about the policies that might enable their greater participation in social and community life. While there is a clear and widely held commitment to greater inclusion across all policy areas, practice often falls far short of these aspirations. In this respect, the issue of inclusive education is perhaps the most widely debated example. The development of inclusive education remains patchy, and disabled children continue to be the most excluded from education and schooling. Yet, in order to understand why disabled children are so disadvantaged, it is important to consider the structural challenge of inclusion and the potential conflict between competitive markets and the celebration of diversity.

QUESTIONS
- Should children have the same 'rights' in society as adults, and if not, why not?
- To what extent do disabled children have 'special' needs or the same needs and rights as other children?
- How would the education system need to change in order to make the goals of inclusive education a reality for disabled children?

EXERCISE: Examine the United Nations Convention on the Rights of the Child as a framework for thinking about disabled childhoods (there is an Internet link at the end of the chapter). One way to do this is to consider each of the main articles in turn, or to divide them between different members in a group. Which of the provisions raise concerns about the rights of disabled children? In each of these specific areas identify the main barriers to the achievement of rights for disabled children. To what extent are these barriers the result of (a) biological differences between children, (b) cultural values in society, or (c) economics?

Summary

The discussion in this chapter develops some of the key themes outlined in chapters 1 and 2. Just as new sociological approaches have redefined childhood as a generational location situated within social and cultural contexts, so the social model of disability highlights the construction and production of that category. In this sense, there is a certain similarity in the way that childhood and disability are revealed in opposition to the supposed normality of (non-disabled) adulthood. In particular, the way we think about adulthood, in terms of autonomy, competence and independence, helps to explain why both children and disabled people have been constructed in terms of dependency and incompetence (this argument is explored further in chapter 5). From a life course perspective, the dominance of developmental theory is also important. When childhood is defined as a period of predictable development towards independence and autonomy in adulthood, children with impairments are more likely to be viewed as a social 'problem'.

As the earlier examples show, disabled children have been addressed through culture, research and policy in quite a limited range of ways. There has been a tendency to focus on impairments, 'vulnerability', the 'burden' of presumed dependency, and the use of services, at the expense of a more nuanced account of everyday lives and identities (Davis and Watson 2001b; Shakespeare and Watson 1998). Thus:

> Preoccupations with impairment have pathologised childhood disability within an individual model. The construction of disabled children as 'vulnerable' and passive has de-sensitised us from their agency as social actors. The preoccupation with services has subjectified disabled children within a discourse of administrative segregation and discipline. Above all, disabled children continue to be constructed within a unitary identity that is largely de-gendered, asexual, culturally unspecific and classless. (Priestley 1998a: 219–20)

Although the emergence of disability activism and disability studies has challenged such perceptions in relation to disabled adults, there has been surprisingly little critical attention to disability issues in childhood. In part, this reflects the lack of children's active representation within the disabled people's movement (bear in mind that parent groups and 'special educators' have also remained largely outside this community). More generally, the absence of a childhood perspective reflects the dominance of adult-centred concerns (such as employment). One of the challenges for disability studies, then, is to bring the voices and experiences of disabled children into contemporary debates about disability equality and disability rights.

SUGGESTIONS FOR FURTHER READING

For an introduction to the 'new sociology of childhood' it may be useful to review some of the key texts, such as *Childhood Matters* (Qvortrup et al. 1994) or *Theorizing Childhood* (James, Jenks and Prout 1998). Although there is little direct reference to disability issues in these books, many of the themes and questions discussed there are relevant to issues raised in this chapter. Regrettably, there is still relatively little published material relating directly to disabled children and written from a critical disability studies perspective. However, the number of articles and research reports is increasing (see e.g. Davis and Watson 2001a, 2001b; Priestley 1998a; Priestley, Corker and Watson 1999). In addition, an excellent overview of international children's rights issues is provided in *Disabled Children's Rights* (International Save the Children Alliance 2001), and the accompanying CD-ROM contains a wealth of source material with examples from around the world. There is also a burgeoning literature on inclusive education, much of it related to disability issues. For an introduction to different approaches, see *Theories of Inclusive Education* (Clough and Corbett 2000) and numerous relevant articles in recent issues of the *International Journal of Inclusive Education* or *Disability & Society*.

INTERNET RESOURCES

- The United Nations Convention on the Rights of the Child: *www.unicef.org/crc/crc.htm* (this version, provided by UNICEF, also includes related commentaries and resources)
- Global Workshop on Children with Disabilities: *www. un.org/esa/socdev/enable/disb971.htm* (a United Nations bulletin from 1997, outlining international policy and development agendas)
- Education for All: *www.unesco.org/education/efa/ed_for_all* (gateway to an extensive collection of materials, including specific country reports)

- Salamanca Statement and Framework for Action on Special Needs Education: *www.unesco.org/education/educprog/sne/salamanc* (influential document discussed earlier in the text)
- Enabling Education Network: *www.eenet.org.uk* (includes materials and case studies relating to different countries)

4

DISABILITY AND YOUTH

This chapter examines the concept of youth and the transitions of young disabled people towards adulthood. The discussion begins with an overview of theoretical perspectives in youth studies, highlighting both structural and cultural explanations. Specific attention is paid to the significance of consumption in young people's agency, cultures and identities, and to the production of 'youth' as a generational category in technological and knowledge societies. The concept of 'youthfulness' is identified as a significant cultural marker in disabling constructions of the perfectible body, and this is linked to the gendered regulation of disabled people's sexuality (e.g. through enforced sterilization). The final part of the chapter examines the institutional management of youth transitions and training, suggesting that an understanding of young disabled people's collective biography requires both structural and cultural explanations. The conclusion highlights some similarities in the location of disability and youth as social categories, and offers a basis for thinking about disability and adulthood (discussed in chapter 5).

Thinking about youth

Youth has become a key theoretical construct within life course and generational studies, particularly as applied to contemporary industrialized societies. However, the current upsurge in youth studies may mask the fact that the concept of 'youth' is a relatively recent construction. More specifically, the generational category of youth can be viewed primarily as a product of rapid cultural and socioeconomic developments associated with late modernity in Western societies, particularly during the second half of the twentieth century. A number of themes seem important.

First, we can think of youth as a significant age category that lies somewhere between childhood and adulthood. But age does not tell the whole story, since young people take on the rights and responsibilities of adulthood at different ages in different societies. It is then the timing, duration and social organization of these transitions that characterize much of what we understand by the term 'youth'.

> Everyone has to make the move from child to adult, but different societies at different times organise the move differently. The transition can take days or years, can mean being collected together with people of the same age or being kept apart from them; it can be a time of relative social freedom or of repression. The task of the sociologist of youth is to show how particular societies organise the process of growing-up. For us, youth is not simply an age group, but *the social organisation of an age group*. (Frith 1984: 467, original emphasis)

From a disability perspective, we might question the assumption that everyone makes such transitions, since there are many barriers to full adult status for young disabled people. There are also some dangers in constructing young people simply as incomplete adults, since youth has its own meanings too. A second view characterizes youth as a distinctive cultural space, between childhood and adulthood, in which young people shape their generational identities as active participants. Third, we might associate youth and youthfulness with a particular construction of the body (both in terms of its physical maturation and as a site of cultural resistance). These different emphases have all been reflected in the emergence of youth studies as an academic sub-discipline. Thus, Coles (1986) distinguishes between approaches based on cultural aspects of youth, identity and agency, and those that emphasize transitions within a structural or policy context. Other authors have made similar distinctions, in the emphasis given to 'process and structure' (G. Jones 1988), 'culture and structure' (Gayle 1998), or 'agency and structure' (Roberts 1997), for example.

Cultural approaches

Cultural approaches have pointed to the emergence of diverse youth cultures and identities, largely defined by consumption (e.g. the consumption of popular music, fashion and leisure). Youth culture, in this sense, is shaped by young people's distinctive consumer choices and short-term leisure consumption (as distinct from the supposedly longer-term goals and investments of adults) and originated in the 'teenage consumers' of the 1950s (Abrams 1959). Young people's display of leisured consumption, and its associated commodities, has thus been central to the development of youth 'subcultures' and changing concepts of 'style' (Brake 1980, 1985). However, young people's agency and consumer choices are not wholly unconstrained. Consumption opportunities are framed by the market interests of powerful multinational industries and the media, and young people themselves have different levels of access to the financial and cultural resources required to take advantage of them. Consequently, 'Leisure activities, in short, are not really "free" – and they relate to people's position in the family and the labour market. Leisure patterns, to put it another way, reflect leisure opportunities, and different groups of young people have different opportunities' (Frith 1984: 23).

This argument has a particular relevance for young disabled people, who may be considerably disadvantaged when it comes to opportunities for leisure consumption or the expression of 'style'. Although there appear to be few differences in the leisure interests of disabled and non-disabled adolescents (Henry 1998), access to consumption and participation varies. On the whole, research points to reduced levels of participation in inclusive leisure activities (e.g. Hayden et al. 1992; L. Kohler 1993). For example, in a survey of young disabled people in England and Scotland, Finch et al. (2001) found that although motivation to participate in sporting activity was not significantly lower than average, participation rates were generally low, and young people with physical impairments were particularly excluded. Lack of money and access barriers played a significant part here. The data also revealed that young disabled people were more likely to participate in sport that took place in school environments than outside (the reverse of patterns for non-disabled young people).

Such patterns are important, because the social spaces where youth subcultures are produced are generally outside the sphere of adult-organized activities. Indeed, the development of youth cultures is frequently associated with participation in 'deviant' or 'risk' behaviours (such as substance use or high risk physical activities), and these activities often provide the context for peer group networks and subcultural youth identities (Engels and Ter Bogt 2001). Thus, Steele et al. (1996) report data showing that young people with physical impairments in Canada were less likely to smoke (both tobacco and mari-

juana) or drink alcohol than their peers, and more likely to participate in 'sedentary leisure activities'.

Participation in youth culture involves the maintenance of peer
friendship networks and close personal relationships. Yet, there may
be many physical and social barriers to such relationships for young
disabled people. As Michalko (2002) points out, personal attitudes
are often more individually disabling than anything else. Thus,
Rowlands (2001) emphasizes the need to support friendship networks
for young disabled people in transition. Drawing on the experiences
of young adults with traumatic brain injuries in rural Australia, she
argues that 'While strategies can be learned and equipment used
to accommodate a range of physical, sensory and cognitive impairments, genuine community participation, and the enjoyment of a web
of caring, reciprocal relationships, often elude young people struggling with the effects of brain injury' (Rowlands 2001: 180).

Interestingly, there is little reference to youth cultures or consumption within disability studies, although the topic of leisure has
attracted attention in the therapeutic literature. Cummings, Maddux
and Cascy (2000) argue that the social significance of leisure is
obscured by an over-focus on employment issues in transitional planning, leading to a lack of meaningful community participation for
many school leavers with learning difficulties. Similarly, Sitlington
(1996) points to a neglect of preparation for the non-employment or
non-educational aspects of adult life. However, leisure has been a key
focus for more formal 'training' and 'instructional' programmes
targeting young disabled people in transition (e.g. Collins, Hall and
Branson 1997; Dattilo and Hoge 1999; Wall, Gast and Royston
1999). In this context, the formalization of leisure opportunities for
young disabled people seems to place greater emphasis on preparation for a 'meaningful life without work' (Committee of Enquiry into
the Education of Handicapped Children and Young People 1978)
than on the potential for participation in youth cultures and consumption. Drawing on an Australian project involving people with
learning difficulties, Fullagar and Owler (1998) show how such
approaches obscure the wider cultural significance of leisure in youth:

> Traditionally, for people with intellectual disability leisure has tended
> to be thought of in quantitative terms, as the 'filling in' of time. It has
> also been constructed through discourses of 'therapy'. As a diversion,
> recreation has been a rationalising of time and space into activities
> which kept people occupied, easily surveilled and thus 'undesir-
> able' behaviour managed. Within such a therapeutic model of leisure,

recreational experiences are assumed to be benign activities rather than an important site for the formation of identity. (Fullagar and Owler 1998: 443)

Since youth identities, subcultures and style rely heavily on the consumption of media imagery, there must also be concern about the historic absence of role models for young disabled people (Hevey 1992, 1993). In this context, the growing profile of disability culture and disability arts appears to offer alternative identities and forms of cultural expression (Peters 2000). Thus, Swain and French (2000) identify the emergence of a more 'affirmative' model of disabled lives and life-style in the disability arts movement, while Morrison and Finkelstein (1993) highlight the empowering potential of disability culture. Similarly, there has been a more long-standing recognition that Deaf culture provides important access to positive identities and role models for young Deaf people growing up in a hearing world (Corker 1996, 1998; Gregory 1995; Padden and Humphries 1988; Sainsbury 1986).

These cultures of resistance and identity have become increasingly significant within the disabled people's movement, generating new cultural spaces and new forms of cultural capital. Their strength has been to challenge the individualized and tragedy-laden discourses of disability in mainstream cultural representation, and to offer a more enabling disability subculture. However, the difficulty from a youth perspective is that disability culture transcends the very generational boundaries on which mainstream youth cultures depend. For young disabled people, then, disability culture offers the affirmation of *disability* identities (irrespective of generation), rather than *youth* identities. Since young people are in the minority of disabled people in Western consumer societies, this gives rise to a certain generational tension or conflict. On the one hand, disability culture offers young disabled people more affirming forms of cultural consumption and expression. On the other hand, identifying with disability culture may mean de-emphasizing the kind of youth identities that are so important in affirming peer group identity and status.

Structural approaches to youth transition

From a structural perspective, youth may be viewed as a generational location that has been produced through processes of modernization. This argument is based on an assumption that the boundaries between childhood and adulthood were perhaps more clear-cut in pre-industrial economies than they are today. For example, it could be argued that there is less space for a concept of youth where the skills and knowledge needed for adult life can be learned 'naturally' by children at home, or where the transition to adulthood can be defined by a single event, such as marriage or a public rite of passage (e.g. Arnett and Taber 1994). Indeed, this kind of argument may help to explain why youth is still so often overlooked as a distinct generational category in developing countries (Cote 1997; Hans 1996). By contrast, the increasingly complex division of labour in modern societies has resulted in a gradual extension of the period of preparation and training required before young people in the West can assume adult roles and responsibilities (Furstenberg 2000).

In this way, we might see 'youth' as a relatively recent, but increasingly significant, generational category, occupying a structural gap that has opened up between childhood and adulthood in industrialized societies. Consequently, there has been much interest in explaining the structuring of youth transitions, highlighting a trend towards extended parental resourcing of young people's lives in Western societies. Irwin (1995), for example, points to an increasing 'deferral' in the timing of young people's transitions towards the economic and social independence traditionally associated with adulthood. The extension of compulsory schooling and the retention of greater numbers of school leavers in full-time education have been particularly significant in this context. Young people in Western societies remain within the parental home for longer, and form households of their own at a later age than was previously the case (Irwin and Bottero 2000).

Arnett and Taber suggest that these extended youth transitions and 'emerging adulthoods' are also characteristic of Western societies because of the high cultural emphasis placed on individualism and adult independence:

> where there is a strong emphasis on independence and individualism, the entrance to adulthood is defined and marked individually. Consequently, it is likely to be based on the achievement of residential and financial independence as well as on the attainment of cognitive self-sufficiency, emotional self-reliance, and behavioral self-control. Thus in the contemporary West the passage from adolescence to young adulthood is a process that is gradual and may take many years. (Arnett and Taber 1994: 517)

These extended pathways, with their focus on the achievement of adult independence and personal autonomy, provide the basis for transitional approaches to youth studies (e.g. Noom, Dekovic and Meeus 2001). But structural transition approaches have also been criticized for failing to represent youth cultures or the diversity and resilience of young people themselves (Newman and Newman 2001). Responding to such criticisms, MacDonald et al. (2001) argue that it is still important to see youth as a key transitional phase in the life course – one that is collectively organized in response to structural change at the macro level. Thus, they argue that 'The concept of transition predisposes us towards a study of youth that is *fundamentally* the study of youth as a life phase. A study of youth remains *essentially* a study of the shifting social, economic and cultural processes that shape this period of the life course: this is what gives "youth" its meaning' (MacDonald et al. 2001: 5.7, original emphasis).

Building on the arguments advanced in chapter 3, this more structural approach to youth is particularly useful in explaining how young people with impairments become disabled through the social organization and regulation of transitions to adulthood. For example, the definition of youth as an extended phase of resourced dependency beyond childhood has much in common with social model analyses of the production of disability in welfare societies. The 'problem' of transition for young disabled people has certainly attracted much attention and social investment, but to what extent do such investments envisage the attainment of future adult status, independent living, or participation in the adult labour market? As the examples later in this chapter show, a structural approach to answering such questions reveals considerable anomalies and concerns in this regard.

Youthfulness and the body beautiful

In addition to explanations based on culture and social structure, it is important to acknowledge the significance of the body as a cultural marker of youth. Indeed, for both young people and society at large the body remains inextricably linked to our understanding of youthfulness. The body is a powerful symbol of identity in consumer culture, and, as Featherstone and Hepworth (1991) point out, the mass marketing of youthful body images has created a near universal attachment to the goal of 'eternal youth'. Thus, Öberg and Tornstam conclude that the cultural ideals of 'youthfulness' and 'fitness' are now widely shared by people of all generations, as the embodiment of more general value-laden norms: 'In consumer society, the body, one focus for youthful consumption, has become a symbol of the true presentation of one's identity. The fit and disciplined body reflects the disciplined and successful person with willpower, energy, self-control' (Öberg and Tornstam 2001: 16).

The consumerist idealization of the youthful body is associated with both its normative construction, as fit and functional, and its aesthetic beauty or sexual potential. Thus, the desirability of youthful bodies is not simply a matter of health, integrity or identity; it also reflects the way we think about the body as an object of sexual desire (Giroux 1998). The normalization of youthful bodily ideals, in terms of functional and sexual desirability, contributes directly to the construction of disability. As B. Hughes (2000) argues, the association between beauty, goodness and power means that 'aesthetic relationships' form an important part of the oppression of disabled people. Disabled people have been particularly disadvantaged by the enforced normalcy of bodily appearance, arising from modernist concerns with measuring and regulating physical characteristics (Davis 1995). Although there has been an apparent diversification of acceptable bodily norms within consumer cultures, aesthetic oppression has been intensified. In particular, contemporary body theorists have highlighted increasing preoccupations with bodily aesthetics and the pursuit of bodily perfection through cultural consumption (e.g. Featherstone 1991a; Glassner 1992; Rojek and Turner 2000; Synott 1993; Welsch 1996). S. Stone (1995) concludes that 'the myth of bodily perfection' is an important, long-standing factor in the construction of people with visible impairments as inferior and disabled.

Hahn notes the success of other minority groups in reclaiming and redefining physical difference as beautiful (notably amongst African-Americans), and asks whether disability can also be 'beautiful'. 'Unlike other minorities, however, disabled men and women have not yet been able to refute implicit or direct accusations of biological inferiority that have often been invoked to rationalise the oppression of groups whose appearance differs from the standards of the dominant majority' (Hahn 1988: 26). This lack of acceptance of disabled bodies, he suggests, reflects an underlying aesthetic anxiety about the threat that they pose to non-disabled norms. Given these concerns, the re-presentation of disabled bodies as potentially beautiful, desirable and sexualized is a significant challenge for disability culture. With this in mind, Hahn offers an alternative perspective on bodily aesthetics, emphasizing the potential beauty of physical difference (an approach that might also be considered advantageous to the non-disabled majority).

By developing awareness of the beauty to be discovered in the physical differences that distinguish human beings rather than the similarities between them and idolized media images, everyone could be
liberated from the conformity perpetuated by these depictions and
acquire a heightened aesthetic appreciation of anatomical variations.
Perhaps even more importantly, by accepting alternative standards for
assessing the aesthetic pleasure of bodily attributes, the nondisabled
might uncover a reciprocal advantage that could sustain an enduring
coalition with the disabled minority. (Hahn 1988: 30)

Shakespeare makes a similar argument in relation to the body,
disability and sexuality:

Rather than struggling to conform and to fit in to stereotypes which
developed on the basis of exclusivity and the body beautiful, and
narrow, limited notions of how to behave and how to look, disabled
people can challenge the obsession with fitness and youth and the body,
and demonstrate that sexual activity and sexual attraction can be
whatever you want it to be. (Shakespeare 2000: 163)

To summarize, the preceding analysis suggests that the trans-
generational ideal of 'youthfulness' has strong cultural links with the
myth of bodily perfection. The aesthetic normalization of youthful
beauty, as a bodily ideal within consumerist culture, is thus a factor
in the oppression of disabled people of all generations, but has a particular resonance for young people with visible differences. Within
this context, disability activists and disability culture have begun to
redefine aesthetic norms in order to challenge the oppression of aesthetic power relationships.

Key points and ideas for further learning

The discussion in the first part of this chapter highlights some of
the theoretical challenges in conceptualizing youth as a generational category. The generic youth literature highlights the value of
cultural and structural approaches, and both have implications for
thinking about the lives of young disabled people. On the one
hand, youth may be viewed as a significant cultural space, in which
young people act reflexively to produce and reproduce youth
subcultures and identities through cultural consumption. This
raises questions about young disabled people's access to cultural

resources and consumption opportunities (e.g. in relation to leisure or 'style'). On the other hand, youth may be viewed as a significant structural space, arising from extended investments in preparing young people for adulthood in industrial societies. This raises questions about the extent and purpose of social investments in young disabled people as human capital. In both cases, the high social value attributed to youthfulness is also expressed through the embodied ideals of fitness and beauty (as fit for productive work and as sexually potent for reproduction). The examples in subsequent sections illustrate this interplay between the body, identity, culture and structure in the lives of young disabled people.

QUESTIONS
- How important are the body, identity, culture and social structure in shaping our understanding of 'youth'?
- What barriers do young disabled people face in accessing youth subcultures and identities?
- Do young disabled people pose a 'problem' for structural models of youth transition?
- How does the myth of youthful bodily perfection contribute to the oppression of disabled people, and can disability be beautiful?

EXERCISE: Think about the way in which young people access and express their generational subcultures and identities. Where does the production of youth culture take place (in what kinds of social spaces)? How do young people access relevant images, icons and role models (through what media)? How do young people express youth identities (e.g. through dress, language and behaviour)? Make a note of examples under each heading, and then consider the potential barriers to participation and expression for young disabled people?

Sex and sexuality

As mentioned previously, the embodied ideals of youthfulness are closely connected with constructions of sexual attractiveness and potency. But the significance of youthful sexuality runs deeper than mere aesthetics. Not only have disabled people been constructed as less attractive or desirable, their potential for expressions of sexuality has been both denied and heavily regulated. While such concerns are not the sole province of youth, young disabled people (and young disabled women in particular) have been most directly subject to institutional discipline and regulation of their sexuality. The following examples illustrate how disabled people have been constructed as both asexual and sexually threatening, how the control of young women's reproductive sexuality has been a key feature of eugenic practices, and how disability culture is challenging sexual stereotypes and taboos.

Myths and realities

Powerful myths surrounding disabled people's sexuality have been reproduced through cultural taboos and the dominance of therapeutic research disciplines (Taleporos and McCabe 2001). These include portrayals of disabled people as asexual, sexually threatening or unquestioningly hetereosexual. For example, Milligan and Neufeldt (2001) note that, although some forms of impairment may alter the performance of certain sex acts, this has little bearing on the desire for romantic attachment or sexual relationships. Yet the myth of asexuality, evident in personal narratives, cultural imagery and re-habilitation programmes, can deny such desires and devalue the worth of disabled people as potential sexual partners. Summarizing the roots of such prejudice, they suggest two lines of thought in traditional discourses:

> First, for people with physical disabilities, because of actual or pre-sumed sexual dysfunction, gratification opportunities are considered so limited that sexual needs are either deemed to be absent or subjugated. Second, although their sexual function is typically intact, individuals with intellectual disabilities and/or psychiatric disorders are thought to have limited social judgement, and therefore, lack the capacity to engage in responsible sexual relationships. (Milligan and Neufeldt 2001: 92)

Pointing to the activism of disabled people in countering these myths, they demonstrate that there is a lack of evidence to support such views, and that disabled people can and do form loving sexual relationships, albeit within a context of taboo and disabling barriers. Understanding how such barriers impact on young disabled people is therefore the key issue.

There is considerable evidence that young disabled people are often excluded from, or receive inferior levels of, sex education. This is particularly evident in the stories of young people residing in institutions, where sexual activity has been both frowned upon and actively dis-couraged through practices of sex segregation and adult surveillance (Shakespeare, Gillespie-Sells and Davies 1996). Such was the denial and control of sexuality amongst people with learning difficulties in traditional institutions that many in the therapeutic professions have only perceived a need for sexual knowledge and information in the light of recent moves towards deinstitutionalization and community living (Redelman 2001). Drawing on her experience of Canadian institutions, Waxman Fiduccia concludes that:

> Mental institutions, nursing homes, intermediate care facilities and the like prohibit in policy/practice any sort of privacy, especially sexual activity by inmates. In fact, most states do not recognize inmates' right to privacy and sexual relationships. In practice, the right to sexual interaction often depends on the whim of line-level staff or on whether such interaction is seen as a feature of the inmate's treatment plan. (Waxman Fiduccia 2000: 173)

Service providers and evaluators have thus been very interested in the 'problem' that disabled people's sexuality poses in service con-texts, and there have been numerous studies of the attitudes of staff (McConkey and Ryan 2001). For example, Wolfe (1997) found that the perceived 'level' of impairment was a key factor in the attitudes of teachers and administrators towards young disabled people's participation in sexual relationships (i.e. staff were more concerned about the sexuality of people they felt had more 'severe' forms of impairment). However, such studies tend to be ill-informed by a more critical disability studies perspective. They are often focused on spe-cific interventions, such as the prevention of public masturbation or dealing with allegations of sexual abuse, rather than with the provi-sion of positive support for loving sexual relationships. Despite a rhetoric of more individualized assessments, policies and legal pro-ceedings have continued to reinforce restrictions on disabled people's sexual relationships (e.g. Levesque 1996).

Similar conclusions could be drawn about the regulation of sexu-ality in the domestic sphere. Here, adult carers (often parents) play an important role in regulating the sexual lives of young disabled people. For example, Shepperdson (1995) found that few young people with Down's syndrome were equipped with sexual knowledge appropriate to the lives they led, often knowing more about events they were less likely to experience (e.g. pregnancy and birth) than those that were most likely (e.g. sexual intercourse). Even adults who held more permissive views often left young people ill-prepared for sexual experiences. Interestingly, the parents of young people living at home were more concerned about the possibility of sexual activity than parents of those living away from home (Pattersonkeels et al. 1994), suggesting an assumption that institutional living would preclude such relationships. However, as the stories revealed by Humphries and Gordon (1992) or Shakespeare, Gillespie-Sells and Davies (1996) show, such assumptions are largely misplaced – young disabled people can and do form sexual relationships, even within the confines of repressive institutions.

The apparently widespread denial of young disabled people's sexuality also conflicts with the preconception that they are more sexually vulnerable than their non-disabled peers (e.g. to sexual abuse). Responding to UK government proposals on curbing sex offences, Mencap, Respond and Voice UK (2001) report an increase in sexual abuse against people with learning difficulties (up to four times that for the general population), and express concern that offenders are rarely prosecuted. In a newspaper interview, a Mencap spokesperson noted: 'When you look at the fact that there are so few prosecutions and the law doesn't provide an effective deterrent, I think society is saying that these acts are trivial compared with those carried out on non-disabled people. You are effectively saying that they should not be treated as seriously' (*Guardian*, 17 September 2001).

In addition to the myth of asexuality, Waxman Fiduccia and Wolfe (1999) suggest that women with learning difficulties and psychiatric survivors are subject to a myth of hypersexuality. Thus, Block (2000) argues that women with learning difficulties in the USA have long been portrayed as 'sexually and socially threatening', requiring professional management and control. To this, O'Toole (2000) adds the myth of disabled women's presumed heterosexuality (see also Tremain 1996). Thus, Tremain (2000) argues that researchers and theorists of disability sexuality should 'open up the conceptual field of possibility', to take account of the fact that 'sex' and 'gender' are the constructions of heterosexist power relationships that emphasize male–female differences at the expense of a more nuanced understanding of sexuality.

Sterilization and the control of sexuality

Perhaps the most graphic example of social intervention to regulate young disabled people's sexuality is that of enforced sterilization (widely practised in a number of states, and particularly targeting young disabled women). The practice of mass eugenic sterilization was begun in the USA early in the twentieth century. There had been attempts to introduce a legal basis for this as early as 1897 (in Michigan), but the first eugenic legislation was almost certainly in Indiana in 1907. Here, 'expert' committees were empowered to sanction the compulsory sterilization of 'confirmed idiots, imbeciles and rapists' in state institutions (see Gardella 1995). By the late 1920s at least twenty-two states had enacted eugenic sterilization laws. In 1927, the US Supreme Court ruled that compulsory sterilization of 'mental defectives' was legal and constitutional (with some safeguards), and during the 1930s more than 25,000 such sterilizations were carried out.

The case of eighteen-year-old Carrie Buck became famous when she was selected as the first person to be forcibly sterilized under US law in 1924 (in the state of Virginia). Her case has been widely debated, and is frequently cited in courses across a range of disciplines (for a fuller discussion of the case and its eugenic implications, see Smith 1993, 1995). Carrie had been admitted to the State Colony for Epileptics and the Feebleminded, near Lynchburg, after giving birth to a child out of marriage (her daughter was taken into foster care, but died nine years later). For Carrie, the timing and location were unfortunate, since the state of Virginia had recently adopted a sterilization law, and she was selected as a test case.

Although the state's right to carry out the operation was appealed through the County, State and Supreme Courts, it was eventually deemed constitutional (by a majority verdict), and Carrie was sterilized, by cutting her Fallopian tubes. She left the Virginia State Colony on parole shortly afterwards, and worked for many years caring for older people, living until 1983 and becoming a prominent public symbol of legal abuses of disabled women. Her case was to have massive repercussions, providing legal precedent for the right of states to intervene directly in the reproductive lives of 'defective' citizens. In delivering the majority opinion of the Supreme Court, Justice Oliver Wendell Holmes argued that:

> We have seen more than once that the public welfare may call upon the best citizens for their lives. It would be strange if it could not call upon those who already sap the strength of the State for these lesser sacrifices, often not felt to be such by those concerned, in order to prevent our being swamped with incompetence. It is better for all the world, if instead of waiting to execute degenerate offspring for crime, or to let them starve for their imbecility, society can prevent those who

are manifestly unfit from continuing their kind. The principle that sustains compulsory vaccination is broad enough to cover cutting the Fallopian tubes.

Early legislation in the USA provided a model for subsequent developments in Europe. Although the Scandinavian countries have often been regarded as pioneers in inclusive welfare provision and disability rights, they were also at the forefront of state-sanctioned sterilization programmes. Denmark was the first country in Europe to introduce eugenic sterilization (in 1929), and within ten years Norway, Sweden, Finland, Estonia and Iceland had enacted similar legislation. Sweden began its programme in 1935, and by the mid-1940s more than a thousand Swedes were being sterilized each year (predominantly young women). As with other countries at the time, Sweden's programme targeted people of 'poor or mixed racial quality', referring primarily to people with learning difficulties and to poor people of non-Nordic heritage. Under the direction of the National Health Board, all 'feeble-minded' people discharged from institutions were routinely assessed for sterilization, justification being required only where this was *not* carried out. The programme did not end until 1975, by which time around 63,000 state-sponsored sterilizations had been officially recorded.

In Germany, the National Socialist government followed the lead of the USA and other European countries by enacting its own sterilization law for the 'Prevention of Hereditary Diseases in Future Generations' in 1934. By 1945, some two million people, mostly teenagers, had been sterilized in Germany (Dahl 2001; Pfafflin and Gross 1982). It was this legislation that paved the way for subsequent eugenic measures, including the systematic murder of millions of Jews, Slavs, disabled people and others (Lifton 1986). Despite the ideological influence of English eugenics (discussed in chapter 2), actual eugenic practices were implemented less there than in North America or mainland Europe. Indeed, forced sterilization was generally illegal in Britain, and state-sanctioned eugenic measures were therefore largely restricted to the control of marriage (Galton and Galton 1998).

The legacy of enforced sterilization remains today. For example, more than 800 disabled people have successfully sued the Canadian government for wrongful sterilization as children or young people in the Alberta Provincial Training School, receiving more than $140 million in total damages (Shea 1999). Yet, such practices continue. For example, particular attention has been drawn to the continuing sterilization of disabled young women in Australia (Brady 2001a; Graycar 1994; Little 1993). Thus, in a report for the Australian Human Rights and Equal Opportunity Commission, Brady, Briton and Grover (2001) review data on unlawful sterilizations and the support available to young women and their parents. Noting the continuing use of sterilization to control menstruation and fertility, they call for reform in the legal process and greater access to information and education.

Challenges to enforced sterilization have begun to find favour in the courts, and there is some evidence of more enlightened approaches. For example, a test case in the British Court of Appeal, in May 2000, overturned a High Court ruling that a twenty-nine-year-old woman with learning difficulties should undergo a hysterectomy to avoid the 'risk' of pregnancy. Here, the judge ruled against the woman's mother, who had expressed concerns that her daughter might have 'unsupervised relationships' when she moved to a community home. In ruling, the judge asserted that 'The patient has the right, if she cannot herself choose, not to have drastic surgery imposed upon her unless or until it has been demonstrated that it is in her best interests'.

As the preceding examples show, past and present practices have been highly gendered, and are most likely to involve young women with the label of learning difficulties (Kallianes and Rubenfeld 1997). Indeed, it is extremely unusual for disabled men to be sterilized by compulsory order. Moreover, traditional therapeutic concerns with the 'problem' of disabled people's sexuality appear to be more concerned with male sexual function than with control. Thus, Waxman Fiduccia (2000) concludes that medico-legal intervention in disabled people's sexuality seeks to control the fertility of 'dangerous women', but to restore the potency of the 'damaged male'.

Challenging stereotypes and taboos

Within an international policy context, sexuality and sexual expression are regarded as disability rights issues. Indeed, the UN Standard Rules on the Equalization of Opportunities for People with Disabilities assert that disabled people 'must not be denied the opportunity to experience their sexuality, have sexual relationships and experience parenthood', and that 'States should promote measures to change negative attitudes towards marriage, sexuality and parenthood of persons with disabilities, especially of girls and women' (United Nations 1993, Rule 9). The examples cited in this chapter raise considerable questions about the implementation of such rights.

Although there has been much discussion of sexuality in the medical and therapeutic literature (dominated by the 'sexual problems' of disabled people), the subject has been somewhat marginalized within critical disability studies, until recently. Thus, early writing on social models of disability tended to emphasize the political and collective significance of discrimination in the public sphere at the expense of issues and debates related to private life and relationships (Crow 1996). Yet, sexual feelings and their expression are a central part of growing up, with a particular significance for the experience of disability in youth. Noting this omission, Finger (1992: 9) suggests an explanation: 'Sexuality is often the source of our deepest oppression; it is also often the source of our deepest pain. It's easier for us to talk about – and formulate strategies for changing – discrimination in employment, education, and housing than to talk about our exclusion from sexuality and reproduction.'

A more critical awareness in this area has been raised by the publication of disabled people's sexual stories (e.g. Shakespeare, Gillespie-Sells and Davies 1996), by the launch of a new journal entitled *Sexuality and Disability*, and through a major international conference in San Francisco on 'Disability, Sexuality and Culture' in March 2000. Such developments, along with a more general awareness amongst disabled activists, leads Waxman Fiduccia (2000) to suggest the emergence of a 'sexuality and disability movement', led by disabled women and activists within the field of queer studies. While some within this movement continue to view sexuality as a 'subset of reproduction' (Waxman Fiduccia 2000) others have taken a broader view, recognizing the importance of sexual pleasure and sexual identities (e.g. Tepper 2000).

However, Shakespeare (2000) cautions that we should not overlook the importance of friendship, love and intimacy in these debates. Thus, he argues that the real 'problems' or barriers to sexual activity for disabled people are not 'how to do it, but who to do it with'. Since young disabled people have often been excluded from the cultural spaces where their generational peers meet sexual partners (e.g. in colleges, bars and night-clubs), the range of options has sometimes been limited. The high levels of adult surveillance experienced by disabled children and young people may also curb expressions of sexuality in peer group settings (such as schools or organized leisure clubs). Additionally, expressing and displaying sexuality within a consumerist youth culture involves both financial expenditure and positive bodily self-esteem, both of which are commonly denied to young disabled people (see Shakespeare, Gillespie-Sells and Davies 1996).

Reflecting on the importance of sexuality and sexual expression to Western youth culture, it is therefore important to consider sexual claims and representations as more than a marginal issue in the disability rights debate.

> In modern life, bodily pleasures are central to consumer culture, and consumption is the key word. As individuals, we demand the right to be sexual and to choose whatever form of sexual expression or fulfilment we can find. We live in the 'market of emotions'. In late modernity, potential sexuality is omnipresent. (Shakespeare 2000: 164)

The recent engagement of the disability movement and disability research with issues of sexuality shows that challenges to traditional stereotypes and taboos are possible. The telling of 'sexual stories' (Plummer 1995) and the high profile achieved by legal test cases has brought these debates further into the public arena. This has led to some uneasiness amongst those who consider that an over-emphasis on personal relationships may detract from wider political strategy (Oliver 1998). However, these are not simply personal struggles, but also significant challenges to institutional discourses of discipline that are enacted on young disabled people throughout the world in very real ways, and which reflect broader structural concerns.

Key points and ideas for learning

The close association between cultural ideals of youthfulness and the myth of bodily perfection in consumer societies raises a number of questions about disabled people's sexuality. Culturally, young disabled people have been constructed as both asexual and as a sexual threat to the moral order. Institutional policies and practices have imposed greater levels of discipline and surveillance on disabled people's sexuality, impacting particularly on young disabled people. Such practices have created barriers to sexual knowledge and to sexual opportunity, particularly in institutional settings (including the family). More directly, there is a considerable history of legal and medical intervention to control reproductive sexuality through state-sanctioned programmes of enforced sterilization. Such interventions have been highly gendered, and young women with learning difficulties have been most affected. These practices have been influenced both by eugenic thinking and by structural concerns to limit the reproduction of disability in future genera-tions. Although issues of sexuality have sometimes been marginal-ized within disability studies, activists and academics have begun to challenge sexual oppression more openly, leading to a wider recognition of diverse sexualities and sexual rights.

QUESTIONS
• Is disabled sexuality a cultural taboo, and why have young dis-abled people been so commonly constructed as 'asexual'?
• Why have young disabled women with learning difficulties been the primary target for institutional regulation and control over sexuality in modern societies?
• How useful is the concept of 'sexual rights' in thinking about barriers for young disabled people?

EXERCISE: Using the examples cited earlier, or similar cases, con-sider the arguments that might be made for and against the control of young disabled people's sexuality. Think about access to sexual knowledge, sexual orientation, access to sexual partners, sex acts and reproductive rights. In each case, make a note of the potential barriers for young disabled people. How far are these the result of (a) individual impairment, (b) identity, (c) cultural values or (d) structural concerns? Consider using these arguments as the basis for a classroom or online debate about young disabled people's sexual rights.

Preparation for what?

The discussion in the first part of this chapter showed how youth has been structurally produced as a 'transitional' generational category between childhood and adulthood. In this context, social invest-ments in young people were considered as investments in future human capital, based on a particular view of what it means to become an independent adult in modern societies. This idealization of autonomous adulthood is discussed at length in chapter 5. However, it is important in the context of the present discussion to look in more detail at the management of youth transitions, in order to examine the kind of adulthoods that young disabled people are being prepared for.

Training for adulthood

Coles (1995) identifies work, housing and the family as the three key themes in the transition to adulthood. Thus the key markers of adult status are often conceived as finding employment, establishing independent living, and creating a family of one's own. Consequently, social and family investments in youth are commonly focused on facilitating successful movement towards these adult status goals. But it is clear that young disabled people face considerable inequalities and barriers in each of these areas. Responding to such concerns, Mitchell (1999) notes the complex interplay between young disabled people's aspirations and the social and economic 'opportunity structure' that governs their choices. More generally, Hodkinson and Sparkes (1997) argue that young people's negotiation of 'careership' involves a balance between unpredictable turning points within the life course, rational decision making, and unequal access to resources.

Mitchell's own research, examining the 'next step' taken by young disabled people leaving special schools, suggests a paradox. While parents and professionals held very low expectations of young people's potential to achieve adult status goals, they were also committed to placing them on training courses with a strong rhetorical focus on those ends. Similarly, Corbett (1989) notes that while moves towards community integration have tended to involve 'an elaborate process of selection of those most easily assimilated', those young people who are rejected are also the most likely to be targeted for 'independence' training. There has been a steady increase in the provision of this type of transitional support for young disabled people, particularly in the area of 'skills training' and college-based 'courses' (C. Hughes 2001). This would seem to reflect increasing social concerns to invest in the progress of young disabled people towards adulthood. Nevertheless, concerns have been raised about the efficacy and social value of such interventions, particularly in the context of 'special' provision. Thus, the rapid expansion of this training sector, often targeted specifically at young people with learning difficulties, reproduces social spaces and discourses that are largely segregated from the mainstream.

In knowledge societies geared towards lifelong learning, the continuing acquisition of recognized skills and competences is an important aspect of young people's careership. Yet, the institutional management of training for young disabled people has focused on less marketable and lower status 'qualifications', primarily concerned with the acquisition of 'life skills' (Riddell, Baron and Wilson 2001). Numerous studies have shown that young disabled people face a disproportionate risk of unemployment and financial dependency (e.g. National Council on Disability and Social Security Administration 2000), with young disabled women less likely to secure post-school employment opportunities than disabled men (Doren and Benz 1998). Thus, Tomlinson and Colquhoun (1995) question the degree to which special provision for young disabled people prepares them for economic participation in the declining youth labour markets of advanced capitalist societies. Reviewing policy developments in the UK, they conclude that those defined as 'special' will find it increasingly difficult to acquire competences that can be exchanged for work:

> A major contradiction revolved around the rhetoric of equipping the young people with skills that would enhance their employability, despite the disappearance of the work they had previously undertaken. ... Colleges invented work-preparation courses that were in effect behaviourally-oriented programmes of personal self-improvement. (Tomlinson and Colquhoun 1995: 195)

Corbett (1989) notes how the development of such programmes has been characterized by a shift of curricular focus, bringing the teaching of life and social skills from the periphery to the core.

> Unlike a vocational training, like hairdressing or nursery nursing, which qualifies the student to move into an area where they can apply the theory they have learnt to their daily practice, these students are learning skills which need constant, repetitive application and which provide their *persona* rather than their *role in society*: a significant distinction. (Corbett 1989: 149, original emphasis)

This personalization of the transitional skills curriculum places the emphasis on highly individualized notions of adult independence and competence. As Corbett notes, 'failing' a course in life skills may be more significant personally and socially than failing a course in, say, biology. More generally, the increased regulation of life skills acquisition may appear to reflect wider concerns with the management of risk in youth transitions. Yet, if this were the case, we would have to ask why non-disabled young people are not formally accredited for their competence to make tea, boil eggs, cross the road, play cards or watch television (e.g. Collins, Hall and Branson 1997). Critiquing such approaches with disabled young people, Kennedy (2001) argues that the teaching of individual skills to promote social inclusion is based on particular assumptions about adult independence, and that a more productive approach would be to promote interventions that foster the sort of relational interdependence which young adults are more likely to need.

The contradictions highlighted above raise a number of questions about the purpose of traditional investments in transitional training for young disabled people. More recently, attention has shifted towards the challenge of including young disabled people in mainstream post-compulsory education. As a result of claims to participation and equality, backed by rights legislation and the removal of disabling barriers, an increasing number of disabled people have begun to access learning and teaching within mainstream higher education (although the situation varies greatly between different countries). For example, Konur (2000) suggests that the legislative approach adopted in the USA has been more effective in securing rights to higher education than in the UK. In particular, he argues that continuing discourses of 'special' needs are less likely to move the agenda beyond incremental change than an approach based on enforceable civil rights. In this context, it is perhaps significant that anti-discrimination law in the UK was initially focused on employment rights, and that access to education (both compulsory and post-compulsory) was initially exempt. Although legal rights to education exist, the provision of opportunities remains subject to the condition that they do not involve 'unreasonable public expenditure' (UK Human Rights Act 1998, Article 2).

The examples outlined so far suggest that the growth of training opportunities for young disabled people has been characterized by an increasing regulation of life skills competences, framed within an idealized and individualist notion of adult autonomy. The production of training for adulthood within 'special' programmes reduces the marketable value of the competences acquired, and reinforces young disabled people's status as devalued human capital. More recent challenges have targeted access to education and training as an equal rights issue. But such initiatives must also be viewed within a structural context of competing claims to limited resources.

The individual and society

There have been two broad approaches to researching youth transitions for disabled people. The first has involved large-scale quantitative studies of outcomes (e.g. to determine the proportion of school leavers who find paid employment). The second has focused on more qualitative studies, engaging with the experiences of young disabled people as they pass through important transitional phases (e.g. between children's services and those for adults). For example, Morris (1999) examined the transitional experiences of young disabled people with complex health and support needs in the UK. She found that this group were particularly at risk of moving into segregated services and accommodation as young adults. Thus, she suggests that they were often 'warehoused' in residential accommodation, with little opportunity for community involvement and an absence of meaningful activity or planning for personal development. In addition, the study raised concerns about access to employment opportunities, financial disincentives and transport (see also Rabiee, Priestley and Knowles 2001).

Such studies have been useful in highlighting the experiences of young disabled people in transition, and their pathways through complex service frameworks. However, the emphasis on improving existing services falls short of an adequate framework for thinking about transition to adulthood more broadly. In particular, such pre-occupations may obscure a structural understanding of the significance of disability in youth transitions. As Tisdall (2001: 175) points out, 'The present approach for young disabled people relies on individual assessment and incessant calls for improved inter-agency collaboration; without a structural perspective. This (expensive) assessment and collaboration lacks purpose when decisions are being made between, at best, a handful of options.'

Following Evans and Furlong (1997), Tisdall argues that young disabled people, and those with learning difficulties in particular, experience a 'collective biographical pattern', in which there are few of the reflexive choices and risk negotiations supposedly characteristic of youth in contemporary consumer societies. She concludes that, while contemporary youth studies have moved on from a traditionally structuralist approach to one based on individuation, culture and risk, young disabled people continue to face significant structural barriers to the achievement of adult status. Similarly, Riddell, Baron and Wilson (2001) suggest that the identities and biographical patterns of young people with learning difficulties in late modernity are more likely to be ascribed than freely 'chosen'. This, coupled with the intersection of gender and class, leads them to argue that more structural explanations are required to explain the life course trajectories of young disabled people in a learning society. That is not say that qualitative investigations of individual life course pathways are not useful – far from it. As G. Hubbard (2000) argues, life history research can be a fruitful way to reveal the interaction between individual agency and structural constraints. Although young people themselves may not consciously articulate the structural context of their life choices, their accounts provide a richly situated lens through which to view structural barriers and social change.

In addition, it is important to acknowledge the cultural significance of disability in youth, and its relationship to idealized constructions of adulthood. Thus, Davies (1998) argues that the categorization of young people with learning difficulties in Western societies is largely incompatible with their achievement of adult social status. Drawing on her own research with young people in transition, she argues that:

> People with learning difficulties challenge Western conceptions of an autonomous and reflective individual self and for this reason may be seen as threatening to basic cultural assumptions. Such a threat is managed in the first instance by categorising and marginalising people with learning difficulties. But it may also be addressed, as in the discourse about adulthood, by trying to provide them with behavioural characteristics which make their self-presentation more consistent with Western cultural expectations. (Davies 1998: 103)

In this context, we might look towards the considerable investment in behaviour modification and 'independence' programmes highlighted earlier. By contrast, the strategies of resistance and resilience that Davies identifies amongst young people and their families suggest an approach to competence and personhood that has less in common with Western constructions of the autonomous self, and more in common with traditionally non-Western networks of relational interdependence. (These ideas are developed further in chapter 5.)

The current cultural and biographical turn in sociology (Rojek and Turner 2000; Rustin 2000) has been reflected in the development of mainstream youth studies, with a corresponding emphasis on young people's agency, identity and subcultures. But it is also important to reiterate the influence of structural mechanisms in producing the transitional space between childhood and adulthood that youth cultures now occupy. Indeed, if the social model of disability has taught us anything, it is not to overlook the influence of structure in producing disability and disabling environments. To convey young disabled people's transitional experiences as simply rooted in culture or identity would be to deny the very real influence of structural forces in shaping their life course pathways and life opportunities.

***

Key points and ideas for learning

To summarize, the preceding sections highlight an apparent contradiction between social investments in preparing young disabled people for adulthood and a widespread denial of their capacity to achieve that end. Young disabled people, particularly those with the label of learning difficulties, have been subject to an increasing institutional regulation of their developing competences. Moreover, such interventions have tended to both formalize and personalize the accreditation of adult status, through idealized notions of individual competence rather than relational interdependency. Challenges to the exclusion of young disabled people, including those based on their own accounts, have highlighted the complex relationship between individual agency, cultural expectations and structural constraints. Despite the emphasis on agency and choice in the mainstream youth literature, young disabled people continue to experience significant forms of collective biography, based on ascribed social roles and produced through social relations of production, that hinder the achievement of future adult social status.

QUESTIONS
- To what extent are investments in transitional support for young disabled people geared towards the expectation of an independent adulthood?
- Are young disabled people subject to a different kind of regulation in the assessment of adult competences compared to their non-disabled peers?
- Does the provision of 'special' programmes devalue the marketability of competences acquired by young disabled people?
- What are the implications for young disabled people of structural changes in the youth labour markets of learning societies?

EXERCISE: Consider the major milestones and turning points that mark the passage from child to adult status in contemporary societies (e.g. in education, work, housing, family responsibilities, mobility, legal rights and citizenship). Draw up a list of these transitions and decide which you regard as most important. For each example, identify the potential barriers for young disabled people, and how these might be challenged.

Summary

As outlined in chapter 1, generational boundaries and life course transitions are highly organized at the collective level in modern societies, and enormous social investments have been made to ensure that citizens make 'proper' transitions from childhood to adulthood. Indeed, major social institutions have emerged to manage the problems arising from 'improper' or 'incomplete' transitions (such as those targeting the perceived 'failure' of young disabled people to achieve an independent adulthood). Although there has been a considerable amount of research into youth issues, particularly in industrialized countries, very little of this has been framed within a critical disability studies perspective. Rather, there has been a tendency for research and thinking about young disabled people to develop within a separate, parallel field, emphasizing transitions within specialist services (e.g. in education, social services or health).

Culturally, there is a sense in which disability has been constructed as a kind of liminal yet enduring adolescence, beyond childhood yet not fully adult. Policies for further education, day centres and employment training have consigned many people (often with learning difficulties or complex impairments) to a nether world of repeated, unresolved transitions in which true adult status is neither envisaged nor attained – described ironically by Baron, Riddell and Wilson (1999) as the 'secret of eternal youth'. At the same time, young disabled people are also constrained from full participation in the consumption of youth subcultures in consumer societies. The related themes of cultural construction and cultural consumption are therefore equally relevant in thinking about disability and youth. Debates around sex and sexuality are significant in this regard, illustrating how young disabled people, and young women with learning difficulties in particular, have been both denied adult sexuality and also regulated as a sexual and reproductive threat to society.

Structurally, the generational category of youth has arisen from social and technological change in learning societies, demanding increased levels of resourced preparation for participation in skilled adult labour markets. Significantly, these processes mirror those identified by social model theorists as producing the social category of disability. For example, it is clear that the structural pressures and knowledge requirements driving the expansion of 'youth' are the same pressures that have led to the rapid expansion of certain 'disability' categories amongst young people (particularly the labelling of more and more young people as having 'learning difficulties'). Thus, as social and structural categories, both youth and disability exist at the margins of adult citizenship, access to which is increasingly regulated by the accreditation of competence, independence and autonomy.

SUGGESTIONS FOR FURTHER READING

Although slightly dated, Frith's (1984) *The Sociology of Youth* provides a quick introduction to some key concepts. For a more thorough analysis in relation to structural and social change, see Irwin's (1995) *Rights of Passage*. For an overview of subsequent developments in youth studies, it might be useful to look briefly at the articles by Roberts (1997) and Furstenberg (2000), or at *Youth Lifestyles in a Changing World* (Miles 2000). In relation to disability issues, Tisdall's (2001) chapter on theorizing transition for young disabled people is a good starting point. Riddell (1998) deals with some similar issues, while Baron, Riddell and Wilson (1999) examine the markers of adult transition in the context of postmodern theories of risk and knowledge societies. There are a large number of specific transition studies, some of which include useful case studies and the perspectives of young disabled people themselves (e.g. Morris 1999; Rabiee, Priestley and Knowles 2001). On the issue of sex and sexuality it would be useful to look at some of the stories in *The Sexual Politics of Disability* (Shakespeare, Gillespie-Sells and Davies 1996) and at the range of recent articles in the journal *Sexuality and Disability*.

INTERNET RESOURCES

- National Council on Disability: *www.ncd.gov/newsroom/publications/transition_11-1-00.html* (detailed report on transition and post-school outcomes for young disabled people in the USA)
- Parents' Guide to Transition: *www.pluk.org/trans.html* (US-based resource with summaries of entitlements and procedures)
- Sexuality Information and Education Council of the United States: *www.siecus.org/pubs/biblio/bibs0009.html* (an annotated bibliography, including both therapeutic and critical sources)

- *Sexuality and Disability*: *www.kluweronline.com/issn/0146-1044* (electronic access to the journal)
- The (Australian) Women with Disabilities Network: *www. wwda.org.au/sexualit.htm* (access to recent debates about the control of young disabled women's reproductive sexuality)

5

DISABILITY AND ADULTHOOD

This chapter highlights some of the core themes of the book, emphasizing how idealized and gendered notions of adulthood underpin the position of disabled people in contemporary societies. In particular, the discussion draws attention to the concepts of adult 'independence', 'competence' and 'autonomy'. Thinking about disability helps to problematize our understanding of what it means to be an adult in society, and reveals more about the way in which both disability and adulthood have been socially produced. In this sense, there is some similarity in the way that the 'non-adult' social categories of disability, childhood, youth and old age have been produced. At the same time it is important to note how changes in technology, gender roles, work, the family and the nation-state have blurred the traditional boundaries of adult citizenship. The discussion draws on the challenges of disability theory and activism to critically examine the concepts of individualism, autonomy and (inter)dependency in a changing world. The specific examples of parenting and employment are used to illustrate an account of disabled adulthoods in the context of citizenship and rights.

Thinking about adulthood

This book examines how the social category of disability intersects with the 'generational system' in contemporary societies, and how the regulation of generational boundaries and the life course impacts on disabled people. As suggested in chapter 1, the concept of adulthood lies at the heart of this generational system, yet it has attracted much less specific theoretical attention than the study of childhood, youth or old age. As a consequence, adulthood remains relatively undertheorized as an analytical or critical concept. There has, for example, been no parallel or sustained attempt to develop a 'new sociology of adulthood' (but see Hudson 1999). Yet, when we look at writing and research on disability, adult issues are core concerns. Although issues like adult independent living and employment are prominent in academic and policy agendas (at the expense of disabled children and older people), there has been little overt recognition of their generational significance. Thinking explicitly about the way that adulthood is constructed and produced helps to address this anomaly. The following sections deal with some of the key concepts. In particular, the discussion illustrates how constructions of adulthood (based on ideas about autonomy, competence and individualism) frame our understanding of citizenship and rights.

Adulthood, disability and the generational system

The first point to consider is that the generational category of adulthood can be both positively and negatively defined. On the one hand, adult social status arises from criteria of inclusion (such as the attainment of a certain chronological age or the achievement of adult roles in relation to employment or parenting, for example). On the other hand, adulthood can be seen as a kind of residual category occupying the territory that is left over when other categories are excluded (in particular, those people exempt from participation in adult labour markets). Thus, while both older people and disabled people of working age may be included in an age-based definition of adulthood, they may also be excluded from the rights and responsibilities normally associated with adult social status.

More generally, adulthood can be viewed as the pivotal organizing concept in a generational system based on the construction and production of dependency. In this sense, other categories (such as children and young people, older people and disabled people) are defined by their perceived dependency on non-disabled adults, as the recipients of adult care or financial resources. By contrast, adults are constructed as independent contributors to the social relations of production and reproduction (e.g. through participation in family work or paid employment). So, there is a sense in which disabled 'adults' excluded from productive and reproductive roles exist as a dependent social category outside the traditional realm of 'adulthood' (in the same way that younger and older people do). This suggests that there is an important generational dimension to the social exclusion of disabled people.

The perceived marginality of children, older people *and* disabled people in Western societies is premissed upon a particular view of adulthood, based on ascriptions of adult independence, competence and autonomy. In addition, the enforced dependency of these other groups on adult labour (in both the public and the private domain) places a generational responsibility on non-disabled adults to engage in productive and reproductive work. These adult responsibilities bring with them the social compensation of adult rights – rights to political participation and citizenship and rights to exercise control over non-adults in caring relationships. There is, then, a close link between the generational responsibilities of independent adulthood and the legitimation of adult rights and power relationships.

Exploring some of these issues, Hockey and James (1993) argue that concepts of personhood and citizenship in Western societies are heavily symbolized in terms of adult autonomy, self-determination and choice. Comparing young childhood and advanced old age, they show how institutional practices of 'caring control or controlling care' deny very young and very old people a proper recognition of their agency and personhood. Hockey and James argue that such practices are culturally specific to Western industrialized societies, where dependency and impairment are regarded as 'childlike' states. Adopting a symbolic approach, they examine how exclusion maintains the dependency of children and older people, and reproduces their generational marginality from adulthood. Making a similar point, Irwin argues that:

> Childhood and later life are positioned, in cultural representations and in social and institutional constructions, as dependent statuses and as social locations that deny children and those in later life full social participation or a proper measure of dignity. In contrast, independent adulthood is positively valued, carrying social status and prestige. . . . There is a clear parallel, in these constructions, with the positioning of disabled experiences in modern society. (Irwin 2001: 18)

This suggests some important parallels in the construction of disability, childhood and old age, as parallel categories marginal to the domain of independent adulthood. In this sense, the generational system that defines childhood and old age has much in common with the system that produces and regulates disability in modern societies (Priestley 1997, 2000). These issues are discussed in more detail later; suffice it to say that just as disabled people have been excluded from participation in adult labour, so they have been excluded from full adult rights and citizenship.

To summarize, although the concept of adulthood remains relatively undertheorized within social science (by comparison with other generational categories), it occupies a pivotal place in the construction and institutional regulation of the life course. This paradox may be explained by thinking of adulthood as a kind of residual category, defined by the exemption of other social groups from adult responsibilities (particularly from adult work). The apparent dependency of these other groups on adult labour then contributes to their maintenance as non-adult social categories. Thus our understanding of independent adulthood may be defined less by intrinsic adult qualities than by the shifting boundaries of neighbouring categories like childhood, youth, old age and disability.

What kind of independence?

As suggested earlier, independence is a key factor in constructions of adulthood, but it can be viewed in a number of ways. For example, independence may be associated with the physical and cognitive functioning of the adult body, with an autonomous sense of adult self-identity, with cultural constructions of adult individualism, or with the successful transcendence of structural dependency upon others. Since each of these themes is relevant to the construction of disabled people as dependent (and in that sense as 'non-adults'), it is important to look critically at adult independence and to examine some of the challenges to its definition arising from generational and disability politics.

For Hockey and James (1993: 142) the construction of adulthood as 'a uniquely work-able condition' is contingent upon an individualist model of adult autonomy in Western societies. Thus, Walker and Leisering (1998) argue that Western individualism has been progressively institutionalized during the era of modernity, and that the regulation of the self and the life course has been increasingly detached from relationships to others or community. Similarly, Giddens (1991) points to the dislocation of lives from their embeddedness within contexts of community, placing more emphasis on individual mobility and reflexivity. Indeed, it is this culture of individualism that frames our current understanding of what it means to be an 'independent' adult. In this sense, adult independence is gauged by the degree to which we are seen to function, both physically and socially, as autonomous actors.

Thinking about adult competence and autonomy within the context of individuation helps to explain the apparent emphasis on narrow, individualist concepts of independence – in particular, the ability to do things for oneself (see Stainton 1994). Clearly, there are parallels here with individual models of disability, which define disabled people's social exclusion as a consequence of their bodily function or 'inability to work'. In particular, medical and therapeutic models of disability have relied heavily on assessments of physical and cognitive function as a measure of actual or potential independence. From this perspective, the presumed dependency of disabled people, like that of children and older people, is defined by the extent to which these groups demand assistance with social and physical tasks.

There have been considerable challenges to the idea that adult independence can be equated with an absence of any need for assistance from within the disability movement. As Oliver notes:

> In common sense usage, dependency implies the inability to do things for oneself and consequently the reliance upon others to carry out some or all of the tasks of everyday life. Conversely independence suggests that the individual needs no assistance whatever from anyone else and this fits nicely with the current political rhetoric which stresses competitive individualism. In reality, of course, no one in a modern industrial society is completely independent: we live in a state of mutual interdependence. The dependence of disabled people therefore, is not a feature which marks them out as different in kind from the rest of the population but different in degree. (Oliver 1989: 83–4)

Redefining adult independence is thus a key goal for the disabled people's movement. Within this political context, disabled people have been more likely to construct adult independence in terms of choice and control than autonomous physical functioning (e.g. Morris 1993; Rock 1988). Two responses are particularly significant. First, much emphasis has been placed on the role of assistive technologies in increasing independent functioning (e.g. Roulstone 1998). Second, the movement for independent living has shown how greater choice and control can be achieved through the self-management of personal assistance (e.g. Priestley 1999). However, some have questioned whether preferences for technological assistance or human assistance reflect different positions in the debate about personal autonomy. For example, Agree distinguishes between these two forms of support, suggesting that people who use assistive technology report lower levels of 'functional limitation' than those using personal assistance: 'The use of assistive technology differs from personal care on a fundamental level. It does not require the ongoing cooperation or coordination of other people and therefore increases the sense of independence with which a disabled individual can meet their long-term care needs' (Agree 1999: 427).

Similarly, Verbrugge, Rennert and Madans (1997) claim that assistive technology offers a more 'efficacious strategy for reducing and resolving limitations' than personal assistance, concluding that the perceived gains to disabled people were greater where they could complete daily living tasks 'by themselves' (see also Hoenig, Taylor and Sloan 2001). Drawing on such findings, and on their own research with older people using mobility aids, Allen, Foster and Berg (2001) note that younger adults in North America are more likely to use equipment and less likely to draw on personal assistance than older people. This, they suggest, may be due to generational norms and expectations about autonomy and independence.

> Older age consistently predicts both having any care and the amount of care received. This finding may reflect greater frailty among older than younger people with disability, as well as greater availability of helping resources. However, it may also reflect the desire for greater autonomy among younger people, as well as perceptions by family members and people with disability themselves that dependency is appropriate for people at older but not younger stages of the life course. (Allen, Foster and Berg 2001: S381)

This kind of reasoning assumes autonomous physical functioning to be the benchmark of adult independence. Within this approach, the achievement of adult independence is directly associated with a lack of reliance on assistance from another *person*. At the same time, increased function or competence achieved by using *non-human* forms of assistance is more highly valued. Such examples highlight the idealized individualism of contemporary adulthood (discussed earlier), and suggest that constructions of dependence and non-adult status tend to devalue the interdependence of supportive personal relationships. Adopting a disability rights perspective, Morris (1997) takes issue with the way people using personal support in their daily lives are constructed as 'dependents' upon their 'carers'. Rather, she emphasizes the importance of choice and control, while recognizing the gender inequalities for disabled women who seek independence through relationships of assistance (Morris 1995). Similarly, Goodley (2000) explores the independence achieved by people with a label of learning difficulties through relationships that promote self-advocacy.

Also from a disability perspective, French (1993) examines the narrow view of independence as autonomous functioning, and asks the more fundamental question, 'What's so good about independence?' As Reindal (1999) notes, the idea of 'being able to do things for oneself, to be self-supporting and self-reliant' is central to thinking about independence in the context of Western industrial societies, grounded in a modernist view of the autonomous subject and arising from European Enlightenment philosophy. This, she argues, limits the discussion of personal autonomy to discussions of an either/or relationship between independence and dependence. By contrast, Reindal argues that a more postmodern understanding of the subject as relational, as 'both embedded and embodied', allows us to deal more openly with the fact that the human condition is ultimately one of interdependence between people. Thus, 'When the human condition is viewed as one of interdependency and vulnerability, this leads to an understanding of independence as "partnership". Departing from a relational view of the subject, independence becomes a two-way responsibility and not solely an individual ability' (Reindal 1999: 364).

Jenkins (1998) makes some similar arguments about competence and incompetence, suggesting that these should be viewed as relational and socially embedded concepts. Reviewing a number of contributions concerned with the situation of people with learning difficulties in different cultural contexts, Jenkins concludes that (in)competence 'is as much an emergent property of social networks and interactional context as it is an endogenous quality of individuals. Perhaps the most basic competence is the capacity for this *sociality*, rooted in the reciprocations of mutually intelligible, complex communication, that characterises human beings and human social life' (Jenkins 1998: 227, original emphasis).

For this reason, he argues that we should broaden our understanding of competence from a narrow, mechanistic property of the embodied individual to one that takes account of its relational character and situated construction. This is quite a complex idea, but in essence it refers to the fact that competence, in the reality of everyday lives, often reflects things that are achieved by people working *together*, rather than in isolation. In this sense, measuring the 'skills' of individuals does not necessarily reveal their competence to perform roles or functions *in collaboration with others*. Thus, Booth and Booth (1998b) suggest that it may make more sense to think about competence as something that is 'distributed' within families and social networks than something located within the individual.

The relational basis of interdependence has been widely employed in feminist debates about disability and health, as a way to reclaim the significance of caring relationships (e.g. Brown and Gillespie 1992). Drawing on similar themes, Gabriel and Gardner (1999) adopt a gendered approach, asking whether there are in fact 'his and hers' versions of interdependence. Reviewing a number of studies, they argue that women are more likely to emphasize the relational aspects of interdependence, while men are more likely to focus on the collective aspects. Similarly, interdependence has been viewed as a key concept in citizenship. As E. Porter (2001) argues, interdependence, arising from experiences of nurturing in our intimate lives, is at the core of responsible citizenship, because it underscores and creates the conditions for connectedness amongst citizens at a political level too.

Key points and ideas for learning

Idealized notions of adulthood occupy the centre or apex of the constructed life course, as it is produced and regulated through policies and institutions. These dominant discourses of adulthood reflect a view of independence and the autonomous self, grounded in individualistic notions of competence and physical functioning. Within the generational system, assistance with daily living becomes synonymous with non-adult forms of dependency. Thus, life course studies have tended to view independence as something that increases during childhood, reaches a peak during adulthood, and declines again during old age. However, this simplistic linear analysis becomes problematic when we consider the situation of disabled adults. Within an individualist paradigm, where adulthood is defined as functional independence, and disability is defined as functional dependence, it is easy to see why disabled people have so frequently been denied adult social status.

Understanding how disability interacts with the generational system, as a social category, is an important step in understanding why disabled adults have been institutionally regulated in such similar ways to children and older people. Expectations about doing things for yourself, doing things on your own, and being independent have been important in defining adult status and citizenship. However, challenges from the disability movement and from feminist critiques suggest that we should reformulate our ideas to take account of the relational nature of human interdependence, both within and between generations. Although many disabled adults (like children and older people) remain structurally dependent on the productive or caring labour of non-disabled adults, it is misleading to suggest that this precludes their ability to exercise adult rights and responsibilities. Indeed, developments within the movements for self-advocacy and independent living suggest that new notions of adult independence can be claimed on the basis of self-determination and relational interdependency.

QUESTIONS
• Why are autonomy and independence so widely viewed as 'adult' characteristics?
• Does the use of support and assistance in daily living under-mine disabled people's claims to adult social status?
• Is there any meaningful difference between independence gained through technological assistance and that achieved through assistance from another person?

EXERCISE: It may be useful to think about adult independence and interdependence in more detail. Begin by thinking about the range of tasks associated with independent living (e.g. personal care, home management, financial management, mobility and travel, parenting, employment and so on). What are the potential barri-ers to independence for disabled adults in these areas, and what is the scope for minimizing such barriers through technology or personal assistance? To what extent are *non-disabled* adults also 'dependent' on or interdependent with others in carrying out these tasks?

Parenting

The opening section of this chapter highlighted the generational significance of adult participation in productive and reproductive labour. In the latter category, we might include a wide range of caring labour within the family, carried out by people across all generations. Here, the issue of parenting is particularly important, because it is a culturally significant, and often overlooked, marker of adult social status. Thinking about parenting exposes the gendered nature of modern adulthoods, and shows how disabled people continue to be obstructed in their claims to parental rights and responsibilities. Building on the discussion of reproductive sexuality in chapter 4, it is clear that disabled women have been particularly subject to disabling practices as parents or prospective parents. The following sections illustrate these arguments, and reveal some of the challenges arising from claims to adult status through parenting roles.

Disabled people and the parenting role

The United Nations Standard Rules on the Equalization for Opportunities for Disabled Persons assert that 'States should promote the full participation of persons with disabilities in family life. They should promote their right to personal integrity and ensure that laws do not discriminate against persons with disabilities with respect to sexual relationships, marriage and parenthood' (United Nations 1993, Rule 9). Examining state practices and disabled people's experiences in this context offers a useful way to think about parenting. Issues of sexuality and romantic relationships are also relevant here, and these were addressed in the preceding chapter on disability and youth (it may be useful to review some of that material in this context). However, the emphasis here is on the specific relationship between adult status and parental rights. In particular, this section highlights examples of legal and policy interventions – notably, through the removal of children from disabled parents into care.

There is a growing body of literature on the experiences of disabled parents, characterized by three main themes. First, there is much work highlighting the perceived incompetence of disabled people in parenting roles, particularly parents with learning difficulties (e.g. Booth and Booth 1994, 1999a; Schofield 1996). Much of this work builds on wider debates about competence and autonomy, similar to those outlined at the beginning of this chapter (see Jenkins 1998). In the most extreme cases, judgements of parental incompetence may result in direct interventions in the reproductive lives of disabled women, through enforced sterilization or abortion (see chapter 4; Brady 2001b; Degener 1992). Much of this literature is grounded in feminist analyses of disabled women's reproductive rights (e.g. Kallianes and Rubenfeld 1997), but tends to highlight the eugenic control of reproduction rather than issues of parental competence *per se*.

Second, there has been a growth in literature that records and celebrates the resilience of disabled parents, particularly disabled mothers, in giving birth and caring for children (e.g. Keith 1994; Morris 1991, 1996; Thomas and Curtis 1997; Wates and Jade 1999).

Here the emphasis has been to record personal accounts of parenting and to draw heavily on disabled people's voices and writings. Third, there have been a number of recent contributions promoting good practice in 'supported parenting' for disabled people within the context of personal assistance, advocacy and independent living (Booth and Booth 1999b; Todd and Shearn 1996; Wates and Tyers 2000). These themes are discussed in more detail later. In addition, research with disabled children, including those 'looked after' outside their birth families, has highlighted the absence of disabled parent role models (e.g. Hintermair 2000; Watson et al. 1999). In this context, it might be suggested that many disabled people would make particularly appropriate parents for the large number of disabled children placed for fostering and adoption (there are parallels here with recent debates, in white Western societies, about the benefits of same culture placements for black, or gay and lesbian young people, such as positive role modelling and the value of shared cultural experience).

Particular attention has been drawn to the situation of Deaf parents. Much of the literature in this area treats Deaf parenting as a problem for hearing children (e.g. in early maternal attachment or language acquisition). The assumption is that, since the vast majority of children born to Deaf parents are themselves functionally hearing, they may be exposed to conflicting cultural influences. For example, Preston's (1995, 1996) research with adult children of Deaf parents in the USA explores their gendered experiences of growing up within both Deaf and hearing cultures. However, there is a considerable danger of pathologizing Deaf parents within this discourse, or at least exposing their parenting to differentially high levels of critique and surveillance (Jones, Strom and Daniels 1989).

More generally, the assessment of disabled adults' fitness to parent has become a considerable concern in policy debates. Campion (1995) addresses the question of who is 'fit to be a parent', highlighting the interaction of legal, medical and social work discourses in shaping our views of the 'ideal' parent, while challenging such constructions as myth (see also Wates 1997). Thus, she draws attention to idealized adult roles in family life, showing how professionals and the media contribute to their reproduction. In constructing her argument, Campion pays particular attention to groups of parents who have been viewed as 'unfit' (e.g. gay parents, teenage mothers, older mothers, single parents, working mothers, black parents and so on). Here, she suggests that disabled parents are perhaps the most significant group.

Campion argues that institutional responses to disabled parents help us to understand the idealized view of the proper parent more clearly – as one who should be physically healthy, expect a long life span, be financially self-sufficient, appear 'normal', and be able to carry out the physical and domestic tasks of caring for children unaided. In judging fitness to parent against these criteria, disabled parents, and people with learning difficulties in particular, are often viewed as inadequate by professionals, the courts and the media:

> Disability and parenthood are words which seem to come together only uncomfortably in our society. The choice of parenthood is withheld from many disabled people through the disapproval of others, through lack of accurate information and lack of role models. If parenthood is embarked upon it is often made more problematic and stressful because of the lack of understanding from professionals. The media reinforce public prejudice, taking little notice of disabled people as parents except to publicise the stories of children being removed from parents deemed unfit or the plight of young children forced into caring for such parents. (Campion 1995: 133)

Thinking about the experiences of disabled parents in this way also helps us to think about the broader relationship between disability and adulthood in contemporary societies. In particular, state and professional interventions in the reproductive lives of disabled people reveal powerful discourses of incompetence and dependency, which are both culturally constructed and socially produced. With specific reference to parents with learning difficulties, Booth and Booth note that:

> Parental competence is not just a matter of possessing adequate parenting skills. It is also an attributed status, which owes as much to the decisions of professionals and the courts as to the behaviour of parents. It is situationally determined by the quality or poverty of the environment in which people live. It is socially constructed in terms of the standards and judgements enforced by the wider society, official agencies and their front-line representatives. (Booth and Booth 1994: 12)

The significance of these constructions and discourses lies in the very real impact that they have in governing and disciplining disabled parents' lives. Thus, Thomas (1997) explores the reproductive experiences of disabled mothers in the UK, highlighting their encounters with medical and professional discourses of risk. She draws particular attention to women's perceptions of pressure to demonstrate their potential as 'good enough mothers', showing how such fears are often driven by the threat of losing parental custody. For example, attempting to live up to idealized notions of autonomy and independence may lead some mothers to become apprehensive about asking for help and support:

> Living with the fear of losing the right to care for their children forces some mothers to go to great lengths to present themselves and their children as managing normally – often at significant personal cost in terms of comfort, and emotional and physical well-being. One consequence is that assistance may not be requested when it is needed because the mother feels that her request may be interpreted to mean that she is not capable. (Thomas 1997: 635)

Success in the parenting role is limited by lack of access to appropriate support. However, professional discourses of 'competence' and 'best interest' tend to place the blame for parental 'failure' on individuals and their impairments, obscuring underlying institutional concerns with the cost of providing support. To summarize, thinking about disabled parenthood provides some useful insights into the wider debate on adult competence and autonomy. Measured against idealized discourses of the fit and proper parent, allegations of incompetence or inappropriateness are easily levelled at disabled people. Such discourses are then formalized within institutions that have powers to remove or regulate parental rights (e.g. in courts or social work agencies). The most striking examples relate to the removal of parental responsibility from disabled adults when children are taken into the legal care of the state, as the following examples show.

Parental rights and child protection

Many states, particularly Western industrialized states, have well-established procedures for determining that children should be removed from their natural parents where there is evidence, or suspicion, of risk, harm or neglect. At the same time, there has been a strengthening of children's rights legislation since the adoption of the United Nations Convention on the Rights of the Child. In particular, child protection agencies and the courts are frequently charged with determining a child's 'best interest' where concerns have been raised about the parents' perceived competence. Yet, there is considerable evidence to suggest that the implementation of such policies discriminates against disabled parents. This evidence is particularly striking in relation to the experience of parents with learning difficulties.

Studies conducted in industrialized countries over the past twenty years indicate that between 40 and 60 per cent of children born into households headed by a parent with learning difficulties are taken into the care of the state (e.g. Accardo and Whitman 1989; Gillberg and Geijer-Karlsson 1983; Mirfin-Veitch et al. 1999; Taylor et al. 1991). Much of this literature accepts the prevalence of child protection orders as evidence that parents with learning difficulties are largely incompetent, or present a danger to their children. However, there are increasing challenges to this reading of the evidence, suggesting that state actions to remove children from disabled parents may also reflect underlying disablist attitudes and barriers. The following example highlights some of these concerns.

McConnell, Llewellyn and Ferronato (2000) examined court records of child protection proceedings over a nine-month period in the Sydney area of New South Wales, Australia. They observed court sittings, and conducted interviews with magistrates, lawyers, child protection workers and community service agencies. Their findings suggest that almost a quarter of all child protection cases involved disabled parents (and that nearly 30 per cent of these cases arose from a formal care order application). There was a considerable gender difference, with disabled mothers accounting for more than 80 per cent of cases and disabled fathers just 4 per cent (the remainder involved couples where both parents were disabled).

The majority of these parents were psychiatric system survivors, many with drug or alcohol dependency issues, and only a very small number of cases involved parents with physical or sensory impairments. Parents with learning difficulties were overrepresented, however, and treated differently by the courts. In particular, they were more likely to have their children made wards of court and placed outside the family home than other parents. McConnell et al. (2000) note six factors contributing to the negative experiences they identified: prejudicial attitudes about disabled people held by agency and court staff; the way in which these influenced definitions of 'risk'; courts' reliance on the opinion of 'experts' (particularly psychologists); a lack of appropriate services to support disabled adults in their parenting role; the bureaucratic constraints of the legal and child protection system; and disabling barriers to participation in the court process itself.

Evidence of similar experiences in other countries, such as the USA, UK, Canada, Germany, Sweden and New Zealand, suggests that children are frequently removed in the absence of any 'real' evidence of actual maltreatment, and that disabled parents are subject to more stringent examinations of their competence and morality than non-disabled parents in similar circumstances (e.g. Tim Booth 2000; Feldman 1998; McConnell and Llwellyn 2000; Pixa-Kettner 1998). Such findings suggest that child protection agencies and the courts commonly attribute difficulties to the parent's impairment, and overlook important contextual factors such as housing, poverty or inadequate support services. In practice, this means that there is often little attempt to arrange adequate support for disabled parents before taking children into care.

Supporting parenting

The concerns raised by such examples have generated greater interest in developing effective supports for disabled adults in their parenting role. The concept of supported parenting recognizes that parental competence is not simply a fixed attribute of individuals. Rather, it is something that develops and is distributed between people in families and social networks (the idea of distributed competence was addressed earlier in the chapter). Supported parenting initiatives are likely to emphasize how individuals, their local networks and service providers can work together to produce better parenting outcomes for everyone concerned (Booth and Booth 1999b). But, in order to challenge existing barriers and disabling practices, considerable investments in advocacy for parents may be required. Thus, Booth and Booth (1998a) evaluate the experiences of parents and advocates in an innovative parenting project in the UK called Parents Together. Here, the aim was to support parents with learning difficulties in a 'non-stigmatising' and 'non-intrusive' way, and to directly challenge the environmental barriers and discrimination that they experienced in parenting their children.

In parallel with such developments, the emergence of disability activism has allowed disabled parents to become more visible, to communicate with one another, and to offer more enabling and diverse narratives of parenthood. Thus, Wates (1997) draws attention to the increasing number of disabled parents (partly as a consequence of medical advance and community living options) and the empowering potential of networking, sharing stories and campaigning together. For example, in the UK such activism led to the formation of a national Disabled Parents Network. Similarly, much has been achieved in the USA by Through the Looking Glass, a community-based organization working with disabled parents to address unmet needs and disabling barriers on the basis of disability culture (see Kirshbaum 2000). In Canada, the Parenting with a Disability Network (PDN) offers peer support and information based within the Centre for Independent Living in Toronto. In the broader international context, Disability Pregnancy and Parenting International also provides a focus for new debates. Contact and communication through such networks has enabled disabled parents, and disabled mothers in particular, to tell new stories that challenge and reclaim notions of the fit parent (e.g. Wates and Jade 1999).

This kind of collective advocacy, in the context of wider claims to full participation and equality by disabled people, has led some states to look again at policies concerning parenting for disabled people. For example, in the UK significant lessons were learned from research into the 'jigsaw of services' that disabled people encounter in their parenting role (Goodinge 2000). This review, involving disabled parent groups, highlighted the positive outcomes of self-directed and family-oriented support systems (particularly in the area of direct payments and independent living). But it also indicated that service agencies still lacked information, and that the rhetoric of social models of disability was not always reflected in practice.

The initial development of disability activism and disability studies focused heavily on adult issues within the public domain (particularly on environmental access and employment opportunities), and it has taken some time for debates on parenting to gain the same kind of recognition. However, there is now a growing disabled parenting movement, and much interest in researching parenting experiences. The emphasis has been to promote independent living solutions that challenge discriminatory attitudes and policies and that recognize parenting as a significant adult status role, particularly for disabled mothers.

Key points and ideas for learning

Parental competence is an important marker of adult social status. Historically, constructions of the fit parent have been highly gendered, impacting particularly on the socially constructed ideals of womanhood. However, disability research and politics have tended to overlook parenting as a rights issue, despite the fact that there are an increasing number of disabled parents. There are many barriers to successful parenting for disabled adults, and these are accentuated when parenting rights are regulated by legal and social institutions. Disabled parents, and young mothers with learning difficulties in particular, have been subject to higher levels of surveillance and to stricter assessments of their parental competence – often resulting in the removal of adult rights and responsibilities when children are taken into care. Recent research and activism illustrate how such practices are framed within a very limited notion of individual competence, thus failing to recognize the levels of distributed competence that can be achieved through social networks and advocacy to support parenting.

QUESTIONS
- What are the requirements of 'good' parenting, and what qualities do 'good parents' need?
- Why are disabled people, and women with learning difficulties in particular, subject to more stringent examinations of their parenting 'competence' than non-disabled people?
- Is there any tension between upholding the rights of disabled parents and the rights of their children?

EXERCISE: Consider some of the legal and moral tensions between disabled adults' parental rights and the 'best interests' of their children. Identify the kinds of argument that might be made for and against the removal of children from families headed by disabled people. It may be useful to consult some of the stories and examples highlighted in the suggested reading and Internet resources at the end of this chapter. What are the main barriers to successful parenting for disabled people, and what kind of policies might support better outcomes?

Work and employment

The preceding discussion suggested that debates on parenting have been marginalized in thinking and research on disabled adulthoods. By contrast, issues of employment have occupied the centre ground of both theoretical development and policy concerns. Indeed, the early development of social models of disability emphasized exclusion from adult labour markets as key to understanding the historical production of disability. The following sections outline the significance of work and employment to constructions of modern adulthood, and their impact on disabled people. Specific attention is then paid to the relative merits of different strategies and policies that seek to increase employment opportunities for disabled adults in contemporary societies.

The social significance of adult employment

There is little doubt that participation in work and employment is a key signifier of adult status in modern societies (and particularly in the historical construction of male adulthoods). Yet disabled people, and disabled women in particular, continue to be disproportionately unemployed, underemployed and underpaid throughout the world. The International Labour Organization (ILO) estimates that some 386 million people of working age are disabled (a majority of the world's disabled population). Yet many, up to 80 per cent in some countries, remain unemployed due to the disabling attitudes of employers, unequal access to education and training, an absence of appropriate support, and disabling barriers in the workplace. Access to economic resources for those who are unemployed is often very limited, and in many developing countries threatens the survival of individuals and their families (Turmusani 2001). Consequently, access to adult paid employment is often seen as the only available mechanism for breaking the link between disability and poverty.

Employment is also significant in the construction of disability as a social category, since 'ability to work' is the primary criterion that states use to define who is disabled. In many ways, this overt focus on adult employment has led to the marginalization of disabled children and older people from disability debates, by focusing research and policy on those 'of working age'. For example, even official figures on the incidence of impairment and disability in European countries are largely restricted to the age range of 16–64 (e.g. European Communities 2001). But it is also important to remember that children and older people outside 'adult' labour markets can and do participate in work throughout the world, and that participation in unpaid labour within the domestic sphere is particularly important in this respect (McDonough 1996).

In developing their ground-breaking discussion on the Fundamental Principles of Disability in the 1970s, the members of UPIAS emphasized that no one aspect of disability discrimination should be treated in isolation. However, they also drew attention to the central significance of employment in creating the social relations of disability in industrialized societies:

the struggle to achieve integration into ordinary employment is the most vital part of the struggle to change the organisation of society so that physically impaired people are no longer impoverished through exclusion from full participation. Only when all physically impaired people of working age are as a matter of course helped to make whatever contribution they can in ordinary work situations, will secure foundations for full integration in society as a whole be laid. All the other situations from which physically impaired people are excluded are linked, in the final analysis, with the basic exclusion from employment. (Union of Physically Impaired against Segregation/Disability Alliance 1976: 15–16)

Following this lead, the development of social model theory emphasized how changes in the structure of adult labour markets were instrumental in the production of disability as a social category in capitalist economies (see chapter 1 and Finkelstein 1975; Oliver 1990; Ryan and Thomas 1980). Indeed, A. Stone (1984) argues that the definition of who is included in the category of disabled people flows directly from state efforts to control the adult labour supply in market economies (see also Priestley 1997). This argument suggests that, while many people with impairments have been historically excluded from competitive wage labour, the exact definition of who is exempt from work obligations changes in response to economic trends and demands. Thus, people who are regarded as 'unable to work' at times of low demand (e.g. during an economic recession) may be brought into the labour market at times of high demand (e.g. during wars or periods of economic growth). In this sense, policy definitions of disabled adults have been revealed as 'elastic' (Gruber 2000), relying more on the changing profitability of their exploitable labour than on fixed biological definitions of their impairment status.

This kind of analysis also suggests that structural changes in future markets may offer new opportunities for disabled adults to participate in economically productive labour. For example, much emphasis has been placed on the potential impact of technology and flexible working in post-Fordist modes of production (see Roulstone 1998). However, technologies are not isolated from the prevailing relations of production, and technology alone can be no guarantor of successful employment. As Michailakis (2001) notes, 'technological optimism' often overlooks the embeddedness of technologies within economic, social and cultural contexts. Similarly, Light (2001) questions uncritical approaches to the role of technology in achieving the employment goals of the Americans with Disabilities Act, expressing concern that technological developments in the information age may actually subvert progressive policies (see also Seelman 2000). Thus, Levine and Nourse (1998) show how an increased reliance on information technology within competitive US labour markets works against the provision of job opportunities for young people with learning difficulties. Thus, rapid economic change brings with it both new opportunities and new forms of exclusion (Jayasooria, Krishnan and Ooi 1997; Landau, Guttmann and Talyigas 1998; Lysack 1997).

To summarize, the emphasis within disability theory on productive paid work, coupled with imperatives for economic survival in countries without established welfare provision, has generated a preoccupation with employment in research and policy. The assumption that entry into employment will promote social inclusion for disabled people is widespread, underlining the significance of socially valued work in constructions of modern adult citizenship. Simply having a job is of course not the whole answer. But the part that work plays in facilitating access to adult social networks and social capital is clearly significant in labour-focused societies (e.g. Chadsey and Beyer 2001). For states too there will be economic benefits in exploiting the economic labour of untapped sections of the population, particularly in times of high demand or where there is pressure on limited welfare resources. Thus, actions to increase employment opportunities for disabled adults have been increasingly promoted by policy makers and disability activists alike, on both economic and social grounds.

Action on employment opportunities

In 1983, the International Labour Organization (ILO) adopted a convention of international standards to promote greater equality of opportunity and treatment for disabled people in employment. Thus:

> The said policy shall be based on the principle of equal opportunity between disabled workers and workers generally. Equality of opportunity and treatment for disabled men and women workers shall be respected. Special positive measures aimed at effective equality of opportunity and treatment between disabled workers and other workers shall not be regarded as discriminating against other workers. (ILO 1983: Article 4)

State and community responses to this challenge have taken a number of different forms. The 1990s saw a rapid expansion of disability employment initiatives, involving a mixture of compulsory and voluntary measures and the proliferation of schemes for support and training. Such responses have emphasized increased flexibility in responding to disabled people's employment needs, and the economic benefits of bringing disabled people into paid work (O'Brien 2001). An alternative strategy has been to facilitate the development of micro-enterprise and entrepreneurship projects run by disabled people in both developing and richer industrialized economies. As Walls, Dowler, Cordingly, Orslene and Greer (2001) argue, the experience of micro-enterprise has enabled many disabled people to 'redefine success' in employment, not simply in terms of income generation, but also in achieving control over the day-to-day management of workloads and workplace environments.

Rhetorically, the presentation of policies has also shifted, from traditional discourses of paternalism and compensatory employment towards arguments based on social inclusion and the 'right to work' (Doyle 1995; Floyd and Curtis 2000; Lonsdale and Walker 1984). While it would be impossible to provide a detailed discussion of these diverse strategies here, it is useful to compare some of the key approaches. There have been a number of cross-cultural studies of policies for supporting and retaining disabled people in employment, although these have focused predominantly on industrialized Western economies. For example, Thornton and Lunt (1997) studied disability employment policies in eighteen countries, building on earlier work in Europe, North America and Australia. Their review suggested an apparently universal commitment to the aims of participation and equality. It also indicated that legislative approaches to this task were becoming more widespread.

In reviewing the data, they identify two broad trends: first, an approach based on anti-discriminatory legislation, in which employment features as one amongst several themes (often a dominant theme), and second, the division of disability policy into departmental concerns, in which employment may be seen as a separate issue. Goss, Goss and Adam-Smith (2000) also argue that there are two distinct approaches in developed countries. Thus, they identify an American tradition, based on anti-discrimination measures and civil rights, and a European tradition, based on compulsory employment quotas and state intervention. Gooding makes a similar distinction, equating quota systems with medical and compensatory models of disability, and rights-based approaches with social models:

> The different approaches are reflected in the contrasting rationales of the two policies. The quota is fundamentally a collective compensation to individuals for loss of capacity. The impetus for this derives

from the state. In contrast impetus for the rights approach derives from the movement of disabled people themselves, and it does not seek to compensate the individual but to change society by opening it up to disabled people as a whole. (Gooding 1996: 65)

Within the rights model, the emphasis has been on anti-discriminatory legislation. However, rights legislation does not automatically alter social contexts and practices that impact on employment opportunities. Employment opportunities continue to be determined by structural factors. For example, Yelin (1997) notes that the raised expectations of disabled people must be balanced against job insecurity in US labour markets, where disabled women are likely to be particularly disadvantaged. Similarly, Schneider, Simons and Everatt (2001) argue that legislative developments may do little to challenge the disadvantage experienced by disabled people in labour markets. In addition, employers and the courts may have a limited understanding of 'reasonable accommodation' in the workplace, focusing on technical changes to work processes rather than the social context of workplaces and work groups (e.g. Grossman 1992). By contrast, when work is viewed as a relational process, involving people in producing through partnerships and groups, work processes are revealed as situated in social spaces, involving more than simply individual workers with individual requirements for accommodation.

Within the compensatory model, traditional approaches were often based on the provision of 'sheltered' employment in segregated workshops or 'training centres'. More recent initiatives have focused on the development of 'supported' placements within mainstream settings. Great optimism surrounded the development of supported employment, and there was rapid growth in this area from the mid-1980s, particularly in North America (Wehman, Revell and Kregel 1997). Although supported employment and training may not always be seen as 'real work' (Black and Meyer 1992), as 'socially valid' (Test 1994) or as 'cost-effective' (Cimera 1998), research suggests that there have been positive outcomes for disabled people. Thus, Thompson, Powers and Houchard (1992) showed how individual placements had a positive impact on disabled people's wages when compared with sheltered employment schemes or group placements (see also Crowther et al. 2001). In addition, there is evidence that disabled people express greater levels of satisfaction with supported employment than with segregated alternatives (Test et al. 2000).

Within the rehabilitation literature, discussion has thus focused on the technical merits of sheltered versus supported employment, and on models of external 'job coaching' versus 'natural supports' in the workplace (see Storey 2000). However, the policy drift from segregated to mainstream employment in Western economies confronts traditional paternalistic services with something of a paradigm shift in thinking and practice. For example, as Saloviita (2000) points out, using examples from Finland, new service paradigms based on employment in open labour markets may be incompatible with the existing policy frameworks of state welfare economies. Reviewing the British government's Supported Employment Programme, Hyde (1998) describes the shift from provision in sheltered workshops towards support for disabled employees in mainstream settings. But he points out that such policies were adopted during the 1980s and 1990s in response to employer interests rather than those of disabled people. Indeed, he concludes that market deregulation and the political emphasis on incentives to work may impact negatively on disabled people (through increased exposure to the disabling social relations of a competitive capitalist labour market).

To summarize, whereas demand-side policies have arisen from disabled people's claims to legislative rights and self-determination through entrepreneurship, supply-side policies have centred on the provision of sheltered or supported employment schemes (targeted at those considered unable to compete in the open labour market). Despite the differing political origins of these traditions, there are some important parallels in their development. In particular, both approaches appear to take an unquestioning view of the centrality of employment status in defining adult citizenship. In this way, both the rights-based approach of disability campaigners and the more revisionist approach of vocational rehabilitation services share a tacit acceptance of the need for as many disabled adults as possible to compete in the labour market of a global capitalist economy. Although laudable in many ways, such aspirations are problematic – particularly given the role of those same capitalist labour markets in the historical creation of disability (Oliver 1990).

Burkhauser (1997) argues that there is unlikely to be any real progress towards independence until there is a culture shift in accepting that disabled people 'can and should be expected to work'. But this raises some fairly fundamental questions about the obligation to work, and about the relationship between work and adult citizenship. Thus, Barnes (1999) argues that a more radical reformulation of the concept of work is required. On the one hand, issues of employment cannot be separated from other dimensions of exclusion (e.g. the environment, transport, housing, attitudes and so on). On the other hand, it is important to understand how work within capitalist economies is underpinned by structural concerns with productivity and profit, based on competition between workers.

In order to develop a more inclusive model of employment, it is therefore necessary to ask whether the notion of work can be reformulated in accordance with an alternative set of principles, such as social obligation and interdependency (e.g. Gleeson 1999). Despite the considerable developments in modes and means of production within post-Fordist economies and information societies, participation in socially valued work remains largely unchallenged as the central marker of adult social status. Yet, an analysis based on competitive wage labour deals with only one side of the work equation, masking the fact that the work of consumption is increasingly significant in the social stratification of contemporary societies (Campbell 1987; Castells 1996). Thus, 'regardless of their role in the "conventional" labour market, people with accredited impairments and labelled "disabled" are both producers and consumers of a vast array of services upon which so many "able bodied" people depend; they are, therefore, an essential component within the context of this equation' (Barnes 1999: 21).

Key points and ideas for learning

The social organization of work and employment has been the key factor in the construction of *both* disability *and* adulthood in modern societies, and disability has been consistently defined by perceived 'inability to work'. Participation in employment is also closely connected with attributions of adult independence and citizenship. Thus both disability and the generational categories of childhood and old age are produced as exemptions from participation in adult labour markets, suggesting certain parallels in the construction of children, older people and disabled people as 'non-adults', or marginal citizens. State interventions to advance employment opportunities for disabled people suggest a move from 'compensatory' schemes towards employment rights and support for disabled workers in competitive labour markets. In many ways, these are positive developments, driven by the activism and claims of the disabled people's movement. However, the political focus on social inclusion through paid employment masks deeper questions about the meaning and ultimate desirability of a citizenship based on 'productivity' and competition. This adult-centred focus reinforces a generational system that marginalizes disabled children and older people from disability debates, and fails to challenge the narrow constructions of work that have produced disability as a social category.

QUESTIONS
• Why have issues of adult employment been so central to the development of social models of disability, and to the citizenship claims of the disabled people's movement?
• Does disabled people's participation in adult labour markets provide greater access to social inclusion and citizenship?
• Should disabled adults be expected to 'work', and who should be exempt?

EXERCISE: Consider the arguments for and against the inclusion of disabled adults in paid employment. For example, what kinds of argument do politicians, employers and disability activists make? What kinds of barriers exist to disabled people's participation in employment? How far are these the result of (a) individual biological differences, (b) disabling attitudes and cultural values, (c) economic imperatives for competition and profit. Addressing each of these areas in turn, identify policies or developments that might lead to greater employment opportunities for disabled adults.

Summary

The discussion in this chapter highlights the central place of adulthood in the construction of disability, generation and the life course. In terms of life course theory and the generational system, adulthood in industrialized Western societies is epitomized by particular constructions of independence, competence and autonomy. By contrast, the generational categories of childhood, youth and old age, and the social category of disability, are constructed as marginal, or non-adult, social statuses. Since discourses of citizenship and social inclusion have also been associated with these same 'adult' characteristics, claims to rights by children and young people, older people and disabled people have been widely contested. However, the construction of these 'non-adult' social categories as dependent obscures the fact that competence and independence are socially situated and relational. Indeed, 'competence' may be better viewed as something that is achieved through social networks and relationships, and theorizing 'interdependence' offers a more useful strategy for understanding how this works. The examples of disabled parenting and employment illustrate the gendered nature of these debates in policy and practice. On the one hand, the political focus on claiming citizenship through access to adult status roles has been very productive, bringing a greater recognition of disabled people's rights to adult social inclusion. On the other hand, these adult-centred claims continue to collude with a generational power system that has been instrumental in the creation of disability as a 'dependent' social category. Rethinking disability from a life course perspective challenges us to rethink the construction of adulthood that underpins this system.

SUGGESTIONS FOR FURTHER READING

For a brief introduction to the way in which disability challenges notions of adult independence, it may be useful to consider the question, 'What's so great about independence?' (French 1993). A more thorough review of debates on competence, in relation to people with the label of learning difficulties, is provided in the edited collection *Questions of Competence* (Jenkins 1998). Discussions of parenting have not been well incorporated into the disability studies literature. However, there are a number of useful contributions, many of which include personal perspectives and experiences. In this context, it may be useful to look at *Bigger than the Sky* (Wates and Jade 1999). The work of Tim and Wendy Booth, such as *Parenting under Pressure* (1994), has been influential in promoting discussion about families headed by people with learning difficulties, while 'Mother Father Deaf' (Preston 1995) raises parallel questions about Deaf and hearing cultures within families. By contrast, there is a great deal of published material dealing with employment for disabled adults, much of it addressing the relative merits of different state policies and interventions. As an introduction, the comparative review of employment policies by Thornton and Lunt (1997) offers a good background, while Storey (2000) provides a more recent summary of arguments for employment in integrated settings. For an analysis of post-war policy developments in the USA see O'Brien (2001).

INTERNET RESOURCES

- Disabled Parents Network: *www.disabledparentsnetwork.org.uk* (UK-based networking and advocacy group)
- Through the Looking Glass: *www.lookingglass.org* (US-based advocacy and development project addressing a range of parenting and family issues)
- Supported Parenting: *www.supported-parenting.com* (focusing on the work of researchers and advocates based at the University of Sheffield, UK)
- Parenting Network: *www.cilt.ca/Parenting/PDN.htm* (peer support and information-sharing network for disabled parents, based at the Centre for Independent Living in Toronto, Canada)
- Parents with Disabilities Online: *www.disabledparents.net/ index.html* (access to a variety of resources and an Internet community of disabled parents, including personal stories)
- Global Applied Disability Research and Information Network on Employment and Training (GLADNET): *www.gladnet.org* (provides access to an extensive international network of research, policy and resources)
- International Labour Organization (ILO): *www.ilo.org/public/ english/employment/skills/targets/disability* (provides details of the ILO's Disability and Work programme with links to a range of related initiatives and resources)

6

DISABILITY AND OLD AGE

In the context of this book, old age is an important area for discussion. Both disability and old age have been produced as structural categories in modern societies through similar processes of social change, primarily through exemption from adult labour markets. There are also similarities in the way that disability and old age have been culturally constructed (e.g. in terms of the impaired body, perceived vulnerability or dependency). Since bodily ageing is closely correlated with impairment, the parallel significance of old age and disability is accentuated by the ageing of world populations. In industrialized societies, the majority of disabled people are over retirement age, and impairment is often considered as a social norm of ageing. Despite this demographic truism, or perhaps because of it, older people with impairments are rarely regarded as 'disabled' in quite the same way as children, young people or adults, and disability activism has tended to focus on issues affecting those of working age or below. There has been much recent debate about the rights of older people, yet their voices and experiences are underrepresented in the disabled people's movement and in disability politics. The discussion addresses some of these tensions and complexities by considering the role of culture and structure, the body and identity, and the political strategy of older and disabled people's movements.

Culture and structure

A recurrent theme in this book has been to examine the way in which disability is constructed and produced in relation to the generational

system, characterizing disability, childhood and youth as social categories marginal to the domain of independent adulthood. In the case
of old age, the parallels with disability are perhaps more striking. Not
only have disability and old age been produced in similar ways, as
dependent social categories; they have also been mutually constructed
as more permanent and inevitable forms of disengagement than childhood or youth. The following sections address some of these parallels, in terms of structural location and the cultural otherness of older
and disabled people.

The structural location of old age and disability

As noted in chapter 1, there has been an increasing interest in theorizing generational divisions as new markers of stratification or
inequality in contemporary societies, reflecting the decline of sociological preoccupations with class (Foner 1988). However, this new
interest in generation has also maintained certain aspects of structural class analysis, by emphasizing the centrality of adult work and
employment. Thus policies to exempt older people from competitive
wage labour have been a driving force in the creation of 'old age' as
a structural and administrative category. This distinction becomes
increasingly significant as fewer older people engage in paid employment. Increased longevity, resulting from social and technological
changes, brings changes not only for older people but also for other
generations, social relations and social norms. Thus, M. Riley
(1988a: 27) concludes that population ageing and social change are
interdependent, each contributing to the transformation of the other.

Structural explanations of old age are then concerned with understanding the kinds of social change that produce this generational
separation, and the kinds of social change that result from it. As
argued in chapters 3 and 4, the increasing technological demands on
modern adult labour produced pressures for compulsory schooling
and youth training that removed younger people from adult labour
markets and placed them in new administrative categories and institutional arrangements. Similarly, the introduction of pension policies
and statutory retirement shaped new 'non-adult' categories of older
people (see Turner 1998). Thus, Townsend (1981) argues that the
structural dependency of older people in Western societies arose from
social policy developments during the twentieth century (see also
Walker 1980). These arguments are very similar to those made by
social model theorists in explaining the emergence of disability as an
administrative category, arising from the dislocation of people with

impairments from participation in competitive adult labour markets under industrial capitalism (Oliver 1989). Linking disability with non-adult generational categories, Hockey and James (1993: 155–6) conclude that 'the economic dependency created through compulsory schooling, compulsory retirement and inflexible working practices produces forms of social marginality or isolation which become recognised as "social problems"'.

Addressing the argument from a disability perspective, Oliver summarizes the similarities of structural location between old age and disability:

> both ageing and disability are produced as an economic problem because of the changes that result in the nature of work and the needs of the labour market within capitalism. The political economy perspective points to the structural dependency of the aged arising from conditions in the labour market and the stratification and organisation of work and society. . . . In other words, old people no longer play a key role in the process of production and no longer participate in the labour market. The same is true of disabled people and has been so, except in times of severe labour shortage, since the time of the industrial revolution. (Oliver 1993: 253)

From a structural perspective, then, old age has been widely viewed as a social category produced through the regulation of adult labour in modern capitalist economies (Minkler and Estes 1991; Phillipson 1982; Phillipson, Bernard and Strang 1986). However, permanent exit from adult work does not always occur at 'retirement age', and many older people, especially in developing countries, continue to labour within families, communities and industries (HelpAge International 1999). Conversely, class, gender and disability are significant factors in decisions to retire 'early' (e.g. Flippen and Tienda 2000). So, defining old age as a stage of permanent exit from adult labour raises some important questions about the generational location of younger disabled adults, who have already been excluded from adult roles in production or reproduction.

This may help to explain the lack of attention to generational identities and transitions for groups of disabled people who appear to age largely *outside* the established generational system. For example, although increasing numbers of adults with learning difficulties survive into old age, many have also been excluded from participation in adult labour and citizenship throughout their lives. Where there is no recognition of adult social status, the generational significance of ageing may also be overlooked: 'for most of the population life is structured into infancy, childhood, working adult life and retirement. For people with learning disabilities, many of the expectations that people have of life are not available. The most striking example is work. . . . Without work or its equivalent there can be no retirement' (Holland 2000: 30).

This lowering of generational significance for older disabled people is reflected in policy and practice. For example, Ashman, Suttie and Bramley (1995) show how older people with learning difficulties in Australia were unable to 'retire' from established work patterns, such as going to a day centre, because the organization and funding of disability services took no account of generational boundaries (see also Hogg and Lambe 1998). Conversely, younger disabled people may be made 'older' through the consumption of services and commodities normally associated with old age (Bernard and Phillips 1998; Vincent 1999; Vincent, Patterson and Wale 2001). Indeed, it is quite common for 'older and disabled people' to be regarded as a single category in policy making and social care.

To summarize, there are some important similarities in the way that disability and old age have been produced and regulated within modern societies. In particular, both have been defined by the work–welfare divide of exemption from adult labour (Irwin 1999). As administrative categories, both have emerged in response to social claims and the changing labour demands of capitalist economies (Irwin 2001). Consequently, disability and old age are parallel structural locations, perceived as 'dependent' and non-adult social categories. This raises some interesting questions about the generational identities and transitions of disabled people who become older (e.g. Zarb and Oliver 1993).

The cultural otherness of old age and disability

In addition to structural similarities, there are also parallels in the cultural construction of disability and old age. In particular, older and disabled people have been subject to similar discourses of dependency and otherness, distinguishing them from the ideals of autonomous adulthood. There is of course a close connection between the cultural distancing of these groups and their structural dislocation from productive and reproductive labour. The cultural distancing of older and disabled people is closely linked to their spatial distancing, and segregation from family work or paid employment reinforces perceptions of cultural difference (Finkelstein 1991). Thus, the perceived 'disengagement' or 'strangeness' of older people with impairments

(Cumming and Henry 1961; Dowd 1986; Maddox 1994) has been underpinned by their systematic removal from families and communities into segregated residential institutions.

In some ways, this distancing of older people (and disabled people) reflects cultural concerns regarding the maintenance of non-disabled adult identities. Thus, 'Just as theories of disability identify cultural fears of distance from the able-bodied ideal, so perceptions of "the elderly" from this ideal generate cultural ambivalence, if not hostility from other age groups. Relatively trivial physical manifestations of difference turn into markers of otherness' (Irwin 1999: 694). For Hevey (1991: 34), the fear and distancing of disabled people, and the threat they pose to non-disabled adult identities, can be explained by the association between impaired bodies, incapacity and death: 'What is happening is that non-disabled people are getting rid of their fear about their mortality, their fear about the loss of labour power and other elements of narcissism. The point I am making is that disabled people are the dustbin for that disavowal.'

Similarly, Shakespeare (1994) draws on feminist approaches to theorizing the 'other' to show how disabled bodies function as conduits for the projection of fears about death and frailty (see Kristeva 1982). In a similar way, Elias (1985) and Marshall (1986) identify links between the distancing of older people and adult denials of death. Thus, there are some parallels in the kind of otherness attributed to disability and old age, as forms of difference and dependence linked to the impaired body and to impending death. Such associations have also been used to argue that the segregation of older people from society is an acceptable prelude to dying (Sankar 1987). Similar arguments have been made about the cultural and physical distancing of disabled people. For example, in their study of the institutional lives of young disabled adults, Miller and Gwynne (1972) pointed to the social death of those segregated from the mainstream (see also Barnes 1990). Thus, they argued that 'by the very fact of committing people to institutions of this type, society is defining them as, in effect, socially dead, then the essential task to be carried out is to help the inmates make their transition from social death to physical death' (Miller and Gwynne 1972: 89).

Picking up this commentary, Finkelstein (1991) argues that institutional segregation is only the final stage in a 'social death model of disability', and that this process begins with the wider construction of disabled people as dependent upon others for permanent care. Thus, modernist discourses of adulthood (emphasizing values such as independence, productivity, youth and progress) have devalued older and disabled people as non-adult dependants. Unsurprisingly, then, resistance to these negative constructions has emphasized the potential for greater independence in later life. 'Sustained personal autonomy' is increasingly viewed as the measure of 'successful ageing' (Ford et al. 2000; Maddox 1994), and this has been expressed in the growing movement for 'active ageing' (Blaikie 1999; Vincent 1999).

Significantly, claims to active ageing have been less concerned with older people's continued participation in adult labour markets (longer working lives) than with participation in new forms of generational consumption (leisured retirement). Indeed, the emergence of a more consumerist culture in late modernity has led some to contend that social status achieved through *consumption* has begun to outweigh that achieved through *production* (Campbell 1987). Indeed, for older people with access to consumption opportunities, the advent of a leisured 'Third Age' offers more in common with the ideals of independent adulthood than with the presumed dependency and physical decline of traditional ageing (Laslett 1989). But such developments also suggest an increasing status divide between older people with and without such opportunities. 'Thus, while the phase of active adulthood expands to embrace many more seniors, stronger taboos form around those in poverty, those whose pastimes lack positive cultural resonances, and those suffering from disability and diseases' (Blaikie 1999: 371).

As 'successful ageing' is increasingly defined with reference to physical fitness, mobility, financial independence and the display of leisured consumption (Tulle-Winton 1999), many older people will benefit from closer associations with adult networks of social capital and citizenship. This is all to the good, for those with opportunities to express consumer choices and adult autonomy. However, positive outcomes for older people at the margins of adulthood do little to challenge the social death of those who do not age 'successfully'. The effect is simply to refocus negative representations onto the most marginalized groups – and particularly on the large number of disabled people amongst the 'very old'.

Key points and ideas for learning

The preceding sections introduce some of the structural and cultural forces relevant to understanding the relationship between disability and old age in contemporary societies. Within the context of modernity, both disability and old age were produced as significant social categories at the margins of independent adulthood. In particular, the exemption of both older and disabled people from competitive wage labour markets created similar kinds of structural dependency for these groups. In contemporary consumer societies, the adult status derived from production must also be weighed against the status derived from consumption. Thus, new spaces have emerged for cultural resistance by older people and for the redefinition of 'successful ageing' (e.g. in terms of leisure consumption, physical fitness or financial independence). This has allowed for an apparent stretching of modernist adulthood, to include more older people at the margins. At the same time, disabling discourses of dependency have been progressively refocused on the oldest of the old, and particularly on those with impairments, thereby accentuating traditionalist associations between the categories of disability and old age.

QUESTIONS
- Do historical exemptions from productive adult labour help to explain the creation of old age and disability as related social categories?
- How significant are the similarities in constructions of old age and disability as forms of 'otherness' and 'social death'?
- What impact are the cultural challenges of 'active' and 'successful' ageing likely to have on older disabled people in consumer societies?

EXERCISE: It may be useful to think further about the ways in which disability and old age are linked through policy and practice, as administrative categories. Think about the provision of institutional support for older people (e.g. in residential and home care, day services, financial benefits, community living options or the family). In each case, identify the reasons why older people might need support, and the kinds of support they might receive. Which of these supports are provided because people are 'older', and which because they are 'disabled'? What does this tell us about the categories of old age and disability?

The body and identity

The preceding sections illustrate how disability and old age have been produced and reproduced through the interplay of structure and culture. Such arguments have been employed to great effect in the development of both critical disability studies and critical gerontology. Indeed, political economy and social constructionism have combined to frame the development of both fields over the past twenty or so years, including the development of social models of disability (Priestley 1998b). However, there is evidence of a new cultural and biographical 'turn' in social theory (Chamberlayne, Bomat and Wengraf 2000; Rojek and Turner 2000; Rustin 2000), and more recent contributions have emphasized issues of identity, biography and the body. The following sections address these themes by reviewing the relationship between impaired bodies and generational identities of old age.

The impaired body as a norm of ageing

The first point to make is that ageing processes are commonly associated with the onset of impairment. For Western industrialized societies in particular, the high incidence of age-related impairments poses a significant challenge. Yet, social theories of ageing have often overlooked this association. Thus, Öberg (1996) draws attention to the paradoxical 'absence of the body' from social gerontology – paradoxical, because cultural representations of old age have played heavily on the imagery of ageing bodies, and because biographical ageing is mediated through embodied experiences (Tulle-Winton and Mooney 1999). Drawing on interviews with older people in Finland, Öberg suggests that the hierarchical separation of mind and body in Western philosophical thought may help to explain why bodily concerns have been devalued in both everyday and theoretical understandings of ageing.

However, more recent theorizing has begun to focus explicitly on the ageing body, as it is both biologically and socially produced. For example, Gilleard and Higgs (1998) note that social constructions of the body are important, because there is no simple relationship between chronological age and the physical 'fitness' of the ageing body (see Featherstone 1995). There are parallels here with attempts to reintroduce the body and impairment into discussions of disability theory (e.g. Hughes and Paterson 1997). Physical and cognitive impairments are not simply biologically caused, but also socially produced, through production and reproduction (see Abberley 1987), while physical ageing arises from lifelong interactions between intrinsic (genetic) and extrinsic (environment and life-style) factors (Evans 2001).

For example, the relationship between ageing and impairment is highly gendered. Women are likely to live longer than men and to spend a larger proportion of their ageing lives with impairment (Kinsella 2000; Leveille, Resnick and Balfour 2000). In addition, women are likely to be relatively disadvantaged due to the gendered nature of disabling barriers – for example, in housing, transport, widowhood and institutionalization (Gibson 1996). In developing countries, poor older women experience additional disadvantages due to massive gender inequalities in literacy, education, employment and nutrition (Prakash 1997). The prevalence of impairment and disability in old age is also related to other social factors, such as social class and education (e.g. Cambois and Robine 2000; Melzer et al. 2001; Melzer et al. 2000), unemployment (Gutierrez-Fisac, Gispert and Sola 2000), and the availability of health care services (e.g. Santana 2000).

There is, then, a sense in which some groups are seen to age 'faster' than others. For example, people with limited access to material and social resources or people with certain kinds of impairment may acquire impairments commonly associated with advanced ageing in younger adulthood (e.g. Holland 2000). The sheer variability of bodily ageing highlights the limitations of biological accounts, and has strengthened more social and political approaches. Yet, at the same time, there is a considerable tension between the view of ageing bodies as socially constructed and concerns with their physical 'finitude' or 'limiting conditions'. This is particularly evident in discussions of resource allocation, where medical aspirations to prolong active life at all costs must be balanced against an acceptance of the body's physical limits (e.g. Longino and Murphy 1995; Moody 1995). Thus:

> Social gerontologists, it is said, face a dilemma when confronted by the physical evidence of ageing bodies and ageing minds. Either they are expected to acknowledge that no amount of money can 'undo' ageing, and accept limits on what is a reasonable level of spend to 'see out' the elderly with dignity or they are asked to acknowledge that the very limited returns from such redistributional strategies will severely restrict the possibilities of redistributing resources to other groups, such as children, young adults, the disabled and so on where the returns may be more rewarding to society as a whole. (Gilleard and Higgs 1998: 3–4)

This suggests an important contrast between the position of the impaired body in old age and that in other generational locations,

illustrating why a generational or life course approach is so important in developing a more overarching theory of disability. For
example, the discussion in chapters 2 and 3 showed how impairment
characteristics at birth and in childhood have long been constructed
as particularly aberrant or untimely. By contrast, impairments and
functional limitations in old age have been more commonly constructed as a generational norm, if not a defining characteristic of
the ageing process. Thus, Zola (1989) argues that the 'specialness' of
impairment and disability is undermined when demographic changes
suggest that they are increasingly a life course norm.

The normalcy of impaired bodies in old age, and particularly
in advanced old age, may help to explain why older people with
impairments are rarely regarded as 'disabled' in the same way that
younger adults or children are. For example, Priestley (2002a) found
that voluntary organizations in the UK did not perceive the older
people they worked with as 'disabled' unless they were unable 'to carry
out what *a normal elderly person* could do' (original emphasis). Many
age-related impairments were thus viewed as consistent with normal
biographies of ageing, as an everyday part of the embodied generational habitus of old age (Turner 1989). To emphasize the point, there
was a tendency to construct older people with impairments as 'disabled' only if their bodily functioning differed markedly from the *generational norms* of their peers. In this way, impairment characteristics
regarded as aberrant in younger bodies are often viewed as 'normal'
in ageing bodies. Significantly, this suggests that constructions of bodily
impairment and disability identity are generationally situated.

Identity and the mask of ageing bodies

It is also possible to view the onset of age-related impairment as an
important factor in triggering identity transitions from adulthood
to old age, and this view has much in common with the character-
ization of impairment as a form of 'biographical disruption' (Bury
1982). From this perspective, the onset of impairment is seen to inter-
rupt previous life course assumptions and narratives, forcing the rene-
gotiation of new biographical identities. However, S. Williams (2000)
contests this view in relation to impairments commonly acquired in
old age, arguing that their onset is in fact widely accepted within
normal narratives of ageing. Thus, he suggests that the biographical
disruption model is inherently adult-centred and has little relevance
to the experience of older disabled people. Indeed, it could be argued
that the onset of impairment in later life *reinforces* the biographical

identity of older people rather than disrupting it (see Carricaburu and Pierret 1995).

Pound, Gomperte and Ebrahim (1998) pursue a similar line of thought in their research with people experiencing stroke in later life. They also note Bury's adult-centred focus, and question his biographical emphasis on 'shattered lives'. Their own research leads them to conclude that the generational and life course context of impairment is a very significant factor, one that has been consistently overlooked in both sociology and disability studies. They suggest two reasons why late life impairment may appear less disruptive to the biography and identity of older people than to those of younger people:

> By the time people have survived into their 70s, 80s and 90s, their experiences may have equipped them with considerable skills which enable them to deal with crises and successfully adapt to new situations such as chronic illness. Alternatively, older people, particularly older working class people, may have lower expectations of health ... and may anticipate illness as inevitable in old age, or meet it with a greater sense of acceptance. (Pound, Gomperte and Ebrahim 1998: 502)

Although the presence of impaired bodies in childhood, youth or adulthood creates tensions with the embodied norms of those generational identities, the prevalence of impaired bodies in old age appears much less disruptive of traditional ageing identities. However, the new cultural challenges of active ageing suggest that such ideas may need to be revised. As mentioned earlier, the transformation of old age from a more structural to a more cultural category in consumer societies has been mirrored by an increasing interest in the identity choices of older people. These developments involve some quite complex arguments, but hinge on the assertion that the identities of older people are becoming less constrained by their structural location and bodily characteristics than they once were. Thus, postmodern identity theories appear to suggest that people can increasingly 'choose' not to be old (Biggs 1997).

Giddens (1991) argues that traditional guidelines for conveying people through the life course have become less clear, and that the uncertainties of high modernity pose certain threats to the maintenance of self-identity in contemporary societies. For other postmodern theorists, such as Featherstone (1991b) and Bauman (1995), such threats are perhaps better viewed as 'opportunities' for consumers to make more diverse and reflexive choices about who they are – drawing on an array of cultural imagery to continually reinvent the way they present themselves to the world. In contrast to the situation under modernity, these identity choices are viewed as largely separate, or at least distanced, from the material conditions of life. In particular, it is claimed that these new identity choices include the possibility of transcending or 'recoding' the limitations of the ageing body (e.g. Featherstone 1995).

For Featherstone and Hepworth (1991) this theme is particularly important in understanding the position of the body in generational identity and the postmodern life course. Thus, they argue that the surface capacities of the ageing body can be conceived as a kind of 'mask' that hides a more youthful or ageless self within. The identity tension for older people is then constructed as the problem of maintaining a youthful sense of self in the face of daily conflicts with the limitations and appearance of the ageing body (see also Öberg and Tornstam 2001). The difficulty from a disability perspective is that the 'mask of ageing' approach sets up an implicitly devalued and generationally specific view of the impaired body. Bodily limitations are equated only with old age, and are seen as inherently problematic.

Other researchers have addressed the supposed malleability of ageing identities with more scepticism, arguing that the limits and appearance of the ageing body impose real constraints on attempts to present the 'youthful self' within. Riggs and Turner (1997), for example, suggest that older people demonstrate rather less reflexivity and choice in practice than might be imagined by identity theory, and that the reality is closer to a 'pragmatic accommodation' of everyday change over the life course. Similarly, Biggs (1997: 566) accepts that while there are some opportunities for 'choosing not to be old', particularly in the rejection of stereotypes, there remains a complex tension between the body, the environment and identity: 'At root the problem would seem to centre on three themes; the nature of what is being hidden by masking, the role of the social environment in which masking takes place, and the importance of the body as a focus for conflict in identity management.'

These are quite complex debates, and require a more extensive resolution than is possible here. But it is clear that disability and impairment pose significant problems for postmodern identity theories that take an uncritical or benevolent view of the consumer environment in which identity choices are made. Social model analyses have consistently suggested that consumer markets do not generally provide enabling or inclusive environments, and that greater interventions and safeguards are required to further the rights of disabled people. Similarly, if the maintenance of 'positive ageing' is focused simply on transcending or modifying impaired bodies, then there is a danger of denying the universality of impairment in advanced old age and reverting to more judgemental and individually based models of disability.

Key points and ideas for learning

To summarize, contemporary theorizing about older people and old age has supplemented structural and cultural perspectives with discussions of the relationship between ageing bodies and ageing identities. However, there has been very little recognition within this debate that 'ageing' bodies are essentially bodies with actual or impending impairments. The close association between advanced chronological age and the onset of impairment means that there is a greater generational prevalence of impaired bodies in old age than in other generational locations. Impairment is, in this sense, part of the everyday generational habitus of old age. Yet, this normalcy also means that older people with impairments are less likely than younger people to be perceived, or to perceive themselves, as 'disabled'.

QUESTIONS
- To what extent is disability 'normal' in old age, and is this socially significant for older people with impairments?
- Does it make sense to think of disability in old age as any less 'disruptive' to biography than disability in adulthood or childhood?
- Does the maintenance of a positive identity in old age require an escape from the impaired body?

EXERCISE: Think about ageing processes and old age identities. What does being older mean, and how do we know that someone is 'old'? What is it that makes us 'feel' old (e.g. in terms of the changing body, the attitudes of others, changing work and family roles, or economic resources)? How important are impairment and disability in these discussions? Now consider the concept of 'successful ageing'. What does it mean, and what strategies might older people adopt to present more positive images of their identity in old age? What are the potential barriers to successful ageing for older disabled people?

The politics of disability and old age

Disability politics and disability rights are relevant to people throughout the life course, and would seem to be particularly significant for the large numbers of people who experience impairment in old age. Yet, when we look at the politics of older people's rights, there has been something of a failure to engage with critical thinking on disability – either in gerontological research or in policies for managing ageing in contemporary societies. Despite recent advances in the field, there remains a tendency to view 'disability' only in terms of individual impairment and physical functioning, rather than environmental limitation or disabling barriers. Similarly, when we look at the political mobilization of the disabled people's movement, and at initiatives against disability discrimination, there is little direct reference to older disabled people. This is surprising, since disability is such an issue for older people, and suggests a lack of cross-over between critical studies of ageing and critical studies of disability. Thinking about the arguments made in chapter 5, it is important to ask how disability rights and identities have been constructed within a generational system that focuses on participation in adult-centred roles.

Population ageing and impairment

That we live in an ageing society is a matter of unquestionable fact, and the increase in world population ageing is dramatic. In general terms, the proportion of people aged over sixty grew from 6.9 per cent in 1900 to 10 per cent in 2000, and is predicted to rise to 28.1 per cent during this century (United Nations 1998). However, there are great regional differences. The largest increases are expected in Asia, Latin America and the Caribbean, with the largest proportions of older people living in Europe. For example, while approximately one in five Europeans are aged over sixty, only one in twenty Africans fall within this age group. Yet the pressures to adapt to population ageing may be greatest in developing countries, where the majority of older people live, because population ageing is more rapid there. At the same time, the proportion of children in the global population continues to decline, to the extent that older people became the larger of the two groups in developed regions at the end of the last century, and will become so in developing regions by 2050 (United Nations Secretariat 1998). Concerns over the 'demographic time bomb' in industrialized societies are perhaps outweighed by the challenges facing older people in the majority of the world, where scarce resources threaten the maintenance of social care (e.g. Jitapunkul, Bunnag and Ebrahim 1993; Kinsella and Suzman 1992; Polivka 2001).

Broadly speaking, we can identify two important trends. First, medical, technological and social developments mean that there has been a dramatic increase in the number of younger disabled adults who survive into old age. The increased longevity of people with long-standing impairments raises questions about the ways in which societies respond to disability issues amongst ageing populations (e.g. Salvatori et al. 1998; Zarb and Oliver 1993). For example, Gething (2000) argues that state policies have largely failed to take account of the substantial number of older people with hearing impairments acquired in younger adulthood, and the cumulative impact of their lifelong disadvantage in education and employment. Similarly, there has been increasing concern about policy responses to the substantially increasing proportion of people with lifelong learning difficulties who now reach older age (e.g. Breitenbach 2001; Patja et al. 2000). Second, the general trend of population ageing means that the number of previously *non-disabled* adults who acquire impairments in later life is also increasing (it is important to remember that previously disabled people will often acquire additional impairments in old age too).

These parallel trends suggest that there is likely to be a convergence of disability status in later life between older people who grew up with impairments and those who acquired them later. For example, Holland (2000) and Janicki, Dalton, Henderson and Davidson (1999) draw attention to parallel increases in the number of people with learning difficulties surviving into old age and the number of previously non-disabled people acquiring cognitive impairments in later life (resulting from dementia or stroke, for example). Similar arguments could be made about convergence in the acquisition of physical or sensory impairments. But it is worth noting that general increases in life expectancy do not always mean an increase in the amount of time that older people can expect to live with impairments (Crimmins, Saito and Ingegneri 1997), and there are regional variations, even between developed countries. For example, on average, a Japanese older person at age sixty might expect to live another twenty-three years and to spend about four and half years of that time with significant levels of impairment (Liu et al. 1995), less time than the equivalent population in the USA (Tsuji et al. 1995).

Acquired cognitive impairments and mental distress account for most impairment worldwide (up to 60 per cent), particularly amongst older people in developed market economies (Jagger et al. 1998), with age-related dementia accounting for a large proportion. Fratiglioni, De Ronchi and Aguero-Torres (1999) report on the global prevalence of dementia, noting its growth in both developing and developed countries, with apparently little regional variation (but see Prince 1997). Although age-related dementia is among the most common forms of impairment in older people, there has been relatively little research in this area from a disability studies or social model perspective. However, researchers working with older people who experience dementia have become increasingly interested in listening to their voices and contextualizing their experiences within relationships of power (e.g. Proctor 2001; Stalker, Duckett and Downs 1999). There is still a considerable amount of work to be done in bringing a social model analysis to these issues.

It is not necessary here to go into extensive detail about the prevalence of impairment in later life. Suffice it to say that global population ageing, including the increased life expectancy of younger disabled adults, means that we are already witnessing a substantial increase in the number of older disabled people, and that we may expect to see this trend continue. Thus, the UN International Strategy for Action on Ageing (2002) draws specific attention to the growing number of older people with impairments throughout the world, and the need to reframe social policies and institutions in response to changing population needs. But, as mentioned previously, such analyses tend to construct the problem of disability only in terms of 'health' and 'functioning'. The real issues and debates are then about the extent that the growing population of older disabled people can be included in discussions of disability rights. If disability policies and debates continue to focus on adult issues, such as employment, then there is a danger that an increasing number of older disabled people will be further marginalized and excluded.

Have disabled elders been left out?

There has been increasing international interest in the rights of older people, and the United Nations has been active in promoting this agenda for at least the past twenty years. For example, the International Plan of Action on Aging, sometimes referred to as the Vienna Plan (United Nations 1983), was endorsed by the UN General Assembly in 1982 (Resolution 37/51), offering an initial framework for thinking about policies on ageing. Its underlying principles emphasized that dignity, equity and commitment between generational age groups should be considered as binding principles in the reproduction of societies: 'The respect and care for the elderly, which has been one of the few constants in human culture everywhere, reflects a basic interplay between self-preserving and society-preserving impulses which has conditioned the survival and progress of the human race' (para. 27).

In pursuing the principles and priorities outlined in the Vienna Plan, the UN later adopted a more comprehensive set of eighteen Principles for Older Persons (United Nations 1991), addressing five core areas of concern: independence, participation, care, self-fulfilment and dignity. These merit some attention, particularly in relation to the discussion of adult independence in the preceding chapter. For example, it is interesting that the six principles relating to the theme of 'independence' refer less to autonomous physical functioning than to choice, self-determination and access to resources (e.g. income maintenance, adaptable environments, and the choice to remain in one's own home). The principles thus resist the common assumption that dependency in old age is biologically determined, and come much closer to the claims and representations of the disabled people's movement. There is also a strong commitment to community integration and participation, including opportunities for older people to mobilize their own associations and movements. In the domain of 'care', the UN Principles stress the importance of individual rights and access to health and social care resources (specific reference to fair treatment and equality of opportunity in relation to disability status is included in Principle 18, under the heading of 'dignity').

Moving on from these developments, 1999 was declared the International Year of Older Persons (UN General Assembly Resolution 47/5). Again, policy makers drew attention to the urgency of finding innovative responses to global population ageing, particularly in developing countries. The International Year also re-emphasized the need to think about older people's experiences within a framework of choices and rights. Within this context, older people have increasingly organized themselves to campaign on issues of equality in areas such as access to health and social care, housing, income, transport and employment (Carter and Beresford 2000; Vincent 1999; Vincent, Patterson and Wale 2001). At the same time, we have seen the emergence of a strong movement of disabled people, campaigning for choices and rights on many similar issues (Barnartt and Scotch 2001;

Barnes 1991; Campbell and Oliver 1996; Fleischer and Zames 2001; Johnson and Shaw 2001). However, while there is some considerable overlap in the issues on which older people and disabled people have campaigned, the ways in which they have represented their claims differ (see Priestley 2002b).

Although such differences of representation may seem small, they belie a certain distancing of older people's political claims from those of disabled people (and vice versa). Clearly, there are some policy issues and claims connected with old age that have less direct relevance to disability *per se* (such as pensions), but there are many more that seem intimately connected with either impairment or disabling barriers. For example, national organizations representing older people in the UK (such as Help the Aged and Age Concern England) have launched campaigns on older people's rights to hospital treatment, inclusive housing, accessible public transport, self-directed care and quality of life. These are just the kinds of issues that have concerned disability activists too. Yet, few of these campaigns make explicit reference to disability rights issues.

Despite the fact that the majority of disabled people in Western societies are over retirement age, older people remain underrepresented within the disability movement, while disability policy making remains focused on the needs of younger adults (and, to a lesser extent, children). For example, despite the high profile given to the role of direct payments and personal assistance in achieving independence for younger disabled adults, there has been some hesitancy about the applicability of such solutions for older people (e.g. Barnes 1997b; Genskow 1986; Keigher 1999). It is certainly evident that many services treat older people very differently from younger adults, and that provision of some of the more progressive developments in services for 'younger disabled people' has not been extended to older people with impairments. In this context, the perceived normalcy of impairment and interdependency in old age may be a factor in the minds of policy makers, as a report into long-term care in the UK concluded:

> Younger people must try to negotiate their lives while disabled and when the vast majority of their peers, who set the standards of normal behaviour, are able-bodied. By comparison, as 7 in 10 people aged 80 or over have some level of disability, being unable to do some things or needing help with others is a common and anticipated experience. This perception may be behind the differences in the policy approach to supporting younger and older disabled people, both in service terms and financially. (Sutherland 1999: §9.7)

Kennedy and Minkler (1998) draw on a review of US policy making to illustrate the distancing of older people's concerns from those of younger disabled people. This leads them to conclude that raised expectations about disability rights, resulting from progressive developments in legislation and policy, are not being applied equally to older disabled people. At the same time, advances in rights for older people are failing to recognize or include those who are also disabled.

> There is a growing appreciation of the potential for reaching goals of autonomy, growth, participation and high life satisfaction on the part of the non-disabled elderly, but these goals tend to be recalibrated dramatically downward for those elders who become disabled. Where 'access' and 'full participation' have become key concepts for the younger disabled population, the sights of families and professionals, and of older disabled persons themselves, tend to be far more circumscribed. In this way, aging professionals [sic], elders, and society in general appear to have traded earlier, limited views of aging for an even more limited view of what it means to be old and disabled. (Kennedy and Minkler 1998: 768–9)

The previous chapter suggested some of the reasons why older people may have been overlooked in the preoccupation of disability theory and policy with adult-centred issues. The argument above suggests that disabled people may also be marginalized from new ways of thinking about old age. The disabled people's movement has gained much ground in terms of representation and rights. But it is important to look critically at the generational significance of these claims (in particular, the emphasis given to younger disabled people's claims to participation in the domain of adult independence and employment). There is, then, a sense in which the political strategy of the movement has sought to distance disability debates from negative associations with old age and dependency by emphasizing adult-centred values and issues. Similarly, older people's movements and movements for the Third Age have advocated 'active ageing' as a way to distance their claims from the negative imagery of disability and dependency (Minichiello, Browne and Kendig 2000).

In this way, the strategy of both older people's movements and disabled people's movements has been to articulate claims for recognition of adult status and citizenship by distancing their struggles from negative associations with the other. These parallel claims may well be benefiting those at the margins of inclusion (i.e. younger disabled people and older adults in their fifties and sixties) by allowing them to liberate themselves from the imagery of frailty, dependence and burden so often attached to very old people with significant impairments. But there is a considerable tension here, one that may be a factor in negotiating future political strategy within the two movements concerned.

> From the point of view of those advocating older people's interests, the disability movement may seem like a model of self-advocacy.... However, there are a number of problems for older people following this route and doubts have been expressed as to whether disabled people are an appropriate comparison. Certainly, many associated with the Third Age movement have sought to disentangle the image of elderly people from illness and disability. (Vincent 1999: 93)

It is tempting to suggest that political alliances and greater understanding could strengthen the claims of both older people and disabled people. Nevertheless, while the two movements have many concerns in common, there are obstacles to such developments. In particular, there may be conflicting issues of identity politics where claims to rights are inseparable from claims to adult social status. It is particularly difficult to envisage how political claims that adopt dominant discourses of adult independence can ultimately benefit those older disabled people who are the most marginalized and excluded.

Key points and ideas for learning

Demographic ageing, and the compression of impairment into later life, raise policy concerns and conflicts of interest in the allocation of resources to meet the citizenship claims of older and disabled people. In this context, there has been a growth of political activism in parallel social movements representing the interests of these two groups. Both have made significant claims to adult rights and citizenship, often focusing on substantively similar areas of policy concern. However, the political strategies and discourses adopted maintain a considerable identity distance between the two constituencies. Thus, whereas disability movements have distanced themselves from old age issues, by focusing on employment and independent living in younger adulthood, movements for the Third Age have advocated 'active ageing', in order to create distance from the perceived dependency of disability in later life. Both forms of activism have been successful where they have made claims at the margins of adulthood, yet both run the risk of further marginalizing the oldest and most disadvantaged of disabled people.

QUESTIONS
- How similar are the political concerns of older and disabled people?
- Why are older people with impairments often not seen to have disability rights in quite the same way that younger adults are?
- What are the potential barriers to greater political alliance between movements of older and disabled people?

EXERCISE: It may be useful to look in more detail at the United Nations Principles for Older Persons. Using the five main headings (independence, participation, care, self-fulfilment and dignity), consider the situation of older disabled people and the potential barriers to their fulfilment of the goals expressed. Now look at the United Nations Rules on the Equalization of Opportunities for People with Disabilities. To what extent does this disability rights agenda accommodate the needs of older disabled people?

Summary

It is possible to think about old age in a number of different ways, all of which have some relevance to understanding disability. Collectively, old age may be viewed as a structural or administrative category deployed to control adult labour supply, and maintained through discourses of ability to work. In this way, old age has been produced and regulated in very similar ways to the category of disability in modern societies. Both have involved categorical exemption from competitive adult markets, resulting in the enforced dependency of older and disabled people on non-disabled adult labour. Old age may equally be viewed as a cultural category, constructed in relation to other generational locations (such as adulthood and childhood). In this context, both older and disabled people have been viewed as non-adult 'others', a construction reproduced through institutional segregation and disciplining forms of care.

It is also possible to think about ageing in terms of the body, and the significance of impairment in defining old age. Since certain impairments are closely associated with advanced ageing, they may become normalized as part of the generational habitus or trappings of old age. This suggests that perceptions of appearance and physical functioning are generationally situated. Whereas impairment in young adulthood is commonly viewed as a disruption of the normative life course, it may be seen as unexceptional to life course trajectories in old age. This has consequences for the negotiation of embodied generational identities and for thinking about disability. In order to explain why older people with impairments are rarely seen as 'disabled', it is necessary to think about both their structural and cultural dislocation from adulthood and about the relative normalcy of impairment in biographies of later life.

The politics of disability in later life is also important, and organizations representing the claims of older people and disabled people have become increasingly active, challenging old assumptions and past policies. However, despite the fact that both movements have campaigned on similar issues, their political strategies highlight differences as well as commonalities. Movements for 'independent living' and 'active ageing' have made increasingly successful claims at the margins of independent adulthood, while distancing themselves further and further from the negative imagery of dependency in deep old age. Developments in rights for older and disabled people have created benefits for many, but there is a risk that those who are already the poorest and most marginalized are being left behind.

SUGGESTIONS FOR FURTHER READING

There is a considerable literature on social theories and approaches to ageing in contemporary societies, and it may be helpful to review some of this material by consulting the contents pages of relevant journals, such as *Ageing and Society*. For a good introduction to theoretical constructions and debates, see Irwin's (1999) paper in the same journal. Townsend's (1981) influential paper on structural dependency remains useful, but see also *Dependency and Interdependency in Old Age* (Phillipson, Bernard and Strang 1986). On the cultural challenges to ageing in consumer societies, it may be useful to look at *Ageing and Popular Culture* (Blaikie 1999), and for a discussion of the debate on embodied identities and the 'mask' of ageing, the article by Biggs (1997) is a good starting point. There are relatively few texts that directly address issues of ageing from a critical disability studies perspective. For some exceptions, see Zarb and Oliver (1993) or Oliver (1993). For a broader discussion of ageing and dependence with some reference to disability politics, see *Ageing,*

Independence and the Life Course (Arber and Evandrou 1993) or *Growing Up and Growing Older* (Hockey and James 1993).

INTERNET RESOURCES

- United Nations Programme on Ageing: *www.un.org/esa/socdev/ageing* (includes a wide range of material and resources relating to population ageing and agendas for action)
- International Year of Older Persons: *www.un.org/esa/socdev/iyop* (includes links to the UN Principles for Older Persons)
- European Sociological Association Research Network on Ageing in Europe: *www.ageing-in-europe.de*
- HelpAge International: *www.helpage.org*

7

DEATH AND DYING

This final chapter completes the review of disability issues and life course transitions by returning to the hotly contested territory of life and death. Taken in a global context and across the life course, disability is very much a life-and-death issue, as illustrated by numerous examples in the preceding chapters. The discussion begins by considering how death and dying have been constructed and produced in contemporary societies and the sociological literature, with an emphasis on the implications for disabled people. In this context, the normalization of life expectancy and increased consumer involvement in dying illustrate the construction of certain kinds of death as 'good', 'natural', 'timely', 'merciful' and so on. The second part of the chapter examines debates about the killing of disabled people, including examples of genocide, euthanasia and physician-assisted death. The discussion pays particular attention to contemporary debates on the worth or 'quality' of disabled lives, and the contribution of the disabled people's movement in challenging disabling practices and constructions of the normal life course.

Thinking about death and dying

The purpose in adopting a life course approach in this book has been to highlight the significance of disability throughout the life span and across all generations, rather than conceding to the dominance of adult-centred approaches. In addition, this framework allows for the inclusion of concerns with the very beginning and end of life. It was important, for example, to include birth and pre-birth issues within the overall framework of the book (in chapter 2). Similarly, the approach would not be complete without attention to the place of disability in thinking about death. Death and dying are an important, and inevitable, part of the way we think about the life course and its normative construction. However, there has been little direct engagement with the sociology of death and dying in the disability studies literature. The following sections introduce these debates by outlining some of the main theoretical approaches, cultural constructions and dying practices in contemporary societies.

Theoretical approaches

Since death is present in all societies, anthropologists and sociologists have looked to its social organization and rituals as a way to reveal how cultures view themselves and their people (e.g. Hockey, Katz and Small 2001; Murray Parkes, Laungani and Young 1997). Indeed, as Kearl (1989) points out, much of what we know about past civilizations comes directly from evidence of funerals and death rites (e.g. Brooks 2001; Demaitre 2001). Thus Drackle (1999: 121) identifies death as 'a central cultural fact which reveals local ideas about social relations, religion and the nature of society'. Studies of bereavement and grieving have certainly yielded substantial theoretical developments. However, Corr, Doka and Kastenbaum (1999) argue that there has been less advance in theories of death and dying itself. Similarly, Kastenbaum and Thuell (1995) suggest that we lack any real theory of dying that can explain the embodied experience of dying people in social contexts.

This is perhaps slightly unfair, given the considerable attention now devoted to death and dying within the sociological literature. For example, J. Riley (1983) draws attention to diverse sociological interests in the self and social existence, bereavement and loss, and the social management of death. Reviewing some of this literature, Corr and colleagues (1999) identify three prominent themes: awareness and communication of dying, processes and trajectories of dying, and coping with dying. They conclude that death should be viewed as unique to individuals, but occurring within particular social contexts, suggesting that the process of dying involves both an objective biological fact and a socially negotiated construction (e.g. in the way that deaths are negotiated between medical practitioners and dying patients). These insights highlight the fact that death is both an event and a process, and that different deaths may follow different 'trajectories' or 'stages' (from momentary or rapid transition to slow physical and mental decline). Thus, Lynn (2001) identifies three distinct pathways of dying: a short and obvious decline, a longer and less predictable chronic illness or disability, and 'a slowly dwindling course to death'.

Such trajectories may also vary depending upon the level of awareness or certainty about death and its timing (see Glaser and Strauss 1965, 1968; Kubler-Ross 1969; Pattison 1977). In this sense, the process of dying will be very different for someone who is aware of their impending death and its timing than for someone who is not (e.g. in the extent to which they are able to involve themselves in planning and negotiating the processes involved). Here, the work of Marshall (1980) was particularly influential in highlighting the need for a more sociological understanding of the self, biography and social consensus within dying processes (in this case, applied to older Americans). Moreover, death and dying will be experienced differently at different ages and points in the life course (Cook and Oltjenbruns 1998).

More generally, demographic changes in richer technological societies have changed the overall pattern of dying trajectories (J. Riley 1983). The decline in child mortality, increased longevity in old age, and reductions in adult death through accident or disease suggest that trajectories of dying are now more predictable (in aggregate terms) than was previously the case. The fact that most dying now takes place in old age rather than in childhood or youth has substantially altered its social significance in relation to the life course. Contemporary dying might thus be viewed as less 'deviant' or destabilizing than that characterized by earlier functional sociologists (such as Parsons 1963), posing less threat to the stability of social organization. Conversely, increasing technological and social control over death may lead to false expectations that dying should always be predictable, suggesting that unplanned deaths are perhaps more socially problematic than in the past.

The 'good death'

From a cultural perspective, it is important to examine how death and dying are socially constructed. In particular, it is useful to think about the way in which different deaths are constructed as more or less desirable. The concept of a 'good death' was initially developed in a religious context (e.g. Taylor 1989), but has now acquired currency as a secular idea. For example, Leichtentritt and Rettig (2000, 2001) used dramatic narrative interviews with older people in Israel to examine the construction of a 'good death'. Drawing on a variety of cultural, structural and individual perspectives, Kearl develops the concept of a good death as one that is timely, that allows for the completion of a successful life project, and that permits those surviving to accommodate their loss.

> Ideally, for the dying, the death should be anticipated, welcomed, non-stigmatizing, and following the completion of one's central social obligations and personal desires or goals. For the surviving, the death should occur neither prematurely nor postmaturely, with the affairs of the deceased in order, with their (the survivors') status at least remaining intact, and having had the opportunity to say or do with the deceased all that was desired and without any regrets. (Kearl 1989: 497)

Developing this argument, Kearl suggests that the potential for good deaths would seem to be increased in societies where dying is more predictable and regulated, and where greater choice exists. However, the construction of good deaths as contingent on the completion of worthwhile life projects leads him to conclude that our social concerns should be with the living: 'The major obstacle is society's ability to provide full, meaningful lives that allow the individual the sense of closure and completeness when the end does arrive. The problem of death remains the problem of life' (ibid.).

Taken in the context of the preceding chapters, this argument has a particular salience in disabling societies that raise barriers to the successful completion of full and meaningful lives for people with perceived impairments. The cumulative evidence of discrimination in important life spheres (such as education, sexuality, cultural consumption, parenting and employment) suggests that it may be particularly difficult for disabled people to achieve equal access to the 'good death' envisaged here. At the same time, the development of the disabled people's movement has enabled increasing numbers of disabled people to reclaim these life domains, while disability culture has challenged us to redefine our constructions of a successful life project.

The perceived timeliness of death in different lives is also significant in defining the desirability or appropriateness of dying. The concept of 'premature' death is important here, conveying the undesirability of deaths that occur 'before their time' (e.g. in the representation of death in childhood or youth as tragedy). As Howarth (1998) points out, the deaths of younger people are more likely to be perceived as traumatic and 'untimely', whereas dying 'of old age' has been constructed as a more natural and less tragic process (Foster et al. 2001). However, it is worth noting that the deaths of younger disabled people are often viewed as more timely, benign or 'merciful' than those of non-disabled people. In such cases, there appears to be less concern with the completion of life projects than with the representation of lives as not worth living (see chapter 2). Clearly, then, the timeliness of the 'good death' has much to do with the social value attributed to individual life projects and their potential for fulfilment.

In addition to being timely and entailing the fulfilment of life projects, good deaths have also been constructed as those that occur 'naturally'. Here, particular attention has been drawn to the role of medical technology. Seymour (1999) examines the way in which natural death has been constructed in the health and social science literature, suggesting that technological intervention has been widely viewed as the marker of unnatural dying. Thus, Mollard (2001) argues that 'technological dying' in medical and palliative care settings detracts from death with dignity, while Harvey (1997) shows how hospital staff attempt to mimic 'natural' processes in the phased withdrawal of technological support from dying people. Basta and Tauth (1996) conclude that high technological intervention can transform dying into a 'medical nightmare', and that natural death is often preferable to resuscitation.

Allied to these technological concerns is the widely held belief that good, natural deaths are more likely to occur at home than in medical settings. Studies consistently show that most people prefer to die at home than in hospital. For example, home deaths may be associated with a sense of comfort, belonging, environmental control, autonomy, privacy or normality (Tang 2000). Yet, when rated against other concerns (such as freedom from pain), dying at home appears to become a lower priority (Steinhauser et al. 2000). Far fewer people in Western industrialized societies die at home than was previously the case, even amongst older people receiving long-term home care (Cobbs 2001). For example, in Canada, most people die in hospital (up to 87 per cent in Quebec), and the proportion dying in special care units is very high, suggesting considerable levels of technological management (Heyland et al. 2000).

However, variations in home deaths also suggest that gender and the availability of support at home are significant factors. For example, Fried, Pollack, Drickamer and Tinetti (1999) found that older women and those living with a child were the least likely to die in hospital, while Richards, Wrubel and Folkman (1999) note the high prevalence of death at home with a partner present in San

Francisco's gay community. In Japan, Yasumura and colleagues (2000) found that the probability of dying at home increased with the availability of home-based care services. In a study of people dying from cancer in the USA, men, people who were unmarried, and those living in lower income areas were more likely to die in institutions; whereas those who were married, women, white or living in higher income areas were more likely to die at home (Gallo, Baker and Bradley 2001).

To summarize, theoretical and lay constructions have tended to construct the 'good death' as one that is both natural and timely. Although the technological management of dying in medical settings has been viewed as less natural than death at home, it has also been seen to allow greater control over the timing and process of dying. Timing has been viewed as particularly important in allowing for the completion of individual life projects prior to death. This, in turn, highlights the negative or tragic construction of deaths that are untimely or 'premature'. There is an important generational context here, with deaths in childhood or young adulthood more likely to be viewed as premature than those occurring in advanced old age. However, impairment and disability also play a significant part in this construction, suggesting that the low social value attributed to disabled life projects may help to explain why the deaths of disabled people are so often viewed as less tragic or more timely than those of non-disabled people.

Involvement in dying

With the growth of consumerism in information and knowledge societies, attention has increasingly turned to the involvement of people in the act of their own deaths. Thus, there have been moves to promote greater awareness about dying and greater communication between patients and professionals (Macleod 2001; Wong, Lee and Mok 2001). Such moves offer a significant counter to institutional traditions of non-disclosure in medically governed settings (Costello 2001), devolving risk negotiations to individuals. The focus has been on providing 'information' to dying patients and their families. However, this may obscure the fact that dealing with death involves not only cognitive awareness but also substantial emotional labour (Mamo 1999).

There is also evidence that access to appropriate and usable information is not equally distributed, and that disabled people are often disadvantaged in this respect. For example, Botsford (2000)

examined the support available to older people with learning difficulties as they confront death and dying, arguing that existing systems
of care continue to disadvantage them up to and including the end
of life. Examining the history of such services, Botsford (2000: 35)
noted how disabled people have often been excluded from 'supportive rituals and education about the end of life'. At the same time,
there is some evidence of more progressive developments in support,
through the increasing availability of grief counselling, bereavement
services, support groups, and 'end of life committees' (see also Read
1999; Botsford and Force 2000).

In addition to claims for information, the consumerist movement
has also articulated desires for 'death with dignity' (e.g. Putnam
2001). The most prominent debates here involve the contested rights
of consumers to choose the manner and timing of their deaths, predominantly through euthanasia and suicide. Ogden (2001), for
example, points to the expansion of technological assistance and
'non-medical death providers' within the euthanasia movement.
Bearing in mind the earlier discussion on good and natural deaths,
there is clearly some tension between the representation of technology as a vehicle for consumer choice in the management of risk and
technology as loss of control in the medicalization of everyday life.

McInerney (2000) reviews claims to choice and control over the
process of dying, characterizing the growth in 'requested death' as a
social movement concerned with identity, the body and resistance to
state control (see also Howarth and Jefferys 1996). Within this movement, two key claims have been significant: the right to die by refusing medical treatment, and the right to die by acting positively to
cause death. Although the ethical debates surrounding these parallel
claims are linked, they have been regarded as legally and morally distinct. This distinction was highlighted recently in two much publi-
cized cases of requested death by adult women in the UK, one
involving a request for assistance with suicide, the other involving a
request for death by cessation of medical treatment.

In 1999, Diane Pretty was diagnosed with motor neurone disease,
a degenerative and terminal condition affecting the nervous system.
Following a period of decreasing physical function, leading to paralysis, she sought assurances that her husband would be allowed to
assist her in dying at a time of her own choosing without fear of pros-
ecution (since she was unable to take her own life without physical
assistance). However, aiding suicide remains an offence in the UK,
and the Director of Public Prosecutions rejected her plea. In August
2001, she brought her case to the High Court, arguing that human

rights legislation provided the right to choose death in order to avoid the 'inhuman and degrading treatment' that she envisaged if her condition deteriorated further. Backing her claim in a television interview, the director of civil liberties group Liberty argued that 'You or I could make a decision to commit suicide, she can't because physically she is unable to do so. . . . We are saying she should be put in the same position as anyone else, and that means her husband having to help her' (John Wadham, BBC News, 20 August 2001).

In rejecting her appeal, the higher courts and the European Court of Human Rights ruled that her legal rights to dignity of life did not extend to choosing death with dignity. However, in March 2002 another British woman, Miss B, also paralysed and who relied on a ventilator to breathe, won the legal right to end her life by arguing her entitlement to refuse 'unwanted medical treatment'. In the light of earlier discussions, the distinction between the two rulings is significant, suggesting that individual claims to a 'natural' death without medical or technological intervention may be seen as more socially acceptable than claims to actively bringing about death by suicide prior to its 'natural' occurrence.

Although medical assistance in voluntary euthanasia is tolerated in some countries (such as Switzerland, Colombia and Belgium), the practice has tended to remain technically illegal. For example, considerable debate ensued in South Korea when a doctor was convicted of homicide in 1998 after ceasing treatment for a terminally ill patient who requested death. In 2002, the Netherlands became the first country to fully legalize active voluntary euthanasia (although the practice had been tolerated for many years previously). The new legislation allows patients to request euthanasia, provided such requests are 'voluntary and well-considered', and where the person experiences 'unbearable suffering'. There have been legislative attempts in other countries too. For example, in Australia's Northern Territory, the 1996 Rights of the Terminally Ill Act allowed four patients to both choose and personally control their own technologically assisted death (using computers to administer lethal injections) before the legislation was overturned by the Australian Federal Government two years later.

The euthanasia debate has been hotly contested, both by the legal, medical and religious establishment, and by disability activists. Public concerns have centred on fears that procedures may be open to abuse, and that disabled people, and older disabled people in particular, may be more heavily targeted for 'voluntary' deaths. There must also be questions about the reality of informed choice where disabled lives are devalued, and where there is pressure to ration health resources (see chapter 2). For example, the British judge in the second case cited above agreed that the life of someone relying on a ventilator to breathe constituted a fate 'worse than death'; yet, disabled people using similar life-sustaining technologies have contributed greatly to their communities and to disability politics. Perhaps the most notable example in this respect is that of pioneering US activist Ed Roberts, who co-founded the World Institute on Disability in California. Commenting on assisted death requests by other paralysed people, Ed argued as follows:

> What's happening is we're killing disabled people in this country and then act like we're doing them a favor. It's outrageous. I've been on a respirator for twenty-six years, and I watch these people's cases. They're just as dependent on a respirator as I am. The major difference is that they know they're going to be forced to live in a nursing home – or they're already there – and I'm leading a quality of life. That's the only difference. It's not the respirator. It's the money. (Quoted in Fleischer and Zames, 2001: 146)

To summarize, the growth of consumerism in health care has been reflected in increasing claims to consultation and involvement in planning the timing and process of dying. In particular, the movement for requested death has focused on claims to choose death through rejection of medical treatment or assistance in dying. Disability issues have figured prominently in these debates, since many of the most contested legal cases have involved people whose impairments limit their functional capacity to take their own lives without assistance. However, the representation of such claims as consumer choices becomes problematic in a cultural and economic context where disabled lives are devalued, and where there is pressure to ration scarce resources.

Key points and ideas for learning

The discussion in the first part of this chapter outlines some of the key theoretical issues and developments in thinking about death and dying in contemporary societies. In addition to traditional concerns with mortality rates, death rituals and bereavement, there has been increasing sociological interest in dying as a situated biographical process. The construction of 'good' deaths emphasizes the importance of timeliness in the completion of a life project and the desirability of dying 'naturally'. In this context, slowly declining trajectories of dying, towards death at home in old age, are viewed as less socially problematic than sudden deaths in younger generations. But technological and social developments in consumerist societies pose significant challenges to this construction. Choice and control over dying have become important themes. People in Western societies are more likely to die in technologically controlled settings, and consumerist claims to involvement in the process of dying have led to debates about the right to choose death. Such developments impact particularly on disabled people, since they have been the most likely to use technologically intensive end-of-life care and the most likely to request legal assistance in ending life.

QUESTIONS
- What constitutes a 'good death'?
- Does it make sense to think of particular deaths as 'untimely' or 'premature'?
- To what extent does increased choice over the process and timing of dying pose a threat to disabled people?

EXERCISE: It may be useful to explore some of the arguments about timely and untimely deaths in more detail before considering the disability debates discussed in subsequent sections. Consider the construction of good and timely deaths and their relationship to the completion of life projects. What kinds of criteria are commonly used to evaluate the success or fulfilment of individual life projects, and how do these relate to the construction of a 'normal' life course (e.g. longevity, productivity, or the value of contributions to family and nation)? To what extent are such criteria reflected in the way that different lives are mourned or celebrated?

Life, death and disability

Building on the review in the first part of this chapter, the following sections explore some of the key debates around disability and dying in more detail. The discussion begins by examining how life expectancy has been constructed and normalized through medical science and knowledge. This knowledge reveals a great disparity between disabled people's life chances and those of non-disabled people, but also illustrates the role of statistical and epidemiological knowledges in devaluing disabled lives. Mirroring the discussion of birth rights and eugenics in chapter 2, the examples of state-sponsored genocide and physician-assisted suicide are then used to illustrate how these values have been enacted in the killing of disabled people.

The normalization of life expectancy

Taking the first of these themes, it is helpful to think briefly about life expectancy and its measurement. Generally speaking, this would seem to be a relatively straightforward, unproblematic concept. Life span is commonly measured as a period of chronological time (from birth to death), and the calculation of life expectancy involves a predictive assessment of how long this period may be. Within modern societies, widespread record keeping has made it relatively easy to determine dates of birth and death with some accuracy and on a large scale. Obtaining measures of life span is therefore a relatively straightforward calculation. Armed with such data, there are almost limitless opportunities to make calculations of life expectancy for different societies and social groups, and to compare these with an array of independent variables (such as gender, social class, occupation, education, income, place of birth and so on). It is unsurprising, then, that chronological measures of life span and life expectancy have been so widely used by statisticians.

Ease of measurement, the availability of data, and the high cultural value placed on longevity mean that life expectancy has also been widely employed as an indicator of the quality of life in different societies. Thus, there has been much concern to highlight disparities in life expectancy between different societies and to promote policies that might increase average life span. For example, World Health Organization figures suggest that life expectancy for men and women in Japan is almost twice as long as in, say, Rwanda. This is a very significant difference, influenced by a variety of factors (such as poverty, diet, public health, war, access to health care, the spread of HIV/AIDS, and so on).

Within individual societies there are also great disparities, between men and women, and in relation to social class, ethnicity, impairment and disability. These disparities raise some questions about the use of aggregate statistical measures in benchmarking our assumptions of life expectancy. Indeed, a simplistic over-emphasis on statistical averages may lead to the legitimation of certain assumptions about the 'normal' life span that fail to recognize the reality of population diversity in dying. In turn, normalized discourses of life expectancy lead us to characterize deaths and life spans that deviate from the norm (statistically speaking) as deviant in other ways too (culturally speaking). Thus, constructions of what it means to have a 'long life' or an 'early death' are entirely dependent upon an underlying construction of the normal life span.

The use of disability adjusted life years (DALYs) offers a particularly useful example here, one that has implications for the valuing of disabled lives. The DALY concept was developed as a means to measure the impact of 'premature' death, impairment and disease. Adopted by the World Bank in 1993 as the principal measure of the global 'disease burden', DALYs became a significant tool for international policy development (World Bank 1993). The calculation of DALYs is quite a complex technical task, but, in essence, it relies on the idea that years of life with certain kinds of impairment can be regarded as years of life lost (even though the person may still be living). For example, where a particular impairment is judged to reduce the quality of life by, say, 50 per cent (e.g. Down's syndrome), then ten years of actual life expectancy might be equated with just five years of 'disability adjusted' life expectancy (i.e. a reduction of 50 per cent).

The use of such measures in research points to great differences in the 'burden' of different impairments in different countries, and between developed and developing countries (see Hyder and Morrow 2000; Melse et al. 2000). However, the use of DALY calculations has been subject to much debate (Barker and Green 1996), raising concerns about the socio-economic and value assumptions involved (Cohen 2000) and about technical or methodological shortcomings (Murray and Lopez 1997; Roberge, Berthelot and Cranswick 1999; Ustun et al. 2001). The calculations themselves are reliant on measures of impairment and functioning derived from panels of 'medical experts'. Thus, DALYs are largely subjective measurements, which fail to adequately theorize disability (Groce, Chamie and Me 1999). Impairment diagnosis alone tells us very little about the expectancy of quality of life for disabled people. Rather, the cultural significance of impairment in different contexts, the availability of enabling support, and the removal of disabling barriers are all much more important factors:

a spinal cord injury resulting in paraplegia may prove far more 'handi-
capping', both socially and economically, to a sugar cane cutter than
to a college professor. The identical loss of sight for an impoverished
washerwoman living in a shanty town and a wealthy urban woman
might produce very different ramifications; indeed the second woman's
need for assistance in home or career may create jobs for one or more
individuals. According to the DALYs, both men with paraplegia and
both women with severe vision loss would be equally burdensome to
their societies – but in the real world, the issues that affect their lives
are economic and social, not medical. (Groce, Chamie and Me 2000)

When we consider disability as a social phenomenon, then, the use
of such calculations raises considerable political and philosophical
issues. Since the DALY calculations rest on an assumption that years
lived with impairment are essentially 'years lost' to life, the implication is that disabled people inhabit a world 'somewhere between life
and premature death' (Groce, Chamie and Me 2000). This in turn
highlights the continuing dominance of statistical and biomedical
knowledge in defining the normal life span, and in perpetuating social
death models of disability (see chapter 6).

However, life expectancy for different population groups is not
only biologically determined and culturally constructed. It is also
socially produced (e.g. as a result of technological and social developments in nutrition and health care). There is certainly considerable
evidence that people with certain impairments are more likely to die
at a younger age than the average within populations, and this may
sometimes be attributed to the biological impact of impairment on
the body's capacity for survival. But it is also evident that differential access to medical treatment, health care, healthy environments
and welfare resources play a large part in the lowered life expectancy
of disabled people throughout the world. Thus, although disabled
children and adults have experienced historically lower levels of life
expectancy than non-disabled people, there have been some dramatic
changes. In particular, research findings have drawn attention to historical increases in the life span of people with the label of learning
difficulties (Patja et al. 2000; Patja and Livanainen 2000).

For example, research on death rates amongst people with learning difficulties in London (Hollins et al. 1998) showed a risk of dying
before the age of fifty that was fifty-eight times higher than the
average for England and Wales. However, in interpreting this data,
the authors focused on the significance of impairment, rather than
investigating the influence of disabling barriers and institutional care.
This kind of medical or impairment focus is problematic if it

promotes a biologically deterministic view of life expectancy, and fails to acknowledge or investigate the social causes of early death. In practice, of course, it is not always easy to differentiate life expectancy findings into impairment effects and disability effects.

To take another example, a study of life expectancy for children and young adults with learning difficulties who had been institutionalized in Greece over a thirty-year period found that mortality rates were twenty to 150 times higher than for the general population (Perakis et al. 1995). Death was particularly high for children under five, and 22 per cent of deaths occurred within one year of being admitted to the institution. Male residents had a better chance of survival than female residents, a finding attributed to culturally based admission criteria. So, several factors are interacting here. Those admitted to the institution, especially young children, often had particularly complex health conditions that influenced the body's capacity for survival (impairment effects). At the same time, resources within the institution were not necessarily allocated to extend life, and some children with life-threatening conditions were 'allowed to die' (disability effects). Overlying these disabling practices, there were also issues of priority associated with gender and family background.

To summarize, the normalization of average life expectancy through statistical and epidemiological knowledge has tended to diminish the value attributed to disabled lives. In addition, the dominance of medical discourse in these constructions lends weight to biologically deterministic explanations of early deaths that fail to account for the influence of disabling barriers or enabling environments. The arbitrary labelling of specific impairments as equivalent to life lost also impacts on disabled people, by bolstering a social death model of disability. This, in turn, perpetuates an approach to policy and resource allocation that places a lower value on disabled people's life expectancy. As the remainder of this chapter shows, such discourses have provided ample justification for the ending of disabled people's lives by more direct means, often with active collaboration from the medical profession.

Disability and genocide

The most graphic example of the wholesale killing of disabled people occurred in Nazi occupied territories before and during the Second World War. Although the remembrance of those who died during this period has emphasized the particular, catastrophic experience of

European Jews, it is less often acknowledged that the genocide programmes began with the killing of disabled people (and that the
numbers who died were substantial). This apparent oversight reflects
both an absence of reliable data and a failure to recognize people
with different impairments as part of a common social group (even
now, disability is largely ignored as a category within the archives of
Holocaust information). However, there is also a danger of collusion
with the underlying eugenic assumption that the killing of disabled
people might be regarded as somehow less outrageous, in its historical and medical context. The recent rediscovery of disability in
the Holocaust is thus long overdue.

> The vicious and systematic persecution of people with disabilities
> during the Nazi era has been overlooked and greatly underestimated
> in historical research and our collective remembrances of the
> Holocaust. The result is widespread public ignorance of these horrors
> – an ignorance often perpetuated by the indifference of politicians, aca-
> demicians and the media. Moreover, restitution measures have been
> virtually non-existent. (Disability Rights Advocates 2001: 1)

As Friedlander (1995) notes, Nazi genocide had its origins in
'euthanasia' programmes targeting disabled people during the mid-
1930s (including the enforced sterilization programmes discussed in
chapter 5). Euthanasia was actively promoted for certain classes of
disabled people from 1933 through propaganda campaigns, resulting in numerous requests from parents for the mercy killing of their
disabled children. The earliest known, and much quoted, case
(around 1938) involved 'Baby Knauer', a boy with a combination of
significant visual, cognitive and physical impairments, whose father
made a personal request to Hitler that his son be allowed to die.
Hitler referred the case to his private physician, Karl Brandt, who
confirmed the baby's impairments, and received the Führer's assent
for doctors to proceed with the killing without fear of recrimination
(for accounts of this case, see Burleigh 1994, 1998; Gallagher 1995;
Lifton 1986).
    Apparently reassured, Hitler signed a secret memo authorizing the
mercy killing of disabled children through medical intervention. The
establishment of the Reich Committee for the Scientific Registration
of Serious Hereditary and Congenital Diseases from 1938 provided
additional medical authority for the programme. This involved the
'registration' of all children under the age of three suspected of having
certain specified impairments, including 'idiocy and mongolism,

microcephaly, hydrocephaly, malformations and paralysis'. Medical experts would then assess whether the child should live or be killed, often in an apparently arbitrary way. It is important to note here the apparently active role of the medical profession in this endeavour – although participation was voluntary, there was no shortage of volunteers (Gallagher 1995; Lifton 1986).

Around 5,000 children were killed in the programme, and at least thirty killing centres were established (in Poland and Austria as well as in Germany), where children were kept before the administration of lethal drugs. Official sanction for euthanasia followed soon after, and a corresponding programme targeting disabled adults was begun under the auspices of the Reich Work Group on Sanatoriums and Nursing Homes, code-named 'T-4'. Adult registration included people suspected of conditions such as schizophrenia, epilepsy, senility, paralysis, 'feeblemindedness' and progressive neurological conditions, but also included those detained as criminally insane, people who had been institutionalized for more than five years, and those who could be employed only in 'simple mechanical work'.

The six killing centres involved in the T-4 programme pioneered the use of lethal gas, later used to such horrifying effect in the concentration camps (Kogon, Langbein and Ruckerl 1993). Although the exact numbers remain uncertain, it is likely that as many as 250,000 disabled people were killed through medical intervention (Disability Rights Advocates 2001; Lifton 1986). Many more died in the concentration camps, or were murdered in Nazi-occupied territories (e.g. in the systematic killing of asylum patients by SS units in Poland and elsewhere). Although Hitler called an end to the T-4 programme in 1941, some doctors continued the practice until after the war (Gallagher 1995), and implicit permission remained for the killing of disabled babies.

As with the state-sponsored murder of Jews and others, the legitimacy of killing disabled people was dependent upon their dehumanization, driven by propaganda that characterized people with a wide range of impairments as lacking the potential to live a worthwhile life. For example, Dahl (2001) reviews the portrayal of disabled children as 'asocial' and 'depraved'. Reviewing the mass killing of disabled people during the Holocaust, Friedlander (1995) argues that this should be regarded as a clear case of genocide, parallel to the racially motivated eugenic killing of other groups. Disabled people were clearly identified as a biologically defined group unworthy of life, and were killed systematically in order to remove that group from the population. The fact that killing took place under the respectable auspices of 'medicine' (rather than in a context of overt political racism) should not cloud the fact that it constitutes a similar form of oppression.

Physician-assisted death, past and present

As discussed in chapters 2 and 5, the mass eugenic programmes of the early twentieth century reflected many of the key characteristics of the modernist nation-state. However, technological and social changes in more postmodern, consumer and knowledge societies suggest that eugenic decision making has become a more individual concern (although still framed by the interests of professions and the state). Thus, the discussion of consumerist trends in requested death included in the first part of this chapter provided examples of end-of-life decisions that involved purposeful negotiations between individual disabled people, doctors and the courts. Such negotiations have attracted much attention and debate, highlighting the increasing practice of legalized euthanasia and 'physician-assisted suicide'.

For example, Cuttini et al. (2000) examined doctors' views on 'end-of-life decisions' for new-born children 'at high risk of death or severe disability' in eight European countries. Most had been involved in such decisions, involving a variety of practices such as the 'non-intensification' or withholding of treatments. Deliberate withdrawal of life support (such as ventilation) was less common, and in only two countries did doctors regularly intervene to end children's lives (in France and the Netherlands). Country-specific regimes were much more significant than the individual attitudes or characteristics of the doctors themselves. However, public concern has often focused on individual cases, particularly in cases of physician-assisted suicide in the USA, as the following more detailed examples illustrate.

Physician-assisted death for disabled people in the USA is not a new phenomenon, and Pernick (1996) describes the largely forgotten case of Harry Haiselden, a prominent physician at the German-American hospital in Chicago during the early part of the twentieth century. Haiselden was an ardent eugenicist, who promoted and pursued euthanasia for 'defective' babies. In his most public case, Haiselden caused the death of a five-day-old disabled baby boy by refusing to perform routine but life-saving surgery. He called a press conference to justify his actions, and produced a full-length silent film, entitled *The Black Stork*, re-enacting the boy's death. He was subsequently involved in the deaths of a number of disabled babies, using a variety of techniques (such as allowing a child to bleed to death from an unstitched umbilical cord or administering lethal doses of opiate drugs). Although Haiselden's actions were widely reported, and attracted much contemporary criticism, he was never prosecuted, and gained substantial support for his campaign from major newspapers and prominent US citizens.

Cheyfitz (1999) picks up on Pernick's account of the Haiselden case, and draws parallels with more recent physician-assisted deaths in the USA. Cheyfitz reviews these cases in their broader context, making comparisons with historical practices of suicide, euthanasia, infanticide, eugenics and genocide. This history, he suggests, is characterized by two consistently recurring moral questions: 'Which lives are not worth living? And who will decide?' In this context, Cheyfitz draws attention to Plato's argument that doctors should not treat people with chronic conditions that prevent them from working, on the grounds that these are examples of 'life not worth living' (see *Republic*, III. 1. 406). Support for medical involvement in 'death assistance' and elective 'mercy killings' was couched in very similar terms in Germany during the 1920s, as a legitimate end to 'life unworthy of life' (Hoche and Binding 1920). This concept was then applied to justify the mass killings of the Nazi Holocaust, described earlier (Glass 1999).

Physician-assisted death would appear to contravene established medical codes of ethics, which emphasize the duty to prolong life, and there has been considerable opposition to such practices within the medical establishment (Meisel, Snyder and Quill 2000; Snyder and Sulmasy 2001). However, the number of cases in which disabled people are assisted to die by physicians appears to be on the increase. There are a number of studies showing that public attitudes towards doctor-assisted deaths in the USA are generally accepting in principle, especially amongst white, liberal men (e.g. Kaplan and Bratman 1999; Lachenmeier, Kaplan and Caragacianu 1999; Muller et al. 1996). A popular vote in the state of Oregon in 1994 provided support for doctor-assisted suicide in the case of terminally ill patients, resulting in the Oregon Death with Dignity Act (which became law in 1997). More than forty people have died in assisted suicides there, although the federal government has moved to restrict the practice (for a discussion of some of these cases, see Lee and Werth 2000). In practice, such cases have aroused considerable public concern – perhaps none more so than the case of Dr Jack Kevorkian, who was sentenced to serve up to twenty-five years for his part in bringing about the deaths of more than 130 people in Michigan state.

Unlike his early US predecessor Haiselden, Kevorkian claimed to assist only patients who had requested to die and sought medical support in that process. Like Haiselden, he sought publicity for this work and to justify his position on the issue. Indeed, this similarity extended to the production of a video recording the actual death of one of his patients, a terminally ill man called Thomas Youk, broadcast on the CBS *Sixty Minutes* programme in November 1998. Reviewing the detailed characteristics of Kevorkian's sixty-nine euthanasia cases, Roscoe, Malphurs, Dragovic and Cohen (2001) compare them with those from the first year of the Oregon project, and with national demographic data from the USA. They conclude that only 25 per cent of Kevorkian's patients were in fact terminally ill (compared to all of those who died in Oregon). Only two of them were in hospice care, and many had prognoses of more than six months. In a small number of cases, no evidence of disease was found in the autopsy.

More generally, the data showed that women were two and a half times more likely to die as Kevorkian patients than would be expected from other known cases (women are less likely than men to commit suicide in the USA, and men and women were equally represented in the Oregan cases). In addition, people who had never married, or who were divorced, appeared more likely to seek euthanasia in both states than would be expected. Roscoe and colleagues argue that more research is required into these findings, suggesting that family support and social environment may be factors in decisions for death. Differential access to relationships of care and support, as well as gendered access to health care, are relevant here. As the authors conclude:

> The availability of a caregiver may also differentially affect the end-of-life decisions made by men and women. Women provide most of the care that is given to dying patients, although women who need care tend to receive less assistance from family members than men, and are more likely to have to pay for assistance even if married. (Roscoe et al. 2001: 439)

Such findings support the social model analysis of disability and interdependency advanced throughout this book, suggesting that the valuing of disabled lives through self-directed support is a key factor in increasing both quality of life and life expectancy. The struggles of the disabled people's movement to create such supports, and to disseminate more enabling narratives of independent living, are thus particularly important in challenging dominant assumptions that disabled lives are less worthy of life.

Advocates of assisted death for disabled people have often based their calls for 'death with dignity' on misplaced assumptions about the supposed inevitability of poor quality of life with impairment. For example, Janet Good (founder of the pro-euthanasia group Hemlock in Michigan state) made the following argument in a newspaper interview during the Kevorkian case.

> Pain is not the main reason we want to die. It's the indignity. It's the inability to get out of bed or get onto the toilet, let alone drive a car or go shopping without another's help. I can speak for literally hundreds of people whose bedside I've sat at over the years. Every client I've talked to – I call them 'clients' because I'm not a medical professional – they've had enough when they can't go to the bathroom by themselves. Most of them say, 'I can't stand my mother – my husband – wiping my butt'. That's why everybody in the movement talks about dignity. People have their pride. They want to be in charge. (*Washington Post*, 11 August 1996)

Yet, such arguments deny the struggles and advances of disabled people within the movement for independent living, who have shown that such dignity can be achieved through choice and control in the self-direction of community-based support services (e.g. Priestley 1999). The real barriers to dignity and quality of life are less connected with impairment than with disabling barriers, such as the way in which resources are allocated to provide support. To advocate the killing of disabled people as an appropriate response to these economic and political problems is highly problematic.

In this context, disability groups have been active in campaigning on right-to-life issues, and in protesting eugenic abuses in cases of child killing, euthanasia and assisted death. For example, the US campaign group Not Dead Yet achieved a high profile for its opposition during the Kevorkian court case by questioning the moral and economic rationale behind the requested death movement. As national organizer Diane Coleman argued: 'The failings of our health care system are not a justification for killing. This right to die epidemic is based on society's extreme prejudice that most of the experts won't even acknowledge, much less try to overcome' (Not Dead Yet press release, 18 June 1996).

Key points and ideas for learning

The examples highlighted in the second half of this chapter illustrate how medical knowledge and authority continue to shape the trajectories of disabled people's dying. On the one hand, the normalization of life expectancy reproduces medical model assumptions about the presumed relationship between impairment and the lowered value of lives. On the other hand, medical practitioners and the courts exercise considerable power in negotiating death with disabled patients. Moves towards greater consumer involvement in adult dying suggest a shift from modernist concerns with state eugenics towards the individual negotiation of death as a life course risk. However, as with the birth decisions of prospective parents (discussed in chapter 2), adult death decisions are framed within a discursive context in which disabling values and economic pressures continue to outweigh more enabling alternatives.

QUESTIONS
- What impact does the normalization of life expectancy have on the value attributed to disabled life projects?
- Is it reasonable to characterize the Nazi persecution of disabled people as an example of 'genocide'?
- To what extent do contemporary examples of physician-assisted suicide for disabled adults reflect new consumerist choices or old eugenic practices?

EXERCISE: Using the examples cited earlier, or similar cases from media reports, consider the case for assisted death involving disabled people. Why do some people with impairments request the right to choose the timing of their own death, and how do others, including disability rights advocates, respond to such requests? Try to identify arguments that might be included under each of the following headings: (a) embodied experiences of illness and impairment, (b) issues of self-identity and life projects, (c) the cultural construction of disabled lives, (d) economic and resource concerns. Consider developing these arguments in a classroom or online debate.

Summary

The discussion in this final chapter highlights the importance of including death and dying in a life course analysis of disability issues. There has been a growing interest in theorizing dying as a situated social process, moving beyond more traditional concerns with death rituals and bereavement. In particular, the sociological literature draws attention to the biographical significance of dying, as a negotiated life course process in knowledge societies. Consumer challenges to the medicalization of everyday life have been mirrored in the emergence of movements claiming death with dignity and greater involvement in dying. Disability issues have figured prominently in these debates, suggesting that disabled people continue to be the primary targets for professional and policy intervention. However, the focus on consumer choice masks the significance of disabling cultural values and resource rationing in these decisions.

The construction of death and dying in contemporary societies reveals a cultural attachment to notions of the 'good' and 'timely' death, emphasizing the importance of longevity in completing life projects. By contrast, the deaths of disabled children and adults are more likely to be constructed as expedient or 'merciful' than premature or untimely, reflecting the low social and economic value attributed to disabled lives as human capital. The normalization of life expectancy and 'disease burden' through medical knowledge reproduces these disabling discourses, and contributes to the maintenance of a social death model of disability.

The examples suggest a move towards more technologically regulated deaths and the greater involvement of state legislatures and the courts in mediating claims to the right to die. Similarly, consumer involvement in adult dying suggests a shift from modernist concerns with state eugenics towards the individual negotiation of death as a life course risk. Yet, public debates are still dominated by disabling discourses that maintain the tragedy-laden association between impairment and negative quality of life. By contrast, disability activism and disability cultures have reclaimed more positive representations of disabled life projects, and have challenged the eugenic assumptions inherent in euphemistic claims to 'death with dignity'. These cultural counter-claims highlight the significance of a social model analysis, illustrating how barriers to successful life projects arise primarily from disabling institutions and relationships of power, rather than embodied experiences of impairment.

SUGGESTIONS FOR FURTHER READING

It may be helpful to contextualize the material in this chapter by reviewing some of the key texts in the sociology of death and dying. In this respect, the most influential account is probably Kubler-Ross's (1969) *On Death and Dying*, although this is now somewhat dated. Kearl's (1989) *Endings* provides an excellent overview of traditional approaches, and prefigures recent developments, while the article by Corr, Doka and Kastenbaum (1999) offers a more succinct and updated review. For other recent analyses, see *Constructing Death* (Seale 1998) or *Beyond the Body* (Hallam 1999). However, this mainstream literature generally fails to engage directly with critical disability debates, and there is no corresponding definitive account that tackles this issue from a disability studies perspective. There are, nevertheless, a number of items that deal with specific issues and examples, such as those cited in this chapter. For example, there are several texts addressing the significance of disability in the Nazi Holocaust (e.g. Burleigh 1998; Disability Rights Advocates 2001; Lifton 1986), while the issue of requested death and physician-assisted suicide has also attracted increasingly critical examination (e.g. Asche 2001; Snyder and Sulmasy 2001).

INTERNET RESOURCES

- Not Dead Yet: *www.notdeadyet.org* (US-based disability group campaigning on right-to-life issues; includes examples of legal arguments from a disability rights perspective)
- Forgotten Crimes: *www.dralegal.org/publications/forgotten_crimes.pdf* (online publication detailing the treatment of disabled people during the Nazi Holocaust)
- The Kevorkian Papers: *www.kevork.org* (access to background material and detailed testimony from the Michigan assisted-suicide debate)
- Exit: *www.euthanasia.org* (extensive gateway to arguments supporting and opposing voluntary euthanasia, UK-based)

CONCLUSION

My aim in writing this book was to explore whether a life course approach could offer a useful analytical frame for understanding current disability debates. My own experiences of research and teaching suggested that such an approach could be useful in accommodating the richness and diversity of the existing field, while offering a coherent way to navigate through it – 'from womb to tomb'. In addition, adopting a life course approach offered a novel way to connect with recent developments in social theory more generally. I was also motivated by the challenges of diversity and underrepresentation within disability studies. These had already been well rehearsed by others in relation to gender, impairment, ethnicity and sexuality. However, it became increasingly apparent that accounts of childhood, youth and old age continued to be produced as 'special cases' or 'add-ons' to a more general account of disability. As I read more about generational divisions, it became evident that disability debates were being conducted within a narrow adult-centred frame, undermining claims to inclusivity.

My approach in this book, like that of most of the disability studies literature, is grounded in social models of disability. As outlined in chapter 1, this perspective emphasizes the way in which disabling barriers (such as environments, attitudes, institutions, discourses, policies and practices) shape the experiences of people with perceived impairments throughout the life course. The diverse material in the preceding chapters shows that these are complex processes. Nevertheless, there are also a number of common strands that run through the book as a whole. In particular, it is useful to return to the four core themes identified as a conceptual framework in chapter 1, relating to the interaction of the body, identity, culture and social structure.

Bodies

The development of critical disability theory has led to a radical transformation in the way we discuss disability issues in contemporary societies. In particular, the emphasis has shifted from historical concerns with the impaired body towards a more social and political view of disability. Within these developing accounts, there has been a tendency to reject discussions of the body, as an apolitical or medical concern, in favour of discussions about social or physical barriers to inclusion. This historic shift of focus, from the body to society, has been both politically expedient and a necessary stage in the development of disability studies. However, the sociological project of refocusing disability debates has also attracted some criticism from those who take a more social view of the body.

It is important to remember that traditional accounts of disability were dominated by biomedical discourses, which reproduced a rather limited view of the body as asocial and biologically determined. By contrast, contemporary social theory has taken a more socially situated and contextual approach, emphasizing the body's social construction and regulation through language, culture and institutions. The initial reticence of some social model theorists to engage with discussions of the body must therefore be seen in its historical and academic context, as a reaction against dominant biomedical models. Thinking about the body in its social and cultural sense is less problematic for disability studies, and has proved useful in understanding more about the relationship between disability, generation and the life course.

For example, chapters 2 and 3 illustrated the intensity of institutional concerns with bodily imperfection in children and the unborn. Here, the continuing dominance of biomedical thinking was underlined by the biological reductionism of new genetic knowledge and technologies. Social theorists have pointed to a greater tolerance of embodied diversity in postmodern consumer societies, yet there is little evidence of such developments in discourses and practices governing the birth of disabled children. Although the pressures on parents and doctors to produce 'normal' children reflect new negotiations of life course risk in knowledge societies, these appear to have less in common with celebrations of diversity than with the modernist concerns of uniformity and the normalization of the body.

The analyses of youth and adulthood (chapters 4 and 5) also high-lighted the social significance of the body in current disability debates. Idealized constructions of youthfulness play heavily on the pursuit of bodily perfection in consumer societies, while constructions of independent adulthood emphasize autonomy in physical and cognitive function. These bodily ideals contribute to disability in two ways. First, they provide cultural scripts for decoding the body's potency as an object of beauty or sexual desire, leading to the aesthetic oppression of those whose bodily characteristics are not usually read in this way. Second, there is the underlying functional imperative that young adult bodies should be fit for production and reproduction in the interests of capital, patriarchy and the state. Thus, the administrative segregation of disabled people in modern societies rests on the definition of disability in terms of bodily function and 'ability to work', while the institutional regulation of disabled sexuality has been enacted through the sterilization of disabled women's bodies.

A recurrent theme in these debates is the representation of impaired bodies as aberrant and abnormal. In the context of the book as a whole, normalizing bodily discourses and practices appear to carry more weight at the beginning of the life course (particularly in the control of diversity before birth and the elimination of diversity through childhood correction). In some ways this seems paradoxical, since impairment poses a greater cultural and structural threat to the supposed functional independence of adulthood than it does to the socially accepted dependence of childhood. However, institutional responses to disability in adulthood have been more concerned with controlling or incarcerating the errant body than correcting it.

The significance of a generational account of the body is also underlined by the discussion of old age (chapter 6). The impaired body has figured prominently in constructions of old age, yet rarely has this been articulated as a disability debate. Indeed, embodied experiences of impairment have been viewed as significantly less disruptive to generational constructions of old age than to those of childhood or young adulthood. It is tempting to conclude that the biographical normality of the impaired body in old age may explain why older people with impairments are rarely seen as disabled in the way that younger adults are. But it is also important to note that older bodies have been increasingly excluded or exempt from the primary sites of productive and reproductive labour in modern societies (from the workplace and the family). As a consequence, older people with impairments have also become less subject to the social processes that give rise to disability.

Disability studies and disability activism pose some significant challenges to the normalization of the body. This resistance has targeted the myth of bodily perfection through the celebration of bodily diversity in human populations. For example, there has been active resistance to the elimination of diversity through genetic technologies and eugenic practices. Similarly, disability culture has offered new representations of the impaired body that place greater value on difference and diversity in constructions of physical beauty or sexual attractiveness. Yet it is also evident that such claims remain rooted in the associations between beauty and youth, thereby failing to challenge the power relationships of a generational system that devalues bodies in later life.

Identities

Sociological analyses of contemporary societies have placed an increasing emphasis on the negotiation of identities and identity politics. Such trends have also been evident within disability studies – for example, in the importance now attached to conveying more authentic firsthand accounts of disabled people's lives. While the analysis in this book has not focused on individual narratives, it does highlight many of the social processes and practices that impact on individual identity and biography. In addition, the adoption of a systematic life course approach reveals much about the interaction of disability and generation in collective identities and identity politics.

First, it is important to acknowledge the potential impact of disabling barriers and practices on negotiations of identity for disabled people. For example, the construction of disabled births as wrongful lives and the eradication of impairment characteristics through new genetic technologies impact on disability identities by devaluing the worth of disabled people in society. Similarly, the normalization of child development and the segregation of children with impairments have reinforced negative associations with developmental delay and abnormality. Barriers to participation in the socially valued labour of production and reproduction have denied many disabled people access to the social networks and citizenship rights upon which autonomous adult identities are premised. These have been further reinforced by institutional practices of controlling care that support continued dependency rather than choice and reflexivity.

Second, institutional responses to disability in modern societies have relied upon categorical definitions that tend to group disabled people according to impairment labels or the convenience of service bureaucracies. This has been reflected in the widespread denial of more nuanced and situated identities for disabled people. For example, there is considerable evidence that disabled children and young people have often been ascribed relatively static identities that privilege their perceived impairment status above attributes of gender, class, ethnicity or sexuality. Here, age and generation are also important, since identification with generational cohort identities is a significant aspect of personal biography over the life course. Yet policies and services often deny disabled people meaningful life course transitions or full participation in the generational transitions of their peers.

In this context, it is relevant to note that many of the resources for identity development over the life course are accessed through particular generational modes of production and consumption. For example, limited access to peer networks and youth cultures may create conflicts of identity management for young disabled people, forcing them to choose between disability identities and generational youth identities. Moves towards more inclusive education may offer greater opportunities for the development of shared cohort experiences and identities in the future. However, there is some concern that young disabled people continue to experience collective biographical patterns that exhibit little of the reflexivity and self-determination suggested by contemporary identity theory.

By contrast, it has been suggested that identity management in old age may be less affected by embodied experiences of impairment or by disabling barriers. That is not to say that older people with impairments are not discriminated against as disabled people – far from it. Rather, the assertion is that impairment and disability in old age may be construed as less disruptive to biographical identity and normal narratives of ageing than, say, impairment in younger adulthood (because disability is more widely anticipated in old age). There are some challenges to this view, however, as new cultural claims to positive ageing place an increasing emphasis on the maintenance of bodily function and leisured consumption opportunities. Although many older people have benefited from these cultural claims, older people with impairments risk increasing exclusion from new generational identities based on 'active' or 'successful' ageing.

The development of disability culture and disability politics has been significant in promoting more positive disability identities. In particular, the development of self-advocacy and independent living offers new opportunities for reflexivity and identity expression that are more empowering than traditionally ascribed roles of passivity and dependence. Thus, the disabled people's movement has created cultural spaces and networks of social capital, from which new identity choices can be forged. Nevertheless, these identity resources remain heavily adult-focused, and children, young people and elders are often conspicuous by their absence. For both younger and older people, then, choosing positive disability identities within the movement may mean losing contact with generational networks and cohort identities. If disability culture is to maintain the inclusive commonality of disability identity, it must also resist the reproduction of an adult-centred generational system within the movement.

Cultures

Cultural analyses have provided a rich strand of theory and research within disability studies, revealing the contextual and embedded nature of disabling relationships in different cultural contexts. In the context of this book, cultural perspectives have also revealed much about the construction of generational categories within modern and contemporary societies. This cultural perspective has been useful in two ways. First, it highlights how disability has been socially constructed in relation to idealized notions of life course progression. Second, it draws attention to the differing cultural significance of impairment and disability in different generational locations. Thus, the various chapters illustrate how disability has been constructed as particularly aberrant at birth and in child development, and as socially problematic in transitions to independence for young adults, yet accepted as a cultural norm in later life and in the negotiation of dying trajectories.

A significant theme throughout the book has been the parallel construction of disability and non-adult generational locations as marginal and dependent social categories. In particular, there are significant similarities in the cultural construction of disability, childhood and old age as dependent social states. Such constructions have been important in the discursive governance of disability through social institutions. For example, the cultural construction of disabled people as childlike (as innocent, asexual or untamed) has been reproduced in the legitimation of adult power relationships based on custodial care and surveillance. Similarly, the infantilization and social death of older people in institutional settings has much in common with that experienced by younger disabled adults.

Cultural constructions have been central to the normalization of the life course. In particular, life course expectations in modern societies have been defined in relation to idealized notions of modern adulthood. Here, the representation of adulthood in terms of independence and competence has also been framed by Western preoccupations with individualism and the autonomous self. Such constructions have been highly gendered, with a traditional emphasis on male and female adult roles centred on participation in productive and reproductive labour respectively. By contrast, children, young people, elders and disabled people of all ages have been constructed as lacking the kind of adult attributes upon which full personhood and citizenship are premissed.

There have also been significant cultural challenges to this adult-centred construction of the life course. The increasing recognition of generational conflict and power relationships has been mirrored in a new generational politics, in which non-adult minority groups have made new claims to adult rights and responsibilities. The emergence of movements for the rights of children and older people places an increasing strain on traditional constructions of citizenship as a uniquely adult-centred concept. Social claims from the disabled people's movement have raised similar challenges, emphasizing self-determination, reflexivity and interdependence over autonomous functioning and individual autonomy. However, these cultural claims have also distanced disabled people from the new generational politics, by focusing almost exclusively on access to the territory of modern adulthood (such as parenting or employment, for example).

Structures

The development of social models of disability has been underpinned by a structural analysis of modern societies, demonstrating how people with perceived impairments become disabled through processes of social transformation. In particular, materialist accounts have pointed to historic changes in the social relations of production and reproduction within Western capitalist economies as a driving force for the creation of disability as a social and administrative category. Here, the changing demands of industrialization, competitive labour markets, new technologies and the patriarchal nation-state have all been important. As the discussion in the various chapters illustrates, this kind of analysis is also helpful in explaining the emergence of an adult-centred generational system in modern societies.

For example, structural analyses help to explain the emergence of childhood and youth as distinct social categories marginal to the domain of independent adulthood. The increasing technological demands of industrialization and individuation in knowledge societies have led to an extension of the compulsory training required of young people before they can participate effectively in productive adult labour. Thus the institutional regulation of childhood and youth as dependent, non-adult states has been driven by economic developments and the structure of adult labour markets. At the same time, increased longevity and the exemption of older workers from competitive labour markets through retirement have created a parallel category of old age. In both cases, generational conflict and power relationships arise because of the structural dependency of these groups on adult labour. Clearly, there are considerable parallels between these processes and those that have produced the structural dependency of disabled people in modern societies.

Indeed, the analysis presented in this book suggests that a structural analysis of disability makes little sense as a 'special case', treated in isolation from the production of this generational system. In order to understand the location of disability in modern societies, it is important to understand its generational significance. In particular, it is important to understand the centrality of adult work and employment in producing both disability and the generational system. This may help to explain why the institutional and political focus of disability debates falls so heavily on adult-centred issues (particularly the productive and reproductive labour of employment and parenting). Whereas disability in younger and older age can be partially accommodated within already dependent generational locations, disability in adulthood stands out as a greater structural challenge.

For instance, the intense institutional focus on correcting or eradicating disabled children reflects the structural imperative for states to invest in children as future human capital. In this sense, social responses to disabled children have had less to do with preserving the cultural integrity of childhood and youth than with structural concerns about their productive participation in future adulthood. Conversely, the distinct lack of any institutional or policy focus on disability in old age reflects the fact that older people are already structurally exempt from participation in productive or caring adult labour.

If structural explanations are important in explaining the historical production of disability and the generational system, it is equally important to review these developments in the light of continuing social transformations in contemporary societies. In particular, structural analyses of both disability and the generational system have been premised on a particular view of the social relations of production in industrializing capitalist economies. But, as the discussion in earlier chapters suggests, this is perhaps an over-simplification, and the kinds of processes and social relations so described might be more broadly defined as representative of modernity. As Meyer concluded:

> The life course in modern societies is itself a construct with deep cultural supports. It is not simply the aggregate product of a series of individual choices, nor is it the accidental construction of institutions organized around other cultural purposes. To a substantial extent, the life course is a conscious and purposive cultural product of the modern system. (Meyer 1988: 57)

Given that much contemporary social theory is now concerned with explaining transitions from modern societies towards late modern or postmodern forms of social organization, it is important to question how this affects our understanding of disability and the generational system. Two themes seem important here. First, processes of individuation have increasingly undermined the apparent uniformity and predictable progressions of modernist life course trajectories (e.g. in the declining significance of class, gender or generational role expectations). As a consequence, the modernist institutional life course has been increasingly redefined in terms of individually negotiated life course risk and the pursuit of 'life projects'. Second, social stratification and social status are increasingly defined by patterns of consumption rather than patterns of production. Since the adult-centred generational system is premised upon social relations of production, this poses an additional challenge (e.g. in the raised social status of leisured consumption in youth and old age).

It is perhaps unsurprising that the increasingly successful claims of disabled people to full participation and equality have occurred at the same time as parallel claims by non-adult generational minorities (particularly children and older people). On the one hand, the progress of such claims suggests that marginal groups can win concessions to social inclusion and adult citizenship. There will be benefits here for some young adults, some older adults and some disabled adults – where they can gain access to valued adult roles and responsibilities. However, there is a danger that such claims may also collude with a generational system that deepens the exclusion of those who are more distantly displaced from traditional adulthood (especially young disabled children and disabled people at the end of life).

On the other hand, the progress of these social movements may suggest a more significant loosening of the institutional life course and its generational system. In this scenario, the parallel claims of children, older people and disabled people may appear more radical. The task of including *all* disabled people is essentially the same task as including the very youngest and the very oldest in society. Both challenge us to reformulate our individualistic, adult-centred notions of competence and autonomy in a more relational way. If disability studies remain committed to more than a partial inclusion of diversity and difference in contemporary societies, then the vision of an enabling society must also be conceived as a society for all ages.

REFERENCES

Abberley, P. (1987). The concept of oppression and the development of a social theory of disability. *Disability, Handicap & Society*, 2(1), 5–19.

Abrams, M. (1959). *The Teenage Consumer*. London: Routledge & Kegan Paul.

Accardo, P., and Whitman, B. (1989). Factors influencing child abuse/neglect in children of mentally retarded parents. *Pediatric Research*, 25, 95.

Adnan, A., and Hafiz, I. (2001). A disabling education: the case of disabled learners in Malaysia. *Disability & Society*, 16(5), 655–69.

Agree, E. (1999). The influence of personal care and assistive devices on the measurement of disability. *Social Science & Medicine*, 48(4), 427–43.

Alanen, L. (1994). Gender and generation: feminism and the 'child question'. In J. Qvortrup, M. Bardy, G. Sgritta, and H. Wintersberger (eds), *Childhood Matters: Social Theory, Practice and Politics*, Aldershot: Avebury, 27–42.

Albrecht, G. (1992). *The Disability Business: Rehabilitation in America*. Newbury Park, CA: Sage.

Albrecht, G., Seelman, K. D., and Bury, M. (eds). (2001). *The Handbook of Disability Studies*. London: Sage.

Alderson, P. (1993). *Children's Consent to Surgery*. Buckingham: Open University Press.

Alderson, P. (2001). Prenatal screening, ethics and Down's syndrome: a literature review. *Nursing Ethics*, 8(4), 360–74.

Alderson, P., and Goodey, C. (1998). *Enabling Education: Experiences in Special and Ordinary Schools*. London: The Tuffnel Press.

Allen, S. M., Foster, A., and Berg, K. (2001). Receiving help at home: the interplay of human and technological assistance. *Journals of Gerontology Series B: Psychological Sciences and Social Sciences*, 56, S374–82.

Arber, S., and Evandrou, M. (eds). (1993). *Ageing, Independence and the Life Course*. London: Jessica Kingsley Publishers.

Ariès, P. (1962). *Centuries of Childhood: A Social History of Family Life*. New York: Vintage Books.

Arnett, J. J., and Taber, S. (1994). Adolescence terminable and interminable – when does adolescence end? *Journal of Youth and Adolescence*, 23(5), 517–37.

Asche, A. (1999). Prenatal diagnosis and selective abortion: a challenge to practice and policy. *American Journal of Public Health*, 89(11), 1649–57.

Asche, A. (2000). *Prenatal Testing and Disability Rights*. Washington, DC: Georgetown University Press.

Asche, A. (2001). Disability, bioethics and human rights. In G. Albrecht, K. D. Seelman, and M. Bury (eds), *Handbook of Disability Studies*, London: Sage, 297–326.

Ashman, A., Suttie, J., and Bramley, J. (1995). Employment, retirement and elderly persons with an intellectual disability. *Journal of Intellectual Disability Research*, 39, 107–15.

Attane, I. (1998). Birth rate and fertility in China: how credible are recent data? *Population*, 53(4), 847–57.

Aylott, J. (1999). Should children with Down's syndrome have cosmetic surgery? *British Journal of Nursing*, 8(1), 33–8.

Bailey, R. (1996). Prenatal testing and the prevention of impairment: a woman's right to choose? In J. Morris (ed.), *Encounters with Strangers: Feminism and Disability*, London: Women's Press, 143–67.

Balaban, E. (1998). Eugenics and individual phenotypic variation: to what extent is biology a predictive science? *Science in Context*, 11(3–4), 331–56.

Baldwin, S., and Carlisle, J. (1994). *Social Support for Disabled Children and their Families*. London: HMSO.

Barker, C., and Green, A. (1996). Opening the debate on DALYs. *Health Policy and Planning*, 11(2), 179–83.

Barnartt, S., and Scotch, R. (2001). *Disability Protests: Contentious Politics 1970–1999*. Washington, DC: Gallaudet University Press.

Barnes, C. (1990). *Cabbage Syndrome: The Social Construction of Dependence*. Lewes: Falmer.

Barnes, C. (1991). *Disabled People in Britain and Discrimination: A Case for Anti-Discrimination Legislation*. London: Hurst/BCODP.

Barnes, C. (1996). Theories of disability and the origins of the oppression of disabled people in Western society. In L. Barton (ed.), *Disability & Society*, London: Longman, 43–60.

Barnes, C. (1997a). A legacy of oppression: a history of disability in Western culture. In L. Barton and M. Oliver (eds), *Disability Studies: Past, Present and Future*, Leeds: Disability Press, 3–24.

Barnes, C. (1997b). *Older People's Perceptions of Direct Payments and Self-Operated Support Systems*. Leeds: Disability Research Unit, University of Leeds.

Barnes, C. (1999). A working social model: disability and work in the 21st century. Paper presented at the Disability Studies Seminar, Apex International Hotel, Edinburgh, 9 December 1999.

Barnes, C., Barton, L., and Oliver, M. (eds). (2002). *Disability Studies Today*. Cambridge: Polity.

Barnes, C., Mercer, G., and Shakespeare, T. (1999). *Exploring Disability: A Sociological Introduction*. Cambridge: Polity.

Baron, S., Riddell, S., and Wilson, A. (1999). The secret of eternal youth: identity, risk and learning difficulties. *British Journal of Sociology of Education*, 20(4), 483–99.

Barton, L., and Slee, R. (1999). Competition, selection and inclusive education: some observations. *International Journal of Inclusive Education*, 3(1), 3–12.

Basta, L., and Tauth, J. (1996). High technology near the end of life: setting limits. *Journal of the American College of Cardiology*, 28(6), 1623–30.

Bauman, Z. (1987). *Legislators and Interpreters: On Modernity, Post-Modernity, and Intellectuals*. Cambridge: Polity.

Bauman, Z. (1989). *Modernity and the Holocaust*. Cambridge: Polity.

Bauman, Z. (1995). *Life in Fragments: Essays in Postmodern Morality*. Oxford: Blackwell.

Bauman, Z. (2001). *The Individualized Society*. Cambridge: Polity.

Beck, U. (1992). *Risk Society: Towards a New Modernity*. London: Sage.

Bengtson, V. L., Burgess, E. O., and Parrott, T. M. (1997). Theory, explanation, and a third generation of theoretical development in social gerontology. *Journals of Gerontology Series B: Psychological Sciences and Social Sciences*, 52(2), S72–88.

Bernard, C. (1999). Child sexual abuse and the black disabled child. *Disability & Society*, 14(3), 325–39.

Bernard, M., and Phillips, J. (1998). *The Social Policy of Old Age*. London: Centre for Policy on Ageing.

Biggs, S. (1997). Choosing not to be old? Masks, bodies and identity management in later life. *Ageing and Society*, 17, 553–70.

Biklen, D. (2000). Constructing inclusion: lessons from critical disability narratives. *International Journal of Inclusive Education*, 4, 337–53.

Black, J., and Meyer, L. (1992). But . . . is it really work? Social validity of employment training for persons with very severe disabilities. *American Journal on Mental Retardation*, 96(5), 463–74.

Blaikie, A. (1999). *Ageing and Popular Culture*. Cambridge: Cambridge University Press.

Bloch, M. N. (2000). Governing teachers, parents, and children through child development knowledge. *Human Development*, 43(4–5), 257–65.

Block, P. (2000). Sexuality, fertility, and danger: twentieth-century images of women with cognitive disabilities. *Sexuality and Disability*, 18(4), 239–54.

Bohme, G. (1997). The structures and prospects of information society. *Social Science Information sur les Sciences Sociales*, 36(3), 447–68.

Booth, Tim (2000). Parents with learning difficulties, child protection and the courts. *Representing Children*, 13(3), 175–88.

Booth, Tim, and Booth, W. (1994). *Parenting under Pressure: Mothers and Fathers with Learning Difficulties*. Buckingham: Open University Press.

Booth, Tim, and Booth, W. (1998a). *Advocacy for Parents with Learning Difficulties: Developing Advocacy Support*. Brighton: Pavilion Publishing.

Booth, Tim, and Booth, W. (1998b). Risk, resilience and competence: parents with learning difficulties and their children. In R. Jenkins (ed.), *Questions of Competence: Culture, Classification and Intellectual Disabilities*, Cambridge: Cambridge University Press, 76–101.

Booth, Tim, and Booth, W. (1999a). *Growing Up with Parents who have Learning Difficulties*. London: Routledge.

Booth, Tim, and Booth, W. (1999b). Parents together: action research and advocacy support for parents with learning difficulties. *Health and Social Care in the Community*, 7(6), 464–74.

Booth, Tony (2000). *Inclusion in Education: Participation of Disabled Learners*. Paris: UNESCO Education for All 2000 Assessment, Thematic: Studies.

Botsford, A. (2000). Integrating end of life care into services for people with an intellectual disability. *Social Work in Health Care*, 31(1), 35–48.

Botsford, A., and Force, L. (2000). End-of-life project: Training staff to address the death and/or dying concerns of older people with developmental disabilities. *Journal of Intellectual Disability Research*, 44, 103.

Brady, S. (2001a). The sterilisation of girls and young women with intellectual disabilities in Australia: an audit of family court and guardianship tribunal cases between 1992–1998. Paper presented at the Disability with Attitude: Critical Issues 20 Years after International Year of the Disabled conference, University of Western Sydney, 16–17 February 2001.

Brady, S. (2001b). Sterilization of girls and women with intellectual disabilities – past and present justifications. *Violence against Women*, 7(4), 432–61.

Brady, S., Briton, J., and Grover, S. (2001). *The Sterilisation of Girls and Young Women: Issues and Progress*. Sydney: Australian Human Rights and Equal Opportunity Commission.

Brake, M. (1980). *The Sociology of Youth Culture and Youth Subcultures: Sex and Drugs and Rock'n'roll*. London: Routledge & Kegan Paul.

Brake, M. (1985). *Comparative Youth Culture: The Sociology of Youth Cultures and Youth Subcultures in America, Britain and Canada*. London: Routledge.

Brannen, J., and O'Brien, M. (1995). Childhood and the sociological gaze: paradigms and paradoxes. *Sociology*, 29(4), 729–37.

Breitenbach, N. (2001). Ageing with intellectual disabilities; discovering disability with old age: same or different? In M. Priestley (ed.), *Disability and the Life Course: Global Perspectives*, Cambridge: Cambridge University Press, 231–9.

Brooks, C. (2001). The Victorian celebration of death. *Interdisciplinary Science Reviews*, 26(2), 144–5.

Brown, G., and Harris, T. (eds). (1989). *Life Events and Illness*. London: Hyman Unwin.

Brown, K., and Gillespie, D. (1992). Recovering relationships – a feminist analysis of recovery models. *American Journal of Occupational Therapy*, 46(11), 1001–5.

Brückner, H. (1995). Poverty in transition? Life course, social policy, and changing images of poverty. In D. Chekki (ed.), *Urban Poverty in Affluent Nations*, Research in Community Sociology no. 5, London: JAI Press, 203–24.

Brush, P. (1998). Metaphors of inscription: discipline, plasticity and the rhetoric of choice. *Feminist Review* 58, 22–43.

Bryman, A., Bytheway, B., Allat, P., and Keil, T. (eds). (1987). *Rethinking the Life Cycle*. London: Macmillan.

Buchanan, A., Daniels, N., Wikler, D., Brock, D. W., and Wilker, D. I. (2000). *From Chance to Choice: Genetics and Justice*. Cambridge: Cambridge University Press.

Burch, S. (2000). Transcending revolutions: the Tsars, the Soviets and Deaf culture. *Journal of Social History*, 34(2), 393–402.

Burkhauser, R. (1997). Post-ADA: Are people with disabilities expected to work? *Annals of the American Academy of Political and Social Science*, 549, 71–83.

Burleigh, M. (1994). *Death and Deliverance: 'Euthanasia' in Germany 1900–1945*. Cambridge: Cambridge University Press.

Burleigh, M. (1998). *Ethics and Extermination: Reflections on the Nazi Genocide*. Cambridge: Cambridge University Press.

Bury, M. (1982). Chronic illness as biographical disruption. *Sociology of Health & Illness*, 4(2), 167–82.

Butler, I., and Shaw, I. (eds). (1996). *A Case of Neglect? Children's Experiences and the Sociology of Childhood*. Aldershot: Avebury.

Caillaud, B., and Cohen, D. (2000). Inter-generational transfers and common values in a society. *European Economic Review*, 44(4–6), 1091–103.

Cambois, E., and Robine, J. M. (2000). Social inequalities in disability-free life expectancy in France: results and methodological issues. *M S-Médecine Sciences*, 16(11), 1218–24.

Campbell, C. (1987). *The Romantic Ethic and the Spirit of Modern Consumerism*. Oxford: Blackwell.

Campbell, J., and Oliver, M. (1996). *Disability Politics: Understanding our Past, Changing our Future*. London: Routledge.

Campion, M. (1995). *Who's Fit to be a Parent?* London: Routledge.

Carricaburu, D., and Pierret, J. (1995). From biographical disruption to biographical reinforcement – the case of HIV-positive men. *Sociology of Health & Illness*, 17(1), 65–88.

Carter, T., and Beresford, P. (2000). *Age and Change: Models of Involvement for Older People*. York: York Publishing Services.

Castells, M. (1996). *The Rise of the Network Society*. Oxford: Blackwell.

Chadsey, J., and Beyer, S. (2001). Social relationships in the workplace. *Mental Retardation and Developmental Disabilities Research Reviews*, 7(2), 128–33.

Chadwick, R., Ten Have, H., Husted, J., Levitt, M., Mcgleenan, T., Shickle, D., and Wiesing, U. (1998). Genetic screening and ethics: European perspectives. *Journal of Medicine and Philosophy*, 23(3), 255–73.

Chamberlayne, P., and Rustin, M. (1999). *From Biography to Social Policy: SOSTRIS Working Paper 9*. London: Centre for Biography in Social Policy, University of East London.

Chamberlayne, P., Bornat, J., and Wengraf, T. (eds). (2000). *The Turn to Biographical Methods in Social Science: Comparative Issues and Examples*. London: Routledge.

Chen, J. H., and Simeonsson, R. J. (1993). Prevention of childhood disability in the People's Republic of China. *Child Care Health and Development*, 19, 71–88.

Cherrington, R. (1997). Generational issues in China: a case study of the 1980s generation of young intellectuals. *British Journal of Sociology*, 48(2), 302–20.

Cheyfitz, K. (1999). Who decides? The connecting thread of euthanasia, eugenics, and doctor-assisted suicide. *Omega – Journal of Death and Dying*, 40(1), 5–16.

Cimera, R. E. (1998). Are individuals with severe mental retardation and multiple disabilities cost efficient to serve via supported employment programs? *Mental Retardation*, 36(4), 280–92.

Clough, P., and Barton, L. (1999). *Articulating the Difficulty: Research Voices in Inclusive Education*. London: Paul Chapman.

Clough, P., and Corbett, J. (2000). *Theories of Inclusive Education*. London: Paul Chapman Publishing.

Cobbs, E. L. (2001). Improving quality in end-of-life care: dying at home. *Journal of the American Geriatrics Society*, 49(6), 831–2.

Cohen, J. (2000). The global burden of disease study: a useful projection of future global health? *Journal of Public Health Medicine*, 22(4), 518–24.

Coles, B. (1986). Gonna tear your playhouse down: towards reconstructing a sociology of youth. *Social Science Teacher*, 15(3), 78–80.

Coles, B. (1995). *Youth and Social Policy: Youth, Citizenship and Young Careers*. London: UCL Press.

Coll, C., Lamberty, G., Jenkins, R., Mcadoo, H., Crnic, K., Wasik, B., and Garcia, H. (1996). An integrative model for the study of developmental competencies in minority children. *Child Development*, 67(5), 1891–914.

Collard, D. (2001). The generational bargain. *International Journal of Social Welfare*, 10(1), 54–65.

Collins, B., Hall, M., and Branson, T. (1997). Teaching leisure skills to adolescents with moderate disabilities. *Exceptional Children*, 63(4), 499–512.

Committee of Enquiry into the Education of Handicapped Children and Young People. (1978). *Special Educational Needs: Report of the Com-*

mittee of Enquiry into the Education of Handicapped Children and Young People. London: HMSO.

Cook, A., and Oltjenbruns, K. (eds). (1998). *Dying and Grieving: Life Span and Family Perspectives*, 2nd edn. Orlando, FL: Harcourt Brace and Company.

Cook, T., Swain, J., and French, S. (2001). Voices from segregated schooling: towards an inclusive education system. *Disability & Society*, 16(2), 293–310.

Corbett, J. (1989). The quality of life in the 'independence' curriculum. *Disability, Handicap & Society*, 4(2), 145–63.

Corbett, J. (1998). *Special Educational Needs in the Twentieth Century: A Cultural Analysis*. London: Cassell.

Corbett, J. (2001). *Supporting Inclusive Education – A Connected Pedagogy*. London: Routledge-Falmer.

Corker, M. (1996). *Deaf Transitions: Images and Origins of Deaf Families, Deaf Communities, and Deaf Identities*. London: Jessica Kingsley Publishers.

Corker, M. (1998). *Deaf and Disabled, or Deafness Disabled? Towards a Human Rights Perspective*. Buckingham: Open University Press.

Corker, M. (2001). *Disabling Language: Analyzing Disability Discourse*. London: Routledge.

Corker, M., and French, S. (eds). (1999). *Disability Discourse*. Milton Keynes: Open University Press.

Corr, C. A., Doka, K. J., and Kastenbaum, R. (1999). Dying and its interpreters: a review of selected literature and some comments on the state of the field. *Omega-Journal of Death and Dying*, 39(4), 239–59.

Corsten, M. (1999). The time of generations. *Time & Society*, 8(2), 249–72.

Costello, J. (2001). Nursing older dying patients: findings from an ethnographic study of death and dying in elderly care wards. *Journal of Advanced Nursing*, 35(1), 59–68.

Cote, J. (1997). A social history of youth in Samoa – religion, capitalism, and cultural disenfranchisement. *International Journal of Comparative Sociology*, 38(3–4), 217–34.

Courbage, Y. (1994). An analysis of population-policy in Egypt – using information from recent surveys. *Population*, 49(4–5), 1041–55.

Crimmins, E., Saito, Y., and Ingegneri, D. (1997). Trends in disability-free life expectancy in the United States, 1970–90. *Population and Development Review*, 23(3), 555–72.

Crow, L. (1996). Including all of our lives: renewing the social model of disability. In J. Morris (ed.), *Encounters with Strangers: Feminism and Disability*, London: Women's Press, 206–26.

Crowther, R., Marshall, M., Bond, G., and Huxley, P. (2001). Helping people with severe mental illness to obtain work: systematic review. *British Medical Journal*, 322(7280), 204–8.

Cumming, E., and Henry, W. (1961). *Growing Old: The Process of Disengagement*. New York: Basic Books.

Cummings, R., Maddux, C., and Casey, J. (2000). Individualized transition planning for students with learning disabilities. *Career Development Quarterly*, 49(1), 60–72.

Cunningham, C., Turner, S., Sloper, P., and Knussen, C. (1991). Is the appearance of children with Down's syndrome associated with their development and social functioning? *Developmental Medicine and Child Neurology*, 33(4), 285–95.

Cunningham, H. (1995). *Children and Childhood in Western Society since 1500*. London: Longman.

Cunningham-Burley, S., and Kerr, A. (1999). Defining the 'social': towards an understanding of scientific and medical discourses on the social aspects of the new human genetics. *Sociology of Health & Illness*, 21(5), 647–68.

Cuttini, M., Nadai, M., Kaminski, M., Hansen, G., De Leeuw, R., Lenoir, S., Persson, J., Rebagliato, M., Reid, M., De Vonderweid, U., Lenard, H., Orzalesi, M., and Saracci, R. (2000). End-of-life decisions in neonatal intensive care: physicians' self-reported practices in seven European countries. *Lancet*, 355(9221), 2112–18.

Cuypers, S. (1991). Is personal autonomy the first principle of education? *Journal of Philosophy of Education*, 26, 5–17.

Dahl, M. (2001). Selection and killing – the treatment of children "not worth living" during the period of National Socialism and the role of child and adolescent psychiatry. *Praxis der Kinderpsychologie und Kinderpsychiatrie*, 50(3), 170–91.

Dattilo, J., and Hoge, G. (1999). Effects of a leisure education program on youth with mental retardation. *Education and Training in Mental Retardation and Developmental Disabilities*, 34(1), 20–34.

Davidson, I., Woodill, G., and Bredberg, E. (1994). Images of disability in 19th century British children's literature. *Disability & Society*, 9(1), 33–46.

Davies, C. (1998). Constructing other selves: (in)competences and the category of learning difficulties. In R. Jenkins (ed.), *Questions of Competence: Culture, Classification and Intellectual Disability*, Cambridge: Cambridge University Press, 102–24.

Davis, J., and Watson, N. (2001a). Countering stereotypes of disability: disabled children and resistance. In M. Corker and T. Shakespeare (eds), *Disability and Postmodernity*, London: Continuum, 159–74.

Davis, J., and Watson, N. (2001b). Where are the children's experiences? Analysing social and cultural exclusion in 'special' and 'mainstream' schools. *Disability & Society*, 16(5), 671–87.

Davis, L. (1995). *Enforcing Normalcy: Disability, Deafness, and the Body*. London: Verso.

Davis, L. (ed.). (1997). *The Disability Studies Reader*. New York: Routledge.

Degener, T. (1992). Sterile without consent. In D. Driedger and S. Gray (eds), *Imprinting Our Image*, Gynergy Books, 119–23.

Delanty, G. (2000). *Modernity and Postmodernity: Knowledge, Power and the Self*. London: Sage.

Demaitre, L. (2001). Death and dying in the Middle Ages. *Bulletin of the History of Medicine*, 75(2), 305–6.

Deng, M., Poon-McBrayer, K., and Farnsworth, E. (2001). The development of special education in China – a sociocultural review. *Remedial and Special Education*, 22(5), 288–98.

Diepstraten, I., Ester, P., and Vinken, H. (1999). Talkin' 'bout my generation. Ego and alter images of generations in the Netherlands. *Netherlands Journal of Social Sciences*, 35(2), 91–109.

Disability Rights Advocates. (2001). *Forgotten Crimes: The Holocaust and People with Disabilities*. Oakland, CA: Disability Rights Advocates.

Disabled People's International Europe. (2000). *The Right to Live and be Different*. Available: www.independentliving.org/docs1/dpi022000.html [20 February 2002].

Dodson, M., and Williamson, R. (1999). Indigenous peoples and the morality of the Human Genome Diversity Project. *Journal of Medical Ethics*, 25(2), 204–8.

Doren, B., and Benz, M. (1998). Employment inequality revisited: predictors of better employment outcomes for young women with disabilities in transition. *Journal of Special Education*, 31(4), 425–42.

Dowd, J. (1986). The old person as stranger. In V. Marshall (ed.), *Later Life: The Social Psychology of Ageing*, London: Sage, 147–90.

Dowling, M., and Dolan, L. (2001). Families with children with disabilities – inequalities and the social model. *Disability & Society*, 16(1), 21–35.

Doyle, B. (1995). *Disability, Discrimination and Equal Opportunities: A Comparative Study of the Employment Rights of Disabled Persons*. London: Mansell.

Drackle, D. (1999). Living and dying – images of death and mourning in the Alentejo (Portugal). *Anthropos*, 94(1–3), 121–40.

Driedger, D. (1989). *The Last Civil Rights Movement*. London: Hurst & Co.

Drouard, A. (1992). The sources of eugenics in France – neo-Malthusianism (1896–1914). *Population*, 47(2), 435–60.

Drucker, P. F. (1993). *Post-Capitalist Society*. Oxford: Butterworth-Heinemann.

Dunham, C. C. (1998). Generation units and the life course: a sociological perspective on youth and the anti-war movement. *Journal of Political & Military Sociology*, 26(2), 137–55.

Dutton, K. (1996). *The Perfectable Body*. London: Cassell.

Eastwood, R., and Lipton, M. (1999). The impact of changes in human fertility on poverty. *Journal of Development Studies*, 36(1), 1–30.

Elias, N. (1985). *The Loneliness of the Dying*. Oxford: Blackwell.

Engels, R., and Ter Bogt, T. (2001). Influences of risk behaviors on the quality of peer relations in adolescence. *Journal of Youth and Adolescence*, 30(6), 675–95.

Erikson, E. (1968). *Identity, Youth and Crisis*. New York: Norton.

Ettorre, E. (2000). Reproductive genetics, gender and the body: 'Please doctor, may I have a normal baby?' *Sociology – the Journal of the British Sociological Association*, 34(3), 403–20.

European Communities. (2001). *Disability and Social Participation in Europe*. Luxembourg: Office for Official Publications of the European Communities.

Evans, J. (2001). Ageing and medicine (reprinted from *Journal of Internal Medicine*, vol. 247, 159–167, 2000). *Journal of Internal Medicine*, 249, 7–15.

Evans, K., and Furlong, A. (1997). Metaphors of youth transition: niches, pathways, trajectories or navigations. In J. Bynner, L. Chisholm, and A. Furlong (eds), *Youth, Citizenship and Social Change in a European Context*, Aldershot: Ashgate, 17–41.

Falkingham, J., and Hills, J. (eds). (1995). *The Dynamic of Welfare: The Welfare State and the Life Cycle*. London: Harvester Wheatsheaf.

Fargues, P. (1997). State policies and the birth rate in Egypt: from socialism to liberalism. *Population and Development Review*, 23(1), 115–38.

Farrant, W. (1985). Who's for amniocentesis? In H. Homans (ed.), *The Sexual Politics of Reproduction*, London: Gower, 96–177.

Featherstone, M. (1991a). The body in consumer culture. In M. Featherstone, M. Hepworth, and B. Turner (eds), *The Body: Social Process and Cultural Theory*, London: Sage, 170–96.

Featherstone, M. (1991b). *Consumer Culture and Postmodernity*. London: Sage.

Featherstone, M. (1995). Post-bodies, aging and virtual reality. In M. Featherstone and A. Wernick (eds), *Images of Aging: Cultural Representations of Later Life*, London: Routledge, 227–44.

Featherstone, M. (ed.). (2000). *Body Modification*. London: Sage.

Featherstone, M., and Hepworth, M. (1991). The mask of ageing and the postmodern lifecourse. In M. Featherstone, M. Hepworth, and B. Turner (eds), *The Body: Social Process and Cultural Theory*, London: Sage.

Feldman, M. (1998). Parents with intellectual disabilities: implications and interventions. In J. Lutzker (ed.), *Child Abuse: A Handbook of Theory, Research and Treatment*, New York: Plenum Press, 401–19.

Ferrari, M., and Sussman, M. B. (eds). (1987). *Childhood Disability and Family Systems*. New York: Howarth.

Finch, N., Lawson, D., Williams, J., and Sloper, P. (2001). *Disability Survey 2000: Survey of Young People with a Disability and Sport*. London: Sport England.

Finkelstein, V. (1975). More on phase 2. *Magic Carpet*, 27(2), 16–17.

Finkelstein, V. (1980). *Attitudes and Disabled People: Issues for Discussion*, Monograph 5. New York: World Rehabilitation Fund.

Finkelstein, V. (1991). Disability: an administrative challenge? (the health and welfare heritage). In M. Oliver (ed.), *Social Work: Disabled People and Disabling Environments*, London: Jessica Kingsley Publishers, 19–39.

Fitzgerald, J. (1998). Geneticizing disability: the Human Genome Project and the commodification of self. *Issues in Law & Medicine*, 14(2), 147–63.

Fleischer, D., and Zames, F. (2001). *The Disability Rights Movement: From Charity to Confrontation*. Philadelphia: Temple University Press.

Flippen, C., and Tienda, M. (2000). Pathways to retirement: patterns of labor force participation and labor market exit among the pre-retirement population by race, Hispanic origin, and sex. *Journals of Gerontology Series B: Psychological Sciences and Social Sciences*, 55(1), S14–27.

Floyd, M., and Curtis, J. (2000). An examination of changes in disability and employment policy in the United Kingdom. *European Journal of Social Security*, 2(4), 303–22.

Foner, A. (1988). Age inequalities: are they epiphenomena of the class system? In M. W. Riley (ed.), *Social Structures and Human Lives*, Newbury Park, CA: Sage, 176–91.

Ford, A., Haug, M., Stange, K., Gaines, A., Noelker, L., and Jones, P. (2000). Sustained personal autonomy: a measure of successful aging. *Journal of Aging and Health*, 12(4), 470–89.

Foster, G., Sherrard, M., Cosbey, J., and Hummel, R. (2001). Dying to be old: a sociological analysis of old age as cause of death. *Journal of Aging and Identity*, 6(3), 165–79.

Foucault, M. (1967). *Madness and Civilisation: A History of Insanity in the Age of Reason*. London: Tavistock.

Foucault, M. (1977). *Discipline and Punish*. New York: Pantheon.

Fratiglioni, L., De Ronchi, D., and Aguero-Torres, H. (1999). Worldwide prevalence and incidence of dementia. *Drugs & Aging*, 15(5), 365–75.

French, S. (1993). What's so great about independence? In J. Swain, V. Finkelstein, S. French, and M. Oliver (eds), *Disabling Barriers: Enabling Environments*, London: Open University Press/Sage, 44–8.

Fried, T., Pollack, D., Drickamer, M., and Tinetti, M. (1999). Who dies at home? Determinants of site of death for community-based long-term care patients. *Journal of the American Geriatrics Society*, 47(1), 25–9.

Friedlander, H. (1995). *The Origins of Nazi Genocide: From Euthanasia to the Final Solution*. Chapel Hill, NC: University of North Carolina Press.

Frith, S. (1984). *The Sociology of Youth*. Ormskirk: Causeway Press Ltd.

Fullagar, S., and Owler, K. (1998). Narratives of leisure: recreating the self. *Disability & Society*, 13(3), 441–50.

Furstenberg, F. (2000). The sociology of adolescence and youth in the 1990s: a critical commentary. *Journal of Marriage and the Family*, 62(4), 896–910.

Gabard, D. (1999). Homosexuality and the Human Genome Project: private and public choices. *Journal of Homosexuality*, 37(1), 25–51.

Gabriel, S., and Gardner, W. (1999). Are there 'his' and 'hers' types of interdependence? The implications of gender differences in collective versus relational interdependence for affect, behavior, and cognition. *Journal of Personality and Social Psychology*, 77(3), 642–55.

Gajdos, P. (2000). The decline of birth rate in Slovakia: the sociological perspective. *Sociologia*, 32(1), 131–4.

Galjaard, H. (1997). Gene technology and social acceptance. *Pathologie Biologie*, 45(3), 250–5.

Gallagher, H. (1995). *By Trust Betrayed: Patients, Physicians, and the License to Kill in the Third Reich*. Arlington, VA: Vandamere Press.

Gallo, W., Baker, M., and Bradley, E. (2001). Factors associated with home versus institutional death among cancer patients in Connecticut. *Journal of the American Geriatrics Society*, 49(6), 771–7.

Galton, D. (1998). Greek theories on eugenics. *Journal of Medical Ethics*, 24(4), 263–7.

Galton, D., and Galton, C. (1998). Francis Galton and eugenics today. *Journal of Medical Ethics*, 24(2), 99–105.

Galton, F. (1869). *Hereditary Genius: An Inquiry into Its Laws and Consequences*. London: Macmillan.

Gannotti, M., Handwerker, W., Groce, N., and Cruz, C. (2001). Sociocultural influences on disability status in Puerto Rican children. *Physical Therapy*, 81(9), 1512–23.

Gardella, J. (1995). Eugenic sterilization in America and North Carolina. *North Carolina Medical Journal*, 56(2), 106–10.

Garland, R. (1995). *The Eye of the Beholder: Deformity and Disability in the Graeco-Roman World*. London: Gerald Duckworth & Co. Ltd.

Gayle, V. (1998). Structural and cultural approaches to youth: structuration theory and bridging the gap. *Youth and Policy*, 61, 59–72.

Genskow, J. (1986). *Independent Living and the Elderly Disabled in Denmark*. Sangamon, IL: Sangamon State University, IL, World Rehabilitation Fund, Inc. International Exchange of Experts and Information in Rehabilitation.

Gething, L. (2000). Ageing with long-standing hearing impairment and deafness. *International Journal of Rehabilitation Research*, 23(3), 209–15.

Gibson, D. (1996). Broken down by age and gender – 'The problem of old women' redefined. *Gender & Society*, 10(4), 433–48.

Giddens, A. (1984). *The Constitution of Society*. Berkeley: University of California Press.

Giddens, A. (1991). *Modernity and Self-Identity: Self and Society in the Late Modern Age*. Cambridge: Polity.

Giele, J., and Elder, G. (eds). (1998). *Methods of Life Course Research: Qualitative and Quantitative Approaches*. Thousand Oaks, CA: Sage.

Giese, S., and Dawes, A. (1999). Child care, developmental delay and institutional practice. *South African Journal of Psychology*, 29(1), 17–22.

Gilger, J. (2000). Contributions and promise of human behavioral genetics. *Human Biology*, 72(1), 229–55.

Gillberg, C., and Geijer-Karlsson, M. (1983). Children born to mentally retarded women: a 1–21-year follow-up study of 41 cases. *Psychological Medicine*, 13, 891–4.

Gilleard, C., and Higgs, P. (1998). Ageing and the limiting conditions of the body. *Sociological Research Online*, 3(4), U56–70.

Giroux, H. (1998). Teenage sexuality, body politics, and the pedagogy of display. In J. S. Epstein (ed.), *Youth Culture: Identity in a Postmodern World*, Oxford: Blackwell, 24–55.

Glaser, B., and Strauss, A. (1965). *Awareness of Dying*. Chicago: Aldine.

Glaser, B., and Strauss, A. (1968). *Time for Dying*. Chicago: Aldine.

Glasper, E., and Powell, C. (1999). Facial surgery and children with Down's syndrome. *British Journal of Nursing*, 8(1), 6.

Glass, J. (1999). *'Life Unworthy of Life': Racial Phobia and Mass Murder in Hitler's Germany*. New York: Basic Books.

Glassner, B. (1992). *Bodies: The Tyranny of Perfection*. Los Angeles: Lowell House.

Gleeson, B. (1999). *Geographies of Disability*. London: Routledge.

Gold, S. (1996). An equality approach to wrongful birth statutes. *Fordham Law Review*, 65(3), 1005–41.

Gooding, C. (1996). Employment and disabled people: equal rights or positive action. In G. Zarb (ed.), *Removing Disabling Barrriers*, London: Policy Studies Institute, 64–76.

Goodinge, S. (2000). *A Jigsaw of Services: An Inspection of Services to Support Disabled Adults in their Parenting Role*. London: Social Services Inspectorate/Department of Health, C1 (2000) 6.

Goodley, D. (1996). Tales of hidden lives: a critical examination of life history research with people who have learning difficulties. *Disability & Society*, 11(3), 333–48.

Goodley, D. (2000). *Self-Advocacy in the Lives of People with Learning Difficulties: The Politics of Resilience*. Buckingham: Open University Press.

Goss, D., Goss, F., and Adam-Smith, D. (2000). Disability and employment: a comparative critique of UK legislation. *International Journal of Human Resource Management*, 11(4), 807–21.

Graves, P., and Tracy, J. (1998). Education for children with disabilities: the rationale for inclusion. *Journal of Paediatrics and Child Health*, 34(3), 220–5.

Graycar, R. (1994). Sterilisation of young women with disabilities: towards a regulatory framework. *Australian Journal of Human Rights*, 1(1), 380–1.

Greely, H. (1998). Legal, ethical, and social issues in human genome research. *Annual Review of Anthropology*, 27, 473–502.

Gregory, S. (1995). *Deaf Young People and their Families Developing Understanding*. Cambridge: Cambridge University Press.

Groce, N. E., Chamie, M., and Me, A. (2000). Measuring the quality of life: rethinking the World Bank's Disability Adjusted Life Year. *Disability World*, 3, http://www.disabilityworld.org/June–July2002/International/DALY.html

Grossman, P. (1992). Employment discrimination law for the learning-disabled community. *Learning Disability Quarterly*, 15(4), 287–329.

Gruber, J. (2000). Disability insurance benefits and labor supply. *Journal of Political Economy*, 108(6), 1162–83.

Gutierrez-Fisac, J., Gispert, R., and Sola, J. (2000). Factors explaining the geographical differences in disability free life expectancy in Spain. *Journal of Epidemiology and Community Health*, 54(6), 451–5.

Haffter, C. (1968). The changeling: history and psychodynamics of attitudes to handicapped children in European folklore. *Journal of the History of Behavioural Sciences*, 4, 55–61.

Hahn, H. (1988). Can disability be beautiful? *Social Policy & Administration*, Winter, 26–32.

Hallam, E. (1999). *Beyond the Body: Death and Social Identity*. London: Routledge.

Hans, G. (1996). Future perspective on the youth policy and programmes. *Indian Journal of Social Work*, 57(3), 461–73.

Hareven, T. (1994). Aging and generational relations – a historical and life-course perspective. *Annual Review of Sociology*, 20, 437–61.

Harper, P., and Clarke, A. (1997). *Genetics, Society and Clinical Practice*. Oxford: Bios.

Harper, P., and Harris, R. (1986). Medical genetics in China: a Western view. *Journal of Medical Genetics*, 23, 385–8.

Harris, J. (1993). Is gene therapy a form of eugenics? *Bioethics*, 7, 178–87.

Harvey, J. (1997). The technological regulation of death: with reference to the technological regulation of birth. *Sociology – the Journal of the British Sociological Association*, 31(4), 719–35.

Hauser-Cram, P., Warfield, M., Shonkoff, J., Krauss, M., Sayer, A., Upshur, C., and Hodapp, R. (2001). Children with disabilities: a longitudinal study of child development and parent well-being – Introduction. *Monographs of the Society for Research in Child Development*, 66(3), 6–21.

Hayden, M., Lakin, K. C., Hill, B., Bruininks, R., and Copher, J. (1992). Social and leisure integration of people with mental-retardation in foster homes and small-group homes. *Education and Training in Mental Retardation and Developmental Disabilities*, 27(3), 187–99.

HelpAge International. (1999). *Ageing and Development Report: Poverty, Independence and the World's Older People*. London: Earthscan.

Henn, W. (2000). Consumerism in prenatal diagnosis: a challenge for ethical guidelines. *Journal of Medical Ethics*, 26(6), 444–6.

Henry, A. (1998). Development of a measure of adolescent leisure interests. *American Journal of Occupational Therapy*, 52(7), 531–9.

Hevey, D. (1991). From self love to the picket line. In S. Lees (ed.), *Disability Arts and Culture Papers*, London: Shape Publications, 23–30.

Hevey, D. (1992). *The Creatures Time Forgot: Photography and Disability Imagery*. London: Routledge.

Hevey, D. (1993). The tragedy principle: strategies for change in the representation of disabled people. In J. Swain, V. Finkelstein, S. French, and M. Oliver (eds), *Disabling Barriers: Enabling Environments*, Milton Keynes: Open University Press/Sage, 116–21.

Heyland, D., Lavery, J., Tranmer, J., Shortt, S., and Taylor, S. (2000). Dying in Canada: is it an institutionalized, technologically supported experience? *Journal of Palliative Care*, 16, S10–16.

Hintermair, M. (2000). Hearing impairment, social networks, and coping: the need for families with hearing-impaired children to relate to other parents and to hearing-impaired adults. *American Annals of the Deaf*, 145(1), 41–53.

Hirschman, C. (1994). Why fertility changes. *Annual Review of Sociology*, 20, 203–33.

Hoche, A., and Binding, K. (1920). *Die Freigabe der Vernichtung lebensunwerten Lebens [The Permission to Destroy Life Unworthy of Life]*. Leipzig.

Hockey, J., and James, A. (1993). *Growing Up and Growing Older: Ageing and Dependency in the Life Course*. London: Sage.

Hockey, J., Katz, J., and Small, N. (eds). (2001). *Grief, Mourning and Death Ritual*. Buckingham: Open University Press.

Hodkinson, P., and Sparkes, A. (1997). Careership: a sociological theory of career decision making. *British Journal of Sociology of Education*, 18(1), 29–44.

Hoenig, H., Taylor, D., and Sloan, F. (2001). Assistive technology is associated with reduced use of personal assistance among disabled older persons. *Journal of the American Geriatrics Society*, 49(4), A40.

Hogg, J., and Lambe, L. (1998). *Older People with Learning Disabilities: A Review of the Literature of Residential Services and Family Caregiving*. Dundee: White Top Research Unit, University of Dundee.

Holland, A. (2000). Ageing and learning disability. *British Journal of Psychiatry*, 176, 26–31.

Hollins, S., Attard, M., Von Fraunhofer, N., McGuigan, S., and Sedgwick, P. (1998). Mortality in people with learning disability: risks, causes, and death certification findings in London. *Developmental Medicine and Child Neurology*, 40(1), 50–6.

Howarth, G. (1998). 'Just live for today'. Living, caring, ageing and dying. *Ageing and Society*, 18, 673–89.

Howarth, G., and Jefferys, M. (1996). Euthanasia: sociological perspectives. *British Medical Bulletin*, 52(2), 376–85.

Hubbard, G. (2000). The usefulness of in-depth life history interviews for exploring the role of social structure and human agency in youth transitions. *Sociological Research Online*, 4(4).

Hubbard, R. (1997). Abortion and disability: who should and who should not inhabit the world? In L. Davis (ed.), *The Disability Studies Reader*, New York: Routledge, 187–200.

Hudson, F. (ed.). (1999). *The Adult Years: Mastering the Art of Self-Renewal*. San Francisco: Jossey-Bass.

Hughes, B. (2000). Medicine and the aesthetic invalidation of disabled people. *Disability & Society*, 15(4), 555–68.

Hughes, B., and Paterson, K. (1997). The social model of disability and the disappearing body: towards a sociology of impairment. *Disability & Society*, 12(3), 325–40.

Hughes, C. (2001). Transition to adulthood: supporting young adults to access social, employment, and civic pursuits. *Mental Retardation and Developmental Disabilities Research Reviews*, 7, 84–90.

Humphries, S., and Gordon, P. (1992). *Out of Sight: The Experience of Disability 1900–1950*. Plymouth: Channel Four/Northcote House.

Hurst, R., and Lansdown, G. (2002). 'We are children too!' Are disabled children included in the rights agenda? In *All Things being Equal: Perspectives on Disability and Development*, Milton Keynes: World Vision UK, 13–18.

Hurt, G. (1981). The handicapped family. In A. Walker and P. Townsend (eds), *Disability in Britain: A Manifesto of Rights*, Oxford: Martin Robertson & Company, 23–6.

Hyde, M. (1998). Sheltered and supported employment in the 1990s: the experiences of disabled workers in the UK. *Disability & Society*, 13(2), 199–215.

Hyder, A. A., and Morrow, R. H. (2000). Applying burden of disease methods in developing countries: a case study from Pakistan. *American Journal of Public Health*, 90(8), 1235–40.

Illich, I. (1975). *Medical Nemesis: The Expropriation of Health*. London: Calder & Boyars.

Ingstad, B., and Reynolds Whyte, S. (eds). (1995). *Disability and Culture*. Berkeley: University of California Press.

International Labour Organization. (1983). *Convention Concerning Vocational Rehabilitation and Employment (Disabled Persons)*. Geneva: ILO, Convention C159.

International Save the Children Alliance. (2001). *Disabled Children's Rights: A Practical Guide*. Stockholm: Save the Children Sweden.

Iredale, R. (2000). Eugenics and its relevance to contemporary health care. *Nursing Ethics*, 7(3), 205–14.

Irwin, S. (1995). *Rights of Passage: Social Change and the Transition from Youth to Adulthood*. London: UCL Press.

Irwin, S. (1999). Later life, inequality and sociological theory. *Ageing and Society*, 19(6), 691–715.

Irwin, S. (2001). Repositioning disability and the life course: a social claiming perspective. In M. Priestley (ed.), *Disability and the Life Course: Global Perspectives*, Cambridge: Cambridge University Press, 15–25.

Irwin, S., and Bottero, W. (2000). Market returns? Gender and theories of change in employment relations. *British Journal of Sociology*, 51(2), 261–80.

Jagger, C., Ritchie, K., Bronnum-Hansen, H., Deeg, D., Gispert, R., Evans, J., Hibbett, M., Lawlor, B., Perenboom, R., Polge, C., and Van Oyen, H. (1998). Mental health expectancy – the European perspective: a synopsis of results presented at the Conference of the European Network for the

Calculation of Health Expectancies (Euro-REVES). *Acta Psychiatrica Scandinavica*, 98(2), 85–91.

Jallinoja, P. (2001). Genetic screening in maternity care: preventive aims and voluntary choices. *Sociology of Health & Illness*, 23(3), 286–307.

James, A., and Prout, A. (eds). (1997). *Constructing and Reconstructing Childhood: Contemporary Issues in the Sociological Study of Childhood*. London: Falmer.

James, A., Jenks, C., and Prout, A. (1998). *Theorizing Childhood*. Cambridge: Polity.

Janicki, M., Dalton, A., Henderson, C., and Davidson, P. (1999). Mortality and morbidity among older adults with intellectual disability: health services considerations. *Disability and Rehabilitation*, 21(5–6), 284–94.

Jayasooria, D., Krishnan, B., and Ooi, G. (1997). Disabled people in a newly industrialising economy: opportunities and challenges in Malaysia. *Disability & Society*, 12(3), 455–63.

Jelas, Z. (2000). Perceptions of inclusive practices: the Malaysian perspective. *Educational Review*, 52(2), 187–96.

Jenkins, R. (ed.). (1998). *Questions of Competence: Culture, Classification and Intellectual Disability*. Cambridge: Cambridge University Press.

Jitapunkul, S., Bunnag, S., and Ebrahim, S. (1993). Health-care for elderly people in developing-countries – a case-study of Thailand. *Age and Ageing*, 22(5), 377–81.

Johnson, M. (1995). Interdependency and the generational compact. *Ageing and Society*, 15, 243–65.

Johnson, M., and Shaw, B. (eds). (2001). *To Ride the Public's Buses: The Fight that Built a Movement*. Louisville: Advocado Press.

Jones, E., Strom, R., and Daniels, S. (1989). Evaluating the success of deaf parents. *American Annals of the Deaf*, 134(5), 312–16.

Jones, G. (1988). Integrating process and structure in the concept of youth: a case study for secondary analysis. *Sociological Review*, 36, 706–32.

Jones, R. (2000). Parental consent to cosmetic facial surgery in Down's syndrome. *Journal of Medical Ethics*, 26(2), 101–2.

Juengst, E. (1999). Genetic testing and the moral dynamics of family life. *Public Understanding of Science*, 8(3), 193–205.

Kalekin-Fishman, D. (2001). The hidden injuries of 'a slight limp'. In M. Priestley (ed.), *Disability and the Life Course: Global Perspectives*. Cambridge: Cambridge University Press, 136–48.

Kallianes, V., and Rubenfeld, P. (1997). Disabled women and reproductive rights. *Disability & Society*, 12(2), 203–21.

Kaplan, K., and Bratman, E. (1999). Gender, pain, and doctor involvement: high school student attitudes toward doctor-assisted suicide. *Omega – Journal of Death and Dying*, 40(1), 27–41.

Kapp, M. (2000). Physicians' legal duties regarding the use of genetic tests to predict and diagnose Alzheimer disease. *Journal of Legal Medicine*, 21(4), 445–75.

Kasnitz, D. (2001). Life event histories and the US independent living movement. In M. Priestley (ed.), *Disability and the Life Course: Global Perspectives*, Cambridge: Cambridge University Press, 67–78.

Kastenbaum, R., and Thuell, S. (1995). Cookies baking, coffee brewing – toward a contextual theory of dying. *Omega – Journal of Death and Dying*, 31(3), 175–87.

Kavale, K., and Forness, S. (2000). History, rhetoric, and reality – analysis of the inclusion debate. *Remedial and Special Education*, 21(5), 279–96.

Kearl, M. (1989). *Endings: A Sociology of Death and Dying*. Oxford: Oxford University Press.

Keigher, S. (1999). The limits of consumer directed care as public policy in an aging society. *Canadian Journal on Aging – Revue Canadienne du Vieillissement*, 18(2), 182–210.

Keith, L. (ed.). (1994). *Mustn't Grumble: Writings by Disabled Women*. London: Women's Press.

Keith, L. (2001). *Take Up Thy Bed and Walk: Death, Disability, and Cure in Classic Fiction for Girls*. London: Routledge.

Kelly, M., and Dickinson, H. (1997). The narrative self in autobiographical accounts of illness. *Sociological Review*, 45(2), 254–78.

Kennedy, C. (2001). Social interaction interventions for youth with severe disabilities should emphasize interdependence. *Mental Retardation and Developmental Disabilities Research Reviews*, 7(2), 122–7.

Kennedy, J., and Minkler, M. (1998). Disability theory and public policy: implications for critical gerontology. *International Journal of Health Services*, 28(4), 757–76.

Kevles, D. (1985). *In the Name of Eugenics*. New York: Knopf.

King, D. (1999). Preimplantation genetic diagnosis and the 'new' eugenics. *Journal of Medical Ethics*, 25(2), 176–82.

Kinsella, K. (2000). Demographic dimensions of global aging. *Journal of Family Issues*, 21(5), 541–58.

Kinsella, K., and Suzman, R. (1992). Demographic dimensions of population aging in developing countries. *American Journal of Human Biology*, 4(1), 3–8.

Kirshbaum, M. (2000). A disability culture perspective on early intervention with parents with physical or cognitive disabilities and their infants. *Infants and Young Children*, 13(2), 9–20.

Kogon, E., Langbein, H., and Ruckerl, A. (eds). (1993). *Nazi Mass Murder: A Documentary History of the Use of Poison Gas*. New Haven, CT: Yale University Press.

Kohler, H. (2000). Social interactions and fluctuations in birth rates. *Population Studies – a Journal of Demography*, 54(2), 223–37.

Kohler, L. (1993). Children with and without disabilities in the Nordic countries – a Nordic project. *Scandinavian Journal of Social Medicine*, 21(3), 146–9.

Konur, O. (2000). Creating enforceable civil rights for disabled students in higher education: an institutional theory perspective. *Disability & Society*, 15(7), 1041–63.

Kristeva, J. (1982). *Power of Horror: An Essay in Abjection.* New York: Columbia University Press.

Kubler-Ross, E. (1969). *On Death and Dying.* New York: Macmillan.

Lachenmeier, F., Kaplan, K., and Caragacianu, D. (1999). Doctor assisted suicide: an analysis of public opinion of Michigan adults. *Omega – Journal of Death and Dying*, 40(1), 61–87.

Landau, R., Guttmann, D., and Talyigas, K. (1998). Eligibility criteria for cash assistance for older and disabled people in Hungary: a model for countries in passage from a planned to a market economy. *British Journal of Social Work*, 28(2), 233–46.

Larson, E. (ed.). (1995). *Sex, Race, and Science: Eugenics in the Deep South.* Baltimore: Johns Hopkins University Press.

Laslett, P. (1989). *A Fresh Map of Life: The Emergence of the Third Age.* London: Weidenfeld and Nicolson.

Laudor, M. (1994). In defense of wrongful life – bringing political-theory to the defense of a tort. *Fordham Law Review*, 62(6), 1675–1704.

Lee, B., and Werth, J. (2000). Observations on the first year of Oregon's Death with Dignity Act. *Psychology Public Policy and Law*, 6(2), 268–90.

Lee, D. (2001). Imperfect conceptions: medical knowledge, birth defects, and eugenics in China. *Pacific Affairs*, 74(1), 110–11.

Leichtentritt, R., and Rettig, K. (2000). The good death: reaching an inductive understanding. *Omega – Journal of Death and Dying*, 41(3), 221–48.

Leichtentritt, R., and Rettig, K. (2001). The construction of the good death – a dramaturgy approach. *Journal of Aging Studies*, 15(1), 85–103.

Leveille, S., Resnick, H., and Balfour, J. (2000). Gender differences in disability: evidence and underlying reasons. *Aging – Clinical and Experimental Research*, 12(2), 106–12.

Levesque, R. (1996). Regulating the private relations of adults with mental disabilities: old laws, new policies, hollow hopes. *Behavioral Sciences & the Law*, 14(1), 83–106.

Levine, P., and Nourse, S. (1998). What follow-up studies say about post-school life for young men and women with learning disabilities: a critical look at the literature. *Journal of Learning Disabilities*, 31(3), 212–33.

Lifton, R. (1986). *The Nazi Doctors.* London: Macmillan.

Light, J. (2001). Separate but equal? Reasonable accommodation in the information age. *Journal of the American Planning Association*, 67(3), 263–78.

Linton, S. (1998). *Claiming Disability: Knowledge and Identity.* New York: New York University Press.

Lisker, R., Carnevale, A., and Armendares, S. (1999). Mexican geneticists' views of ethical issues in genetics testing and screening. Are eugenic principles involved? *Clinical Genetics*, 56(4), 323–7.

Little, H. (1993). Non-consensual sterilisation of the intellectually disabled in the Australian context: potential for human rights abuse and the need for reform. *Australian Yearbook of International Law*, 1993, 203.

Liu, X., Liang, J., Muramatsu, N., and Sugisawa, H. (1995). Transitions in functional status and active life expectancy among older people in Japan. *Journals of Gerontology Series B: Psychological Sciences and Social Sciences*, 50(6), S383–94.

Lloyd, C. (2000). Excellence for all children – false promises! The failure of current policy for inclusive education and implications for schooling in the 21st century. *International Journal of Inclusive Education*, 4(2), 133–51.

Loeppky, R. (1998). Control from within? Power, identity, and the human genome project. *Alternatives – Social Transformation and Humane Governance*, 23(2), 245–66.

Longino, C., and Murphy, J. (1995). *The Old Age Challenge to the Biomedical Model*. New York: Baywood Publishing Co.

Lonsdale, S., and Walker, A. (1984). *A Right to Work: Disability & Employment*. London: Disability Alliance and Low Pay Unit.

Lubeck, S. (1996). Deconstructing 'child development knowledge' and 'teacher preparation'. *Early Childhood Research Quarterly*, 11(2), 147–67.

Luken, P., and Vaughan, S. (1999). Life history and the critique of American sociological practice. *Sociological Inquiry*, 69(3), 404–25.

Luo, H. (1988). Medical genetics in China. *Journal of Medical Genetics*, 25, 253–7.

Lynn, J. (2001). Serving patients who may die soon and their families – the role of hospice and other services. *JAMA (Journal of the American Medical Association)*, 285(7), 925–32.

Lysack, C. (1997). Modernity, postmodernity and disability in developing countries. *International Journal of Rehabilitation Research*, 20(2), 121–8.

Macdonald, R., Mason, P., Shildrick, T., Webster, C., Johnston, L., and Ridley, L. (2001). Snakes and ladders: in defence of studies of youth transition. *Sociological Research Online*, 5(4), U86–103.

Macleod, R. (2001). On reflection: doctors learning to care for people who are dying. *Social Science & Medicine*, 52(11), 1719–27.

Maddox, G. (1994). Lives through the years revisited. *Gerontologist*, 34(6), 764–7.

Mamo, L. (1999). Death and dying: confluences of emotion and awareness. *Sociology of Health & Illness*, 21(1), 13–36.

Mannheim, K. (1952). *Essays in the Sociology of Knowledge*. London: Routledge & Kegan Paul.

Mao, X. (1998). Chinese geneticists' views of ethical issues in genetic testing and screening: evidence for eugenics in China. *American Journal of Human Genetics*, 63(3), 688–95.

Mao, X., and Wertz, D. (1997). China's genetic service providers' attitudes towards several ethical issues: a cross-cultural survey. *Clinical Genetics*, 52(2), 100–9.

Markham, I. (1998). Ethical and legal issues. *British Medical Bulletin*, 54(4), 1011–21.

Marshall, V. (1980). *Last Chapters: A Sociology of Aging and Dying.* Belmont, CA: Wadsworth.

Marshall, V. (1986). A sociological perspective on aging and dying. In V. Marshall (ed.), *Later Life: The Social Psychology of Ageing,* London: Sage, 125–46.

Mayer, K., and Tuba, N. (1990). *Event History Analysis in Life Course Research.* Madison: Wisconsin University Press.

Mazumdar, P. (1992). *Eugenics, Home Genetics and Human Failings: The Eugenics Society, its Sources and its Critics in Britain.* London: Routledge.

McConkey, R., and Ryan, D. (2001). Experiences of staff in dealing with client sexuality in services for teenagers and adults with intellectual disability. *Journal of Intellectual Disability Research,* 45, 83–7.

McConnell, D., and Llwellyn, G. (2000). Disability and discrimination in statutory child protection proceedings. *Disability & Society,* 15(6), 883–95.

McConnell, D., Llewellyn, G., and Ferronato, L. (2000). *Parents with a Disability and the NSW Children's Court.* Lidcombe, NSW: University of Sydney, Family Support and Services project.

McDaniel, S. (2001). Born at the right time? Gendered generations and webs of entitlement and responsibility. *Canadian Journal of Sociology – Cahiers Canadiens de Sociologie,* 26(2), 193–214.

McDonough, P. (1996). The social production of housework disability. *Women & Health,* 24(4), 1–25.

McInerney, F. (2000). 'Requested death': a new social movement. *Social Science & Medicine,* 50(1), 137–54.

Mehler, B. (1997). Beyondism: Raymond B. Cattell and the new eugenics. *Genetica,* 99(2–3), 153–63.

Meijer, C., and Jager, B. (2001). Population density and special needs education. *European Journal of Special Needs Education,* 16(2), 143–8.

Meisel, A., Snyder, L., and Quill, T. (2000). Seven legal barriers to end-of-life care – myths, realities, and grains of truth. *JAMA,* 284(19), 2495–501.

Melse, J., Essink-Bot, M., Kramers, P., and Hoeymans, N. (2000). A national burden of disease calculation: Dutch disability-adjusted life-years. *American Journal of Public Health,* 90(8), 1241–7.

Melzer, D., Izmirlian, G., Leveille, S., and Guralnik, J. (2001). Educational differences in the prevalence of mobility disability in old age: the dynamics of incidence, mortality, and recovery. *Journals of Gerontology Series B: Psychological Sciences and Social Sciences,* 56(5), S294–301.

Melzer, D., McWilliams, B., Brayne, C., Johnson, T., and Bond, J. (2000). Socioeconomic status and the expectation of disability in old age: estimates for England. *Journal of Epidemiology and Community Health,* 54(4), 286–92.

Mencap, Respond, and Voice UK. (2001). *Behind Closed Doors: Preventing Sexual Abuse against Adults with a Learning Disability.* London: Mencap.

Meyer, J. (1988). Levels of analysis: the life course as a cultural construction. In M. W. Riley (ed.), *Social Structures and Human Lives*, Newbury Park, CA: Sage, 49–62.

Michailakis, D. (2001). Information and communication technologies and the opportunities of disabled persons in the Swedish labour market. *Disability & Society*, 16(4), 477–500.

Michalko, R. (2002). *The Difference that Disability Makes*. Philadelphia: Temple University Press.

Middleton, L. (1996). *Making a Difference: Social Work with Disabled Children*. Birmingham: Venture Press.

Miles, S. (2000). *Youth Lifestyles in a Changing World*. Buckingham: Open University Press.

Miller, E., and Gwynne, G. (1972). *A Life Apart: A Pilot Study of Residential Institutions for the Physically Handicapped and the Young Chronic Sick*. London: Tavistock Publications.

Miller, H. (1992). Not the only game in town – zooepistemology and ontological pluralism. *Synthese*, 92(1), 25–37.

Milligan, M., and Neufeldt, A. (2001). The myth of asexuality: a survey of social and empirical evidence. *Sexuality and Disability*, 19(2), 91–109.

Minichiello, V., Browne, J., and Kendig, H. (2000). Perceptions and consequences of ageism: views of older people. *Ageing and Society*, 20, 253–78.

Minkler, M., and Estes, C. (eds). (1991). *Critical Perspectives on Aging: The Political and Moral Economy of Growing Old*. Amityville, NY: Baywood Press.

Mirfin-Veitch, B., Bray, A., Williams, S., Clarkson, J., and Belton, A. (1999). Supporting parents with intellectual disabilities. *New Zealand Journal of Disability Studies*, 6, 60–74.

Misztal, B. (1998). New times, new social movements and new theories in sociology – generational determinants for professing the critical theory of society. *Sociologia*, 30(6), 557–86.

Mitchell, W. (1999). Leaving special school: the next step and future aspirations. *Disability & Society*, 14(6), 753–70.

Mollard, D. (2001). *On Death without Dignity: The Human Impact of Technological Dying*. Amityville, NY: Baywood Publishing Company.

Moody, H. (1995). Ageing, meaning and the allocation of resources. *Ageing and Society*, 15, 163–84.

Morgan, D. (1998). Sociological imaginings and imagining sociology: bodies, auto/biographies and other mysteries. *Sociology*, 32(4), 647–63.

Morgan, J. (1996). A defence of autonomy as an educational ideal. *Journal of Philosophy of Education*, 30, 239–53.

Morita, K. (2001). The eugenic transition of 1996 in Japan: from law to personal choice. *Disability & Society*, 16(5), 765–71.

Morris, J. (1991). *Pride Against Prejudice: Transforming Attitudes to Disability*. London: Women's Press.

Morris, J. (1993). *Independent Lives? Community Care and Disabled People*. Basingstoke: Macmillan.

Morris, J. (1995). Creating a space for absent voices – disabled women's experience of receiving assistance with daily living activities. *Feminist Review*, 51, 68–93.

Morris, J. (ed.). (1996). *Encounters with Strangers: Feminism and Disability*. London: Women's Press.

Morris, J. (1997). Care or empowerment? A disability rights perspective. *Social Policy & Administration*, 31(1), 54–60.

Morris, J. (1998a). *Accessing Human Rights: Disabled Children and the Children Act*. London: Barnardo's.

Morris, J. (1998b). *Don't Leave Us Out: Involving Children and Young People with Communication Impairments*. York: Joseph Rowntree Foundation.

Morris, J. (1999). *Hurtling into a Void: Transition to Adulthood for Young Disabled People with 'Complex Health and Support Needs'*. York: Pavilion Publishing/Joseph Rowntree Foundation.

Morrison, E., and Finkelstein, V. (1993). Broken arts and cultural repair: the role of culture in the empowerment of disabled people. In J. Swain, V. Finkelstein, S. French, and M. Oliver (eds), *Disabling Barriers: Enabling Environments*, Milton Keynes: Open University Press/Sage, 122–7.

Morton, N. (1998). Hippocratic or hypocritic: birth pangs of an ethical code. *Nature Genetics*, 18, 18.

Muller, M., Onwuteakaphilipsen, B., Kriegsman, D., and Vanderwal, G. (1996). Voluntary active euthanasia and doctor-assisted suicide: knowledge and attitudes of Dutch medical students. *Medical Education*, 30(6), 428–33.

Murray, C., and Lopez, A. (1997). Regional patterns of disability-free life expectancy and disability-adjusted life expectancy: global burden of disease study. *Lancet*, 349(9062), 1347–52.

Murray Parkes, C., Laungani, P., and Young, B. (eds). (1997). *Death and Bereavement across Cultures*. London: Routledge.

Najman, J., Bor, W., Morrison, J., Andersen, M., and Williams, G. (1992). Child developmental delay and socioeconomic disadvantage in Australia – a longitudinal study. *Social Science & Medicine*, 34(8), 829–35.

National Council on Disability and Social Security Administration. (2000). *Transition and Post-School Outcomes for Youth with Disabilities: Closing the Gaps to Post-Secondary Education and Employment*. Washington, DC: National Council on Disability.

Newell, C. (2000). Biomedicine, genetics and disability: reflections on nursing and a philosophy of holism. *Nursing Ethics*, 7(3), 227–36.

Newman, B., and Newman, P. (2001). Group identity and alienation: giving the we its due. *Journal of Youth and Adolescence*, 30(5), 515–38.

Nikolaraizi, M., and Reybekiel, N. (2001). A comparative study of children's attitudes towards deaf children, children in wheelchairs and blind children in Greece and in the UK. *European Journal of Special Needs Education*, 16(2), 167–82.

Nirje, B. (1969). The normalisation principle and its human management implications. In R. Kugel and W. Wolfensberger (eds), *Changing Patterns in Residential Services for the Mentally Retarded*, Washington, DC: President's Committee on Mental Retardation, 179–95.

Noom, M., Dekovic, M., and Meeus, W. (2001). Conceptual analysis and measurement of adolescent autonomy. *Journal of Youth and Adolescence*, 30(5), 577–95.

Norrie, K. (1991). Wrongful birth and the Supreme-Court of South-Africa. *International and Comparative Law Quarterly*, 40, 437–42.

Öberg, P. (1996). The absent body – a social gerontological paradox. *Ageing and Society*, 16, 701–19.

Öberg, P., and Tornstam, L. (2001). Youthfulness and fitness – identity ideals for all ages? *Journal of Aging and Identity*, 6(1), 15–29.

O'Brien, C. (1996). China urged to delay 'eugenics' law. *Nature*, 383(6597), 204.

O'Brien, R. (2001). *Crippled Justice: The History of Modern Disability Policy in the Workplace*. Chicago: University of Chicago Press.

Ogden, R. (2001). Non-physician assisted suicide: the technological imperative of the deathing counterculture. *Death Studies*, 25(5), 387–401.

Oldman, D. (1994). Adult–child relations as class relations. In J. Qvortrup, M. Bardy, G. Sgritta, and H. Wintersberger (eds), *Childhood Matters: Social Theory, Practice and Politics*, Aldershot: Avebury, 43–58.

Oliver, M. (1983). *Social Work and Disabled People*. Basingstoke: Macmillan.

Oliver, M. (1989). Disability and dependency: a creation of industrialised societies. In L. Barton (ed.), *Disability and Dependency*, London: Falmer Press, 6–22.

Oliver, M. (1990). *The Politics of Disablement*. Basingstoke: Macmillan.

Oliver, M. (1993). Societal responses to long term disability. In G. Whiteneck, S. Charlifue, K. Gerhart, D. Lammertse, S. Manley, R. Manter, and K. Seedroff (eds), *Ageing with Spinal Cord Injury*, New York: Demos Publications, 251–62.

Oliver, M. (1996). *Understanding Disability: From Theory to Practice*. Basingstoke: Macmillan.

Oliver, M. (1998). The sexual politics of disability: untold desires (book review). *Disability & Society*, 13(1), 150–2.

Opie, I. (1993). *The People in the Playground*. Oxford: Oxford University Press.

Opie, I., and Opie, P. (1959). *The Lore and Language of Schoolchildren*. Oxford: Oxford University Press.

O'Toole, C. (2000). The view from below: developing a knowledge base about an unknown population. *Sexuality and Disability*, 18(3), 207–24.

Otsubo, S., and Bartholomew, J. (1998). Eugenics in Japan: some ironies of modernity, 1883–1945. *Science in Context*, 11(3–4), 545–65.

Padden, C., and Humphries, T. (1988). *Deaf in America: Voices from a Culture*. Cambridge, MA: Harvard University Press.

Painton, D. (ed.). (1997). *Antenatal Screening and Abortion for Fetal Abnormality: Medical and Ethical Issues*. London: Birth Control Trust.

Parsons, T. (1951). *The Social System*. London: Free Press/RKP.

Parsons, T. (1963). Death in American society: a brief working paper. *American Behavioural Scientist*, 6, 61–5.

Patja, K., and Livanainen, M. (2000). Life expectancy of people with intellectual disability: a follow-up study from 1963 to 1997. *Journal of Intellectual Disability Research*, 44, 907.

Patja, K., Livanainen, M., Vesala, H., Oksanen, H., and Ruoppila, I. (2000). Life expectancy of people with intellectual disability: a 35-year follow-up study. *Journal of Intellectual Disability Research*, 44, 591–9.

Pattersonkeels, L., Quint, E., Brown, D., Larson, D., and Elkins, T. E. (1994). Family views on sterilization for their mentally-retarded children. *Journal of Reproductive Medicine*, 39(9), 701–6.

Pattison, E. (1977). *The Experience of Dying*. Englewood Cliffs, NJ: Prentice-Hall.

Pecheux, M. (1999). Parental representations of early development. *Année psychologique*, 99(4), 709–30.

Perakis, A., Kolaitis, G., Kordoutis, P., Kranidioti, M., and Tsiantis, J. (1995). Mortality among institutionalized people with learning disabilities in Greece – a 30-year survey at the Leros Pikpa Asylum. *British Journal of Psychiatry*, 167, 70–7.

Pernick, M. (1996). *The Black Stork*. New York: Oxford University Press.

Peters, S. (2000). Is there a disability culture? A syncretisation of three possible world views. *Disability & Society*, 15(4), 583–601.

Petersen, K. (1997). Medical negligence and wrongful birth actions: Australian developments. *Journal of Medical Ethics*, 23(5), 319–22.

Pfafflin, F., and Gross, J. (1982). Involuntary sterilization in Germany from 1933 to 1945 and some consequences for today. *International Journal of Law and Psychiatry*, 5(3–4), 419–23.

Pfeiffer, D. (2000). The devils are in the details: the ICIDH2 and the disability movement. *Disability & Society*, 15(7), 1079–82.

Phillipson, C. (1982). *Capitalism and the Construction of Old Age*. London: Macmillan.

Phillipson, C., Bernard, M., and Strang, P. (1986). *Dependency and Interdependency in Old Age: Theoretical Perspectives and Policy Alternatives*. London: Croom Helm in association with the British Society of Gerontology.

Philp, M., and Duckworth, D. (1982). *Children with Disabilities and their Families: A Review of Research*. Windsor, Berks: NFER-Nelson.

Piaget, J. (1959). *The Language and Thought of the Child*, 3rd edn. London: Routledge.

Pixa-Kettner, U. (1998). Parents with intellectual disability in Germany: results of a nation-wide study. *Journal of Applied Research in Intellectual Disabilities*, 11(4), 355–64.

Plummer, K. (1995). *Telling Sexual Stories*. London: Routledge.

Polivka, L. (2001). Globalization, population, aging, and ethics. *Journal of Aging and Identity*, 6(3), 147–63.

Porter, D. (2000). The problem of mental deficiency: eugenics, democracy, and social policy in Britain, c.1870–1959. *Isis*, 91(4), 802–4.

Porter, E. (2001). Interdependence, parenting and responsible citizenship. *Journal of Gender Studies*, 10(1), 5–15.

Potts, M. (1997). Sex and the birth rate: human biology, demographic change, and access to fertility-regulation methods. *Population and Development Review*, 23(1), 1–39.

Pound, P., Gompertz, P., and Ebrahim, S. (1998). Illness in the context of older age: the case of stroke. *Sociology of Health & Illness*, 20(4), 489–506.

Prakash, I. (1997). Women and ageing. *Indian Journal of Medical Research*, 106, 396–408.

Preston, P. (1995). Mother father deaf – the heritage of difference. *Social Science & Medicine*, 40(11), 1461–7.

Preston, P. (1996). Chameleon voices: interpreting for deaf parents. *Social Science & Medicine*, 42(12), 1681–90.

Priestley, M. (1997). The origins of a legislative disability category in England: a speculative history. *Disability Studies Quarterly*, 17(2), 87–94.

Priestley, M. (1998a). Childhood disability and disabled childhoods – agendas for research. *Childhood – A Global Journal of Child Research*, 5(2), 207–23.

Priestley, M. (1998b). Constructions and creations: idealism, materialism and disability theory. *Disability & Society*, 13(1), 75–94.

Priestley, M. (1998c). Discourse and resistance in care assessment: integrated living and community care. *British Journal of Social Work*, 28(5), 659–73.

Priestley, M. (1999). *Disability Politics and Community Care*. London: Jessica Kingsley Publishers.

Priestley, M. (2000). Adults only: disability, social policy and the life course. *Journal of Social Policy*, 29, 421–39.

Priestley, M. (ed.). (2001). *Disability and the Life Course: Global Perspectives*. Cambridge: Cambridge University Press.

Priestley, M. (2002a). 'It's like your hair going grey', or is it? Impairment, disability and the habitus of old age. In S. Riddell and N. Watson (eds), *Disability, Culture and Identity*, London: Longman.

Priestley, M. (2002b). Whose voices? Representing the claims of older disabled people under New Labour. *Policy & Politics*, 30(3), 361–72.

Priestley, M., Corker, M., and Watson, N. (1999). Unfinished business: disabled children and disability identity. *Disability Studies Quarterly*, 19(2), 90–7.

Prince, M. (1997). The need for research on dementia in developing countries. *Tropical Medicine & International Health*, 2(10), 993–1000.

Proctor, G. (2001). Listening to older women with dementia: relationships, voices and power. *Disability & Society*, 16(3), 361–76.

Putnam, C. (2001). New information on 'death with dignity'. *Hastings Center Report*, 31(4), 8.

Qvortrup, J. (1994). Childhood matters: an introduction. In J. Qvortrup, M. Bardy, G. Sgritta, and H. Wintersberger (eds), *Childhood Matters: Social Theory, Practice and Politics*, Aldershot: Avebury, 1–23.

Qvortrup, J., Bardy, M., Sgritta, G., and Wintersberger, H. (eds). (1994). *Childhood Matters: Social Theory, Practice and Politics*. Aldershot: Avebury.

Rabiee, P., Priestley, M., and Knowles, J. (2001). *Whatever Next? Young Disabled People Leaving Care*. Leeds: First Key.

Rao, S. (2001). 'A little inconvenience': perspectives of Bengali families with children with disabilities on labelling and inclusion. *Disability & Society*, 16(4), 531–48.

Read, S. (1999). *Bereavement and People with a Learning Disability*. London: Nursing Times Books.

Redelman, M. (2001). Sexuality and the intellectually disabled. *Current Therapeutics*, 42(5), 63–7.

Reindal, S. (1999). Independence, dependence, interdependence: some reflections on the subject and personal autonomy. *Disability & Society*, 14(3), 353–67.

Reindal, S. (2000). Disability, gene therapy and eugenics – a challenge to John Harris. *Journal of Medical Ethics*, 26(2), 89–94.

Richards, T., Wrubel, J., and Folkman, S. (1999). Death rites in the San Francisco gay community: cultural developments of the AIDS epidemic. *Omega – Journal of Death and Dying*, 40(2), 335–50.

Riddell, S. (1996). Theorising special educational needs in a changing political climate. In L. Barton (ed.), *Disability & Society: Emerging Issues and Insights*, Harlow: Longman, 83–106.

Riddell, S. (1998). The dynamic of transition to adulthood. In K. Stalker and L. Ward (eds), *Growing Up with Disability*, London: Jessica Kingsley Publishers, 189–209.

Riddell, S., Baron, S., and Wilson, A. (2001). The significance of the learning society for women and men with learning difficulties. *Gender and Education*, 13(1), 57–73.

Riggs, A., and Turner, B. (1997). The sociology of the postmodern self: intimacy, identity and emotions in adult life. *Australian Journal on Ageing*, 16(4), 229–32.

Riley, J. (1983). Dying and the meanings of death – sociological inquiries. *Annual Review of Sociology*, 9, 191–216.

Riley, M. (1988a). On the significance of age in sociology. In M. W. Riley (ed.), *Social Structures and Human Lives*, Newbury Park, CA: Sage, 24–45.

Riley, M. (ed.). (1988b). *Social Structures and Human Lives*. Newbury Park, CA: Sage.

Roberge, R., Berthelot, J. M., and Cranswick, K. (1999). Adjusting life expectancy to account for disability in a population: a comparison of three techniques. *Social Indicators Research*, 48(2), 217–43.

Roberts, K. (1997). Structure and agency: the new youth research agenda. In J. Bynner, L. Chisholm, and A. Furlong (eds), *Youth, Citizenship and Social Change in a European Context*, Aldershot: Ashgate, 17–41.

Rock, P. (1988). Independence: what it means to six disabled people living in the community. *Disability, Handicap & Society*, 3, 27–35.

Rock, P. (1996). Eugenics and euthanasia: a cause for concern for disabled people, particularly disabled women. *Disability & Society*, 11(1), 121–7.

Rohrlich, F. (2001). Cognitive scientific realism. *Philosophy of Science*, 68(2), 185–202.

Rojek, C., and Turner, B. (2000). Decorative sociology: towards a critique of the cultural turn. *Sociological Review*, 48(4), 629–48.

Roscoe, L., Malphurs, J., Dragovic, L., and Cohen, D. (2001). A comparison of characteristics of Kevorkian euthanasia cases and physician-assisted suicides in Oregon. *Gerontologist*, 41(4), 439–46.

Rosman, E., and Knitzer, J. (2001). Welfare reform: the special case of young children with disabilities and their families. *Infants and Young Children*, 13(3), 25–35.

Roulstone, A. (1998). *Enabling Technology: Disabled People, Work and Technology*. Milton Keynes: Open University Press.

Rousso, H., and Wehmeyer, M. L. (eds). (2001). *Double Jeopardy: Addressing Gender Equity in Special Education*. Albany, NY: State University of New York Press.

Rowlands, A. (2001). Breaking my head in the prime of my life: acquired disability in young adulthood. In M. Priestley (ed.), *Disability and the Life Course: Global Perspectives*, Cambridge: Cambridge University Press, 179–91.

Russell, P., John, A., and Lakshmanan, J. (1999). Family intervention for intellectually disabled children – randomised controlled trial. *British Journal of Psychiatry*, 174, 254–8.

Rustin, M. (2000). Reflections on the biographical turn in social sciences. In P. Chamberlayne, J. Bornat, and T. Wengraf (eds), *The Turn to Biographical Methods in Social Science: Comparative Issues and Examples*, London: Routledge, 33–52.

Ryan, J., and Thomas, F. (1980). *The Politics of Mental Handicap*. Harmondsworth: Penguin.

Sainsbury, S. (1986). *Deaf Worlds: A study of Integration, Segregation and Disability*. London: Hutchinson.

Salisbury, P. (1998). Factors affecting birth rates among white women 20–24 years of age: a trend analysis (January 1972–March 1992). *Social Indicators Research*, 43(3), 261–89.

Salisbury, P. (1999). Factors affecting birth rates among black women 20–24 years of age: a trend analysis (January 1972–March 1992). *Social Indicators Research*, 48(1), 1–38.

Saloviita, T. (2000). Supported employment as a paradigm shift and a cause of legitimation crisis. *Disability & Society*, 15(1), 87–98.

Salvatori, P., Tremblay, M., Sandys, J., and Marcaccio, D. (1998). Aging with an intellectual disability: a review of Canadian literature. *Canadian Journal on Aging – Revue Canadienne du Vieillissement*, 17(3), 249–71.

Sandieson, R. (1998). A survey on terminology that refers to people with mental retardation developmental disabilities. *Education and Training in Mental Retardation and Developmental Disabilities*, 33(3), 290–5.

Sankar, A. (1987). The living dead. In P. Silverman (ed.), *The Elderly as Modern Pioneers*, Bloomington: Indiana University Press, 345–56.

Santana, P. (2000). Ageing in Portugal: regional iniquities in health and health care. *Social Science & Medicine*, 50(7–8), 1025–36.

Saviolonegrin, N., and Cristante, F. (1992). Teachers' attitudes towards plastic surgery in children with Down's syndrome. *Journal of Intellectual Disability Research*, 36, 143–55.

Savulescu, J. (2001). Is current practice around late termination of pregnancy eugenic and discriminatory? Maternal interests and abortion. *Journal of Medical Ethics*, 27(3), 165–71.

Schneider, J., Simons, K., and Everatt, G. (2001). Impact of the national minimum wage on disabled people. *Disability & Society*, 16(5), 723–41.

Schofield, G. (1996). Parental competence and the welfare of the child: issues for those who work with parents with learning disabilities and their children. *Child and Family Social Work*, 1(2), 87–92.

Scott, J. (2000). Is it a different world to when you were growing up? Generational effects on social representations and child-rearing values. *British Journal of Sociology*, 51(2), 355–76.

Scott, S., Jackson, S., and Backett-Milburn, K. (1998). Swings and roundabouts: risk anxiety and the everyday worlds of children. *Sociology*, 32(4), 689–705.

Seale, C. (1998). *Constructing Death: The Sociology of Dying and Bereavement*. Cambridge: Cambridge University Press.

Seelman, K. (2000). Science and technology policy: is disability a missing factor? *Assistive Technology*, 12(2), 144–53.

Selden, S. (1999). *Inheriting Shame: The Story of Eugenics and Racism in America*. New York: Teachers' College Press.

Selden, S. (2000). Eugenics and the social construction of merit, race and disability. *Journal of Curriculum Studies*, 32(2), 235–52.

Seymour, J. (1999). Revisiting medicalisation and 'natural' death. *Social Science & Medicine*, 49(5), 691–704.

Shakespeare, T. (1994). Cultural representation of disabled people: dustbins for disavowal? *Disability & Society*, 9, 283–99.

Shakespeare, T. (1998). Choices and rights: eugenics, genetics and disability equality. *Disability & Society*, 13(5), 665–81.

Shakespeare, T. (1999). 'Losing the plot'? Medical and activist discourses of contemporary genetics and disability. *Sociology of Health & Illness*, 21(5), 669–88.

Shakespeare, T. (2000). Disabled sexuality: towards rights and recognition. *Sexuality and Disability*, 18(3), 159–66.

Shakespeare, T., and Watson, N. (1998). Theoretical perspectives on research with disabled children. In K. Stalker and L. Ward (eds), *Growing Up with Disability*, London: Jessica Kingsley Publishers, 13–27.

Shakespeare, T., Gillespie-Sells, K., and Davies, D. (1996). *The Sexual Politics of Disability: Untold Desires*. London: Cassell.

Shamgar-Handelman, L. (1994). To whom does childhood belong? In J. Qvortrup, M. Bardy, G. Sgritta, and H. Wintersberger (eds), *Childhood Matters: Social Theory, Practice and Politics*, Aldershot: Avebury, 249–66.

Shapira, A. (1998). 'Wrongful life' lawsuits for faulty genetic counselling: should the impaired newborn be entitled to sue? *Journal of Medical Ethics*, 24(6), 369–75.

Sharp, K., and Earle, S. (2002). Feminism, abortion and disability: irreconcilable differences? *Disability & Society*, 17(2), 137–46.

Shea, G. (1999). *Redress Programs Relating to Institutional Child Abuse in Canada*. Ontario: Law Commission of Canada.

Shepherd, L. (1995). Protecting parents' freedom to have children with genetic differences. *University of Illinois Law Review*, 4, 761–812.

Shepperdson, B. (1995). The control of sexuality in young people with Down's syndrome. *Child Care Health and Development*, 21(5), 333–49.

Simon, A. (2000). A right to life for the unborn? The current debate on abortion in Germany and Norbert Hoerster's legal-philosophical justification for the right to life. *Journal of Medicine and Philosophy*, 25(2), 220–39.

Sitlington, P. (1996). Transition to living: the neglected component of transition programming for individuals with learning disabilities. *Journal of Learning Disabilities*, 29(1), 31–9.

Smith, J. (1993). *The Eugenic Assault on America: Scenes in Red, White and Black*. Fairfax, VA: George Mason University Press.

Smith, J. (1995). The Bell-curve and Carrie Buck: eugenics revisited. *Mental Retardation*, 33, 60–1.

Smith, P. (1999). Drawing new maps: a radical cartography of developmental disabilities. *Review of Educational Research*, 69(2), 117–44.

Snyder, L., and Sulmasy, D. (2001). Physician-assisted suicide. *Annals of Internal Medicine*, 135(3), 209–16.

Stainton, T. (1994). *Autonomy and Social Policy*. Aldershot: Avebury/Ashgate.

Stalker, K., Duckett, P., and Downs, M. (1999). *Going with the Flow: Choice, Dementia and People with Learning Difficulties*. Brighton: Pavilion Publishing.

Steele, C., Kalnins, I., Jutai, J., Stevens, S., Bortolussi, J., and Biggar, W. (1996). Lifestyle health behaviours of 11- to 16-year-old youth with physical disabilities. *Health Education Research*, 11(2), 173–86.

Steinbicker, J. (2001). Soziale Ungleichheit in der Informations- und Wissensgesellschaft [Social inequality in the information and knowledge society]. *Berliner Zeitschrift für Soziologie*, 11(4), 441–58.

Steinhauser, A., Christakis, N., Clipp, E., McNeilly, M., McIntyre, L., and Tulsky, J. (2000). Factors considered important at the end of life by patients, family, physicians, and other care providers. *JAMA* 284(19), 2476–82.

Stepanuk, N. (1998). Genetic information and third party access to information: New Jersey's pioneering legislation as a model for federal privacy protection of genetic information. *Catholic University Law Review*, 47(3), 1105–44.

Stobel-Richter, Y., and Brahler, E. (2001). Children – why not . . . Results of a representative survey in East and West Germany. *Zentralblatt für Gynäkologie*, 123(1), 64–7.

Stone, D. (1984). *The Disabled State*. Philadelphia: Temple University Press.

Stone, E. (1996). A law to protect, a law to prevent: contextualising disability legislation in China. *Disability & Society*, 11(4), 469–84.

Stone, E. (ed.). (1999). *Disability and Development: Learning from Action Research on Disability in the Majority World*. Leeds: Disability Press.

Stone, S. (1995). The myth of bodily perfection. *Disability & Society*, 10(4), 413–24.

Stoneman, Z. (2001). Supporting positive sibling relationships during childhood. *Mental Retardation and Developmental Disabilities Research Reviews*, 7(2), 134–42.

Storey, K. (2000). Why employment in integrated settings for people with disabilities *International Journal of Rehabilitation Research*, 23(2), 103–10.

Stott, F., and Bowman, B. (1996). Child development knowledge: a slippery base for practice. *Early Childhood Research Quarterly*, 11(2), 169–83.

Strickland, S., and Tuffrey, V. (1997). Parental investment theory and birth sex ratios in Nepal. *Journal of Biosocial Science*, 29(3), 283–95.

Sutherland, S. (1999). *With Respect to Old Age: Long Term Care – Rights and Responsibilities: A Report by the Royal Commission on Long Term Care*. London: Stationery Office, Cm 4192-I.

Swain, J., and French, S. (2000). Towards an affirmation model of disability. *Disability & Society*, 15(4), 569–82.

Synott, A. (1993). *The Body Social: Symbolism, Self and Society*. London: Routledge.

Takala, T., and Gylling, H. (2000). Who should know about our genetic makeup and why? *Journal of Medical Ethics*, 26(3), 171–4.

Taleporos, G., and McCabe, M. (2001). Physical disability and sexual esteem. *Sexuality and Disability*, 19(2), 131–48.

Tang, S. (2000). Meanings of dying at home for Chinese patients in Taiwan with terminal cancer – a literature review. *Cancer Nursing*, 23(5), 367–70.

Tangwa, G. (1999). Globalisation or westernisation? Ethical concerns in the whole big-business. *Bioethics*, 13(3–4), 218–26.

Taylor, C., Norman, D., Murphy, J., Jellinek, M., Quinn, D., Poitrast, F., and Goshko, M. (1991). Diagnosed intellectual and emotional impairment among parents who seriously mistreat their children: prevalence, type, and outcome in a court sample. *Child Abuse*, 15, 389–401.

Taylor, J. (1989). *Holy Living and Holy Dying*, ed. P. G. Stanwood. Oxford: Oxford University Press.

Tepper, M. (2000). Sexuality and disability: the missing discourse of pleasure. *Sexuality and Disability*, 18(4), 283–90.

Test, D. (1994). Supported employment and social validity. *Journal of the Association for Persons with Severe Handicaps*, 19(2), 116–29.

Test, D., Carver, T., Ewers, L., Haddad, J., and Person, J. (2000). Longitudinal job satisfaction of persons in supported employment. *Education and Training in Mental Retardation and Developmental Disabilities*, 35(4), 365–73.

Thomas, C. (1997). The baby and the bath water: disabled women and motherhood in social context. *Sociology of Health and Illness*, 19(5), 622–43.

Thomas, C., and Curtis, P. (1997). Having a baby: some disabled women's reproductive experiences. *Midwifery*, 13, 202–9.

Thomas, N., and Price, N. (1996). The evolution of population policy in rural China. *Health Policy and Planning*, 11(1), 21–9.

Thompson, L., Powers, G., and Houchard, B. (1992). The wage effects of supported employment. *Journal of the Association for Persons with Severe Handicaps*, 17(2), 87–94.

Thornton, P., and Lunt, N. (1997). *Employment Policies for Disabled People in Eighteen Countries: A Review*. York: Social Policy Research Unit, University of York.

Tisdall, K. (2001). Failing to make the transition? Theorising the 'transition to adulthood' for young disabled people. In M. Priestley (ed.), *Disability and the Life Course: Global Perspectives*, Cambridge: Cambridge University Press, 167–78.

Todd, S., and Shearn, J. (1996). Time and the person: the impact of support services on the lives of parents of adults with intellectual disabilities. *Journal of Applied Research in Intellectual Disabilities*, 9(1), 40–60.

Tomlinson, S., and Colquhoun, R. (1995). The political economy of special educational needs in Britain. *Disability & Society*, 10(2), 191–202.

Tooley, M. (1983). *Abortion and Infanticide*. New York: Oxford University Press.

Topliss, E. (1979). *Provision for the Disabled*. Oxford: Blackwell/Martin Robertson.

Townsend, P. (1981). The structural dependency of the elderly: the creation of social policy in the twentieth century. *Ageing and Society*, 1(May), 28.

Tremain, S. (ed.). (1996). *Pushing the Limits: Disabled Dykes Produce Culture*. Toronto: Women's Press.

Tremain, S. (2000). Queering disabled sexuality studies. *Sexuality and Disability*, 18(4), 291–9.

Trent, J. W. (1998). Defectives at the World's Fair – constructing disability in 1904. *Remedial and Special Education*, 19(4), 201–11.

Tsuji, I., Minami, Y., Fukao, A., Hisamichi, S., Asano, H., and Sato, M. (1995). Active life expectancy among elderly Japanese. *Journal of Gerontology Series A: Biological Sciences and Medical Sciences*, 50(3), M173–6.

Tulle-Winton, E. (1999). Growing old and resistance: towards a new cultural economy of old age? *Ageing and Society*, 19, 281–99.

Tulle-Winton, E., and Mooney, E. (1999). Managing old bodies: the body in social gerontological theorising. *Zeitschrift für Gerontologie und Geriatrie*, 32(2, suppl. 2), 835.

Turmusani, M. (2001). Work and adulthood: economic survival in the majority world. In M. Priestley (ed.), *Disability and the Life Course: Global Perspectives*, Cambridge: Cambridge University Press, 192–205.

Turner, B. (1989). Ageing, politics and sociological theory. *British Journal of Sociology*, 40(4), 588–606.

Turner, B. (1998). Ageing and generational conflicts: a reply to Sarah Irwin. *British Journal of Sociology*, 49(2), 299–304.

Turney, J., and Turner, J. (2000). Predictive medicine, genetics and schizophrenia. *New Genetics and Society*, 19(1), 5–22.

Ulrich, M. (2000). *Life Courses in the Transformation of East Germany*. Madrid: Instituto Juan March de Estudios e Investigaciones.

Um, Y. (2000). A critique of a 'wrongful life' lawsuit in Korea. *Nursing Ethics*, 7(3), 250–61.

Union of Physically Impaired against Segregation/Disability Alliance. (1976). *Fundamental Principles of Disability*. London: UPIAS/Disability Alliance.

United Nations. (1983). *Vienna International Plan of Action on Aging*. New York: United Nations.

United Nations. (1991). *Principles for Older Persons*. New York: United Nations.

United Nations. (1993). *Standard Rules on the Equalization of Opportunities for People with Disabilities*. New York: United Nations.

United Nations. (1998). *The Sex and Age Distribution of the World Populations: 1998 Revision, Volume II: Sex and Age*. New York: United Nations.

United Nations Educational Scientific and Cultural Organization and Ministry of Education and Science. (1994). The Salamanca Statement and Framework for Action on Special Needs Education. Paper presented at the World Conference on Special Needs Education: Access and Quality, Salamanca, Spain, 7–10 June 1994.

United Nations Secretariat. (1998). *World Population Prospects, the 1998 Revision, Volume II: Sex and Age*. New York: The Population Division, Department of Economic and Social Affairs, United Nations Secretariat.

Ustun, T., Chatterji, S., Bickenbach, J., Trotter, R., Room, R., Rehm, J., and Saxena, S. (eds). (2001). *Disability and Culture: Universalism and Diversity*. Kirkland, WA: Hogrefe & Huber Publishers/World Health Organisation.

Verbrugge, L., Rennert, C., and Madans, J. H. (1997). The great efficacy of personal and equipment assistance in reducing disability. *American Journal of Public Health*, 87(3), 384–92.

Vierzigmann, G., and Kreher, S. (1998). 'Zwischen den Generationen' – Familiendynamik und Familiendiskurse in biographischen Erzählungen ['Between generations' – family dynamics and family discourses in biographical accounts]. *Berliner Zeitschrift für Soziologie*, 8(1), 23–38.

Vincent, J. (1999). *Politics, Power and Old Age*. Buckingham: Open University Press.

Vincent, J., Patterson, G., and Wale, K. (2001). *Politics and Old Age: Older Citizens and Political Processes in Britain*. Aldershot: Ashgate.

Vintzileos, A., Ananth, C., Fisher, A., Smulian, J., Day-Salvatore, D., and Beazoglu, T. (1998). An economic evaluation of the first-trimester genetic sonography for prenatal detection of Down's syndrome. *Obstetrics and Gynecology*, 91, 535–9.

Waksler, F. (1991). Studying children: phenomenological insights. In F. Waksler (ed.), *Studying the Social Worlds of Children*, London: Falmer Press, 60–9.

Wald, N., Kennard, A., Densem, J., Cuckle, H., Chard, T., and Butler, L. (1992). Antenatal maternal screening for Down's syndrome: results of a demonstration project. *British Medical Journal*, 305, 391–4.

Waldman, H., Swerdloff, M., and Perlman, S. (1999). A 'dirty secret': the abuse of children with disabilities. *Journal of Dentistry for Children*, 66(3), 197–202.

Waldman, M. (1990). Prenatal injuries: wrongful life, birth, or conception. *American Jurisprudence, 2nd ser.*, 62A, 393–518 (and supplement).

Walker, A. (1980). The social creation of poverty and dependency in old age. *Journal of Social Policy*, 9, 49–75.

Walker, R., and Leisering, L. (eds). (1998). *The Dynamics of Modern Society: Poverty, Policy and Welfare*. Bristol: Policy Press.

Wall, M., Gast, D., and Royston, P. (1999). Leisure skills instruction for adolescents with severe or profound developmental disabilities. *Journal of Developmental and Physical Disabilities*, 11(3), 193–219.

Walls, R., Dowler, D., Cordingly, K., Orslene, L., and Greer, J. (2001). Microenterprising and people with disabilities: strategies for success and failure. *Journal of Rehabilitation*, 67(2), 29–35.

Ward, L. (1997). *Seen and Heard: Involving Disabled Children and Young People in Research and Development Projects*. York: Joseph Rowntree Foundation.

Wates, M. (1997). *Disabled Parents: Dispelling the Myths*. London: Radcliffe Medical Press/National Childbirth Trust.

Wates, M., and Jade, R. (eds). (1999). *Bigger than the Sky: Disabled Women on Parenting*. London: Women's Press.

Wates, M., and Tyers, H. (2000). Supporting Disabled Parents: A Sample Protocol for Good Practice in Social Services Departments. Unpublished research paper.

Watson, N., Shakespeare, T., Cunningham-Burley, S., Barnes, C., Corker, M., Davis, J., and Priestley, M. (1999). *Life as a Disabled Child: A Qualitative Study of Young People's Experiences and Perspectives*. Edinburgh and Leeds: Universities of Edinburgh and Leeds.

Wattanapitayakul, S., and Schommer, J. C. (1999). The Human Genome Project: benefits and risks to society. *Drug Information Journal*, 33(3), 729–35.

Waxman Fiduccia, B. (2000). Current issues in sexuality and the disability movement. *Sexuality and Disability*, 18(3), 167–74.

Waxman Fiduccia, B., and Wolfe, L. (1999). *Women and Girls with Disabilities: Defining the Issues*. Washington, DC: Center for Women's Policy Studies and Women and Philanthropy.

Wehman, P., Revell, G., and Kregel, J. (1997). Supported employment: a decade of rapid growth and impact. In P. Wehman, G. Revell, J. Kregel, and M. West (eds), *Supported Employment Research: Expanding Competitive Employment Opportunities for Persons with Significant Disabilities*, Richmond, VA: Rehabilitation Research and Training Center on Supported Employment, Virginia Commonwealth University.

Welsch, W. (1996). Aestheticization processes – phenomena, distinctions and prospects. *Theory, Culture & Society*, 13(1), 1–24.

Werner, D. (1993). Meeting the needs of disabled village children. *Tropical and Geographical Medicine*, 45(5), 229–32.

Wertz, D. (1998). Eugenics is alive and well: a survey of genetic professionals around the world. *Science in Context*, 11(3–4), 493–510.

Wertz, D., and Gregg, R. (2000). Genetics services in a social, ethical and policy context: a collaboration between consumers and providers. *Journal of Medical Ethics*, 26(4), 261–5.

Westcott, H., and Cross, M. (1996). *This Far and No Further: Towards Ending the Abuse of Disabled Children*. Birmingham: Venture Press.

Williams, G. (1984). The genesis of chronic illness: narrative reconstruction. *Sociology of Health & Illness*, 6, 175–200.

Williams, S. (2000). Chronic illness as biographical disruption or biographical disruption as chronic illness? Reflections on a core concept. *Sociology of Health & Illness*, 22(1), 40–67.

Wirz, S., and Lichtig, I. (1998). The use of non-specialist personnel in providing a service for children disabled by hearing impairment. *Disability and Rehabilitation*, 20(5), 189–94.

Wolbring, G. (2001). Where do we draw the line? Surviving eugenics in a technological world. In M. Priestley (ed.), *Disability and the Life Course: Global Perspectives*, Cambridge: Cambridge University Press, 38–49.

Wolfe, P. (1997). The influence of personal values on issues of sexuality and disability. *Sexuality and Disability*, 15(2), 69–90.

Wolman, C., and Basco, D. (1994). Factors influencing self-esteem and self-consciousness in adolescents with spina-bifida. *Journal of Adolescent Health*, 15(7), 543–8.

Wong, F., Lee, W., and Mok, E. (2001). Educating nurses to care for the dying in Hong Kong – a problem-based learning approach. *Cancer Nursing*, 24(2), 112–21.

World Bank. (1993). *World Development Report 1993*. Washington, DC: World Bank.

World Conference on Education for All. (1990). World Declaration on Education for All: Meeting Basic Learning Needs. Paper presented at the World Conference on Education for All, Jomtien, Thailand, 5–9 March 1990.

Wu, J. (1994). Population and family planning in China. *Verhandelingen-Koninklijke Academie voor Geneeskunde van Belgie*, 56, 383–400.

Wu, Z. (1994). Conflicts between Chinese traditional ethics and bioethics. *Cambridge Quarterly of Healthcare Ethics*, 3(3), 367–71.

Yasumura, S., Haga, H., Shibata, H., Iwasaki, K., Nakamura, Y., Ahiko, T., Ihara, K., Oiji, A., Fujita, M., Imuta, H., Abe, H., and Fukao, A. (2000). Factors relating to place of death of Japanese people from a small town in a rural area. *Aging – Clinical and Experimental Research*, 12(6), 449–54.

Yelin, E. (1997). The employment of people with and without disabilities in an age of insecurity. *Annals of the American Academy of Political and Social Science*, 549, 117–28.

Yell, M., Rogers, D., and Rogers, E. (1998). The legal history of special education – what a long, strange trip it's been! *Remedial and Special Education*, 19(4), 219–28.

Zarb, G., and Oliver, M. (1993). *Ageing with a Disability: What do they Expect after all these Years?* London: University of Greenwich.

Zimmerman, S. (1998). The use of genetic tests and genetic information by life insurance companies: does this differ from the use of routine medical information? *Genetic Testing*, 2(1), 3–8.

Zinkin, P., and McConachie, H. (eds). (1995). *Disabled Children & Developing Countries*. Cambridge: Cambridge University Press.

Zola, I. (1977). Healthism and disabling medicalisation. In I. Illich (ed.), *Disabling Professions*, London: Marion Boyars, 41–67.

Zola, I. (1989). Towards a necessary universalizing of disability policy. *Millbank Memorial Quarterly*, 67(2), 401–28.

INDEX